Producing Desire

STUDIES ON THE HISTORY OF SOCIETY AND CULTURE

Victoria E. Bonnell and Lynn Hunt, Editors

# Producing Desire

## *Changing Sexual Discourse in the Ottoman Middle East, 1500–1900*

Dror Ze'evi

UNIVERSITY OF CALIFORNIA PRESS
*Berkeley · Los Angeles · London*

University of California Press, one of the most distinguished university presses in the United States, enriches lives around the world by advancing scholarship in the humanities, social sciences, and natural sciences. Its activities are supported by the UC Press Foundation and by philanthropic contributions from individuals and institutions. For more information, visit www.ucpress.edu.

University of California Press
Berkeley and Los Angeles, California

University of California Press, Ltd.
London, England



Library of Congress Cataloging-in-Publication Data

Ze'evi, Dror, 1953–
Producing desire : changing sexual discourse in the Ottoman Middle East, 1500–1900 / Dror Ze'evi.
p. cm.—(Studies on the history of society and culture)
Includes bibliographical references and index.
ISBN 13: 978-0-520-24564-8 (cloth : alk. paper)
ISBN 13: 978-0-520-24563-1 (pbk. : alk. paper)

1. Sex customs—Middle East. 2. Desire.
I. Title. II. Series.
HQ18.M52Z44 2006
306.7'0956'0903—dc22 2005013949

Manufactured in the United States of America
15 14 13 12 11
10 9 8 7 6 5 4 3 2

This book is printed on New Leaf EcoBook 50, a 100% recycled fiber of which 50% is de-inked post-consumer waste, processed chlorine-free. EcoBook 50 is acid-free and meets the minimum requirements of ANSI/ASTM D5634-01 *(Permanence of Paper)*.⊗

*In memory of my father,*
*Benny,*
*a man of integrity and love*

# Contents

# Illustrations

# Tables

# Acknowledgments

This voyage began more than a decade ago in Princeton's Firestone Library, when a seventeenth-century treatise on sexuality caught my eye. Since then this book has gone through many ports, storms, and upheavals in its quest, and the end product is very distant from the port of origin. My first thanks are due to my family, Amira, David, Lior, and Omer, who accompanied me on the voyage and stood by me all this time.

Along the way I was helped by many people who read drafts, argued, disagreed, showed me the way forward, and encouraged me to sail on. I owe a special debt of gratitude to my dear departed friend Mine Ener, with whom I spent four wonderful months in Istanbul, on the shores of the Bosphorus. Working on her research alongside me, she had some wonderful suggestions, including the title of this book. May her soul rest in peace.

At the newly established Department of Middle East Studies at Ben Gurion University in Beer Sheva, a dedicated faculty shared their thoughts and ideas with me. Thanks are due to Nimrod Hurvitz and Sam Kaplan for their continued engagement and support. I am also indebted to my students Dafna Poremba, Salih Biçakçı, and Ben Okyere, who contributed their time and energy to help me cope with the burdens of research, and to our administrator, Aliza Ouzan-Suissa, whose assistance was invaluable.

Many thanks to Afsaneh Najmabadi, Leslie Peirce, Amy Singer, Nikki Keddie, and Gabriel Piterberg for their ideas, valuable comments, and support. My deepest gratitude is to Naghmeh Sohrabi, whose love I cherish and whose incisive observations made me rewrite entire sections.

Sheila Levine, Laura Harger, Madeleine Adams, Randy Heyman, and the editors, readers, and staff at the University of California Press navigated the book to its port of destination with patience and wisdom. It was a privilege and a learning experience to work with such professionals.

Finally, I would like to thank the Israel Academy of Science, the American Research Institute in Turkey, Ben Gurion University of the Negev, the Crown Center for Middle East Studies at Brandeis University, and Harvard University's Center for Middle East Studies for their financial support and hospitality.

# Note on the Transliteration of Arabic and Turkish

This book is based mainly on Arabic and Ottoman Turkish sources. Since Ottoman was written in Arabic script, many of the words share the same spelling. Turkish pronunciation, however, is markedly different from Arabic. In transliteration I have tried to follow the original language of the source or sources.

Arabic terms are transliterated according to the rules of the *International Journal of Middle East Studies.* Terms in Turkish are rendered in modern Romanized Turkish orthography. In this system, *c* is pronounced as *j* in English; *ç* is pronounced as *ch; ğ* is usually unvocalized and lengthens the preceding vowel; and *ı* (undotted *i*) is pronounced as the vowel *u* in the word *turn.*

Where words in Ottoman do not have a well-known modern equivalent, or when the text relies heavily on Arabic, I have used Arabic diacritics in transliteration of Turkish.

In many cases, the same term is transliterated from both Ottoman and Arabic sources. As a rule, the transliteration follows the Arabic when Arabic sources were quoted and Turkish in the case of Ottoman Turkish sources. In other cases, when specified, the transliteration is used to make temporal or spatial distinctions. For instance, the term for Islamic law is transliterated as *sharīʿa* when referring to non-Ottoman practices, and as *şeriat* when referring to the system as practiced and elaborated under the Ottomans.

# Introduction

*Sex as Script*

> One day, the tribe of ʿAbd al-Qays, residing on the eastern coast of the Arabian Peninsula, sent a delegation to meet the Prophet Muhammad. As they were being seated in his presence, he observed among them a young boy of radiant beauty. The Prophet immediately instructed the boy to leave his place and find a seat behind his back. When asked by his disciples for the reason, he said, "David's rebellion was caused by none other than sight."[1]

This story is ascribed to al-Shaʿbi, a scholar and legal expert from the city of Kūfa, who was known for, among other things, his fashionable silk attire and his red hair, carefully dyed with henna. Born a few years after the Prophet's death, he was not one of the Companions but appeared to remember hundreds of the Prophet's sayings and deeds, which he duly transmitted to his disciples and contemporaries.[2]

This was not a well-documented tradition in the early centuries, and many doubted its veracity. Though appreciated as a jurist, al-Shaʿbi did not have a very good reputation as a transmitter of tradition, and quite a few of his stories were found to be false. But in later centuries the story suddenly became popular and was told, with minute variations, by many scholars, among them a certain Abu al-Fatḥ al-Dajjāni, a scholar living in Jerusalem in the seventeenth century, whose version is given here.

The sense of incomprehension elicited by this story reflects our feelings of confusion when faced with the sexual world of a distant culture. Why would the Prophet ask the boy to move and disappear from view?

Could it be that he feared temptation, or was he concerned about the sexual inclinations of other people at this gathering and was trying to shield them from sin? And what about the reference to David (Dāwūd)? Clearly, the Prophet was referring to the story of the prophet David gazing at Bathsheba from the rooftop of his palace and inviting her over, which resulted in his having sexual relations with a married woman. How could this story be applicable to the case of the Qaysi youth?

These are some of the difficulties we may encounter when trying to understand the meaning of historical texts relating to sexuality. Like peeling an onion, the outer layer of mystery relates to the veracity of the story itself. It might be wise to ignore this layer and discard it altogether. It does not really matter for our purposes whether the events in the story happened. The second layer would refer to the world of al-Shaʿbi. Why would he be interested in telling this story, and why would those around him be interested in hearing it or in denying its veracity? A further layer would be the seventeenth-century Ottoman author al-Dajjāni. Why did he, along with so many of his contemporaries, decide to reproduce this old forgotten story, and what does the telling of this story teach us about their sexual world?

One answer to these questions, as we shall see, may be that in al-Dajjāni's Ottoman world, and perhaps in that of al-Shaʿbi too, homoerotic or pederastic passion did not bear the stigma of abnormal behavior that it came to bear in modern Western cultures, and the reason for bringing it up probably had very little to do with sexual deviation. The impetus for summoning it from forgotten scriptures more than a thousand years after the death of the Prophet had much more to do with the great dispute in religious circles between those who believed admiring beauty—male or female—to be a credible path to experiencing the divine, and those who thought it a terrible travesty. But in order to follow this line of reasoning, we should first look at developments in the history and historiography of sexuality in the Islamicate world.[3]

## CURRENT RESEARCH ON SEX AND SEXUALITY IN ISLAMICATE SOCIETIES

From hesitant beginnings in Arab and Western literature, a substantial body of research on sexuality in Islamicate societies has evolved in recent years.[4] Early attempts to discuss sexuality in Islam are marked by the effort to present Islam in a more positive light, and have to do with the struggle of intellectuals to promote the liberation of women and to address common misconceptions. In this intellectual environment, it is no wonder that scholars who sought to depict Islam as a religion compatible with modernity accepted the basic premises of modern psychology and the depiction of many Islamicate societies as sexually flawed. In an attempt to redress the bias, they offered apologetic explanations. Taking as their point of departure the essentialized depiction of an Islam formulated by the Koran and the *ḥadīth* (the deeds and sayings of the prophet Muhammad, as recorded by his friends and followers), one of the main arguments in this type of scholarship was that true Islam was a sexually enlightened religion. Through the centuries, as a result of incomprehension and distortion, its message was corrupted and gave rise to a sexually depraved society. Observe the concluding remarks of Abdelwahab Bouhdiba in his pathbreaking *Sexuality in Islam:*

> One can even speak of degradation, which began at a very early date, of an ideal model. The open sexuality, practiced in joy with a view to the fulfillment of being, gradually gave way to a closed, morose, repressed sexuality. The discovery of one's own body and that of another, the apprehension of self through the mediation of otherness, turned in the end into male selfishness. Furtive, secretive, hypocritical behaviour assumed an ever more exorbitant place. Sexual division turned into an inhuman, untenable social dimorphism and a source of untold suffering. . . . The price paid by women and by the young in the maintenance of this social status quo was a terrible one. This reification of being deprived it of all autonomy, freedom and value.[5]

What I would like to highlight here is not the claim of degradation, nor even the depiction of an entire civilization as one linear projection of its holy scriptures. It is the assumption that there must of necessity be an ideal model. What Bouhdiba refers to as an "open sexuality, practiced in joy with a view to the fulfillment of being" is, of course, an ideal of heterosexual and monogamous perfection, supposedly ordained by the Koran. Its degradation, apart from being the product of patriarchal and misogynistic forces in Islamic society, is also the process by which it is said to have given way to homoerotic tendencies and to other unorthodox sexual practices.

Bouhdiba's book, originally published in French in 1975, was the first major attempt to survey the entire field of sexuality in the world of Middle Eastern and North African Islam. A sociologist by training, Bouhdiba chooses the Koran as his point of departure and Arabo-Muslim society as his social-temporal space. The holy scriptures, he says, are based on the concept of unity and duality. The original unity (of God) evolves toward duality, manifested in the male-female couple only to be united once again in the sexual act. Marital sex is therefore the true path to sanctity, harmony, and devotion. In that context, sex is seen not only as vital, but also as constituting worship. It is part and parcel of a person's obligation toward God and in no way connotes sin for the Muslim believer as it does in Christianity. As the relation between man and woman is one of complementarity, although it recognizes the supremacy of men, true Islam honors women and does not see them, or sex with them, as impure.

This reified, original, true "Islam" thus offers a perfect sexuality, based on the union of one man and one woman, preferably joined in matrimony. All other forms of sexuality are frowned upon:

> Islam remains violently hostile to all other ways of realizing sexual desire, which are regarded as unnatural purely and simply because they run counter to the antithetical harmony of the sexes. As a result a divine curse embraces both the boyish woman and the effeminate man, male and female homophilia, auto-eroticism, zoophilia etc. All these deviations involve the same refusal to accept the sexed body and to assume the female or male condition. Sexual deviation is a revolt against God.[6]

Of all these travesties, says Bouhdiba, the Koran considers male homosexuality the worst. In a sense it stands for the essence of all perversions. The story of the prophet Lot (Lūṭ) and of his city, Sodom, destroyed by God for the sexual sins of its people, assumes central importance as a warning against this kind of atrocity. It is a violation of the order of the world and may lead to its destruction. For fear of committing the abomination of male intercourse, the segregation of the sexes almost ends up embracing the segregation of the age groups. The mere sight of pretty boys is considered too much of a danger for adult men.

But "what was unified in revelation fell apart at the historical level," Bouhdiba claims.[7] Fear of transgression and the need to set clear boundaries between the sexes, so that women and men will never assume each other's roles and subvert the sacred concord, finally led to the segregation of women and even to the devirilization of young men. This culminated in a deformed society, based on a fear of women that sometimes bordered on hatred. Islamic culture in later centuries is at base an attempt to flee from women into a homosocial male companionship and, finally, into homosexuality.

Emplotted almost as a tragedy in Bouhdiba's book, Arabo-Muslim sexuality gradually degraded, finally becoming a stage for widespread homosexuality and pederasty. The many treatises against homoerotic love, written by the *ulema* (legal scholars), only prove how widespread it was and how it pervaded society through the ages. Instead of reversing the tide, modernity continues the process of corruption of tradition, and Western colonialism has even exacerbated the situation by forcing the colonized to retreat into traditional stances as a last bastion of defense against colonial penetration. The result, according to Bouhdiba, is that modern sex in the Arabo-Muslim world is mechanical; it has broken the bond between sex and divinity and replaced it with meaningless pornography.

Perhaps in an effort to flee apologetic, sometimes homophobic, explanations such as that suggested by Bouhdiba, most other discussions of premodern Islamic sexuality center on literature. One of the most interesting discussions is found in Fedwa Malti-Douglas's book *Woman's Body, Woman's Word.* Malti-Douglas brilliantly analyzes Arabic literature from the famous *Thousand and One Nights* to the works of Nawwāl al-Saʿdāwi and Fadwa Tūqān. A succession of vivacious images and people are paraded before us: Shahrazād and Shahriyār, Hayy Ibn Yaqẓān and his adventures on a mysterious island, as well as modern protagonists and their stories. Malti-Douglas carefully examines woman's place in this literature: the metaphors and underlying assumptions governing her sexuality, her body, and her words.

Although the stories and periods vary, a common thread unites them all: the fear of woman's sexuality and her demonic power that finally results in male preference for male companionship. Betrayed by women time and time again, Shahzamān and his brother Shahriyār, the male protagonists of the frame story in *A Thousand and One Nights*, decide to avoid social contact with women and to maintain their friendship instead. They use women for sexual pleasure and then execute them, and cease these actions only when Shahrazād restores their confidence in the female sex. But even the famous Shahrazād, a symbol of female virtue and power, falls prey to this powerful homosocial world. At the end of *A Thousand and One Nights,* Shahriyār, who has now become her husband, appropriates the power of public speech. Shahrazād now takes on the traditional role of a silent wife, while the bonds between the male protagonists are preserved.

Another medieval hero, Ḥayy Ibn Yaqẓān, chooses to seclude himself with his male companion, Asāl, on an island rather than live in the world of women and their hazardous sexuality. Indeed, in a related story, the island of Waqwāq offers the ideal solution to men's problems: women who grow on trees like fruit, to be plucked, used, and thrown away, "the ultimate disposable woman."[8] Even in the later twentieth century, when women retrieved their power of speech and authors such as Nawwāl al-Saʿdāwi and Fadwa Tūqān used their own words instead of being spoken for by men, their description of society is much the same: a misogynistic male-centered society that fears women and abhors their sexuality. In the last analysis, even though very different methodologies and sources are involved, Malti-Douglas's conclusions are analogous to Bouhdiba's. Although there is no degradation here from an ideal model, there is hardly any development either. Men in modern Arab literature always prefer the company of men. Women, in contrast, are still imprisoned in their own world, are taught to worship men, and are hated by them. Their prose and poetry are essentially a cry for help and for sexual liberation. Women are marginalized, and men prefer homosocial bonds, which may sometimes lead to homosexuality.

In contrast to Bouhdiba and Malti-Douglas, whose perceptions cannot be divorced from the hetero-normal context in which they write, a recent development in studies of Islamic conceptions of sex emerges mainly from American gay studies. It is characterized by works that center on homoerotic literature (mostly male, for lack of sources discussing female homoeroticism).[9] This time the subject is treated in a more positive light. A serious study in this vein is J. W. Wright and Everett K. Rowson's edited volume *Homoeroticism in Classical Arabic Literature.*[10] A series of essays by different authors present aspects of homoerotic prose and poetry in Arabic literature from the Abbasid to the Mamluk period.

Rowson's article in the volume describes two Mamluk works written in the 1300s by Ibn Dāniyāl and al-Ṣafadi.[11] Al-Ṣafadi's work, more reserved in its tone, depicts a (probably) consummated love affair between two men that ends with the tragic departure of the beloved. The more audacious Ibn Daniyāl, in a stylish play intended for the shadow theater, also describes a homoerotic quest, but in this story the lover's ploys are to no avail. His beloved refuses his advances and flees. Instead, the forlorn lover encounters a series of people with different sexualities offering their favors: effeminate men, catamites, gropers, and masturbators. It is interesting to note that in both stories the beloved, though young, is not a beardless boy but a fully developed young man. Although both writers pay lip service to morality, they are also straightforward in their discussion of homoerotic love.

In his analysis of the stories, Rowson, like other contributors to the volume, considers the relationship of this literature to the historical context that enabled its production:

> As for the reality that lies behind these excursions, both texts presuppose a society in which male erotic attraction to males, in some form, is assumed to be natural and, if not universal, sufficiently widespread to be treated on its own terms rather than as a "marked" minority version of an "unmarked" heterosexual eroticism. At the same time, this society puts constraints on homosexual eroticism (again, not presented as differing in either intensity or nature from those on heterosexual eroticism) that encourage its treatment in terms of either sublimated frustration or antinomian indulgence.[12]

In the works of Bouhdiba, Malti-Douglas, and Wright and Rowson, historical research has moved from an apologetic mode to a more balanced one or even to one that is more empathetic to Arabo-Muslim sexual culture. Whereas Bouhdiba described Islamic sexuality in terms of continuing degradation, Malti-Douglas characterizes it as static and fundamentally misogynistic, and Rowson describes it perhaps as more liberal. Otherwise, all seem to agree on some basic premises. Heterosexuality was a matter of necessity, perhaps, but not lauded. Love was more frequently conceived as a homosocial or homoerotic pursuit than a heteroerotic one, and in the sexual scheme women were marginalized.

## METHODOLOGICAL CONSIDERATIONS

When discussing sex, one approach is to look at actual cases of sexual behavior: anecdotes about kings and sultans, court cases describing sexual transgressions, and the like. But interesting though they may be, such anecdotes rarely provide insight into the way society viewed these acts and transgressions, and, more important, what exactly about them was seen as peculiar, deviant, or as violating the law.[13] Rather than try to describe how people actually behaved in bed, a hardly viable task in many cases, the historian can look at practices in the light of discussions of sex: at questions that bothered authors, at power relations that made sense or nonsense of sexual preferences, and at the sets of belief that permitted certain things and prohibited others.

Although works of fiction, such as *A Thousand and One Nights,* are as valid a source as any for cultural research, they present some pitfalls for researchers who try to look for historical "reality" in the texts. The relations are complex, certainly where a topic such as sexuality is concerned. Praise for the beauty of young boys was a common trope, at which poets were expected to excel regardless of their own sexual inclinations. Descriptions of male love were sometimes used as a metaphor for religious devotion or even as an attempt to criticize strict moralists in society. Tropes and poetic license, style and convention, all serve to obfuscate social reality and to produce a discourse that distorts as much as it reveals. J. W. Wright discusses this point in his article examining poetry in the Abbasid court.[14] He notes that in many studies of this type of literature, a misunderstanding of the cultural context may lead to false conclusions. For one thing, he says, there is reason to believe that reference to women was considered more scandalous than reference to boys and was sometimes avoided in order to refrain from touching on delicate matters. There was also a stylistic appeal that a naïve reading of the text may fail to yield, of equating text with antitext, moral with immoral:

> In the end we see that Abu Nuwās and his contemporaries [Abbasid poets] used homoerotic conventions, symbols and motifs to create satirical chaos in the early ʿAbbāsid courts. Speculating about the poets' personal proclivities may be of interest to some, but it is time poorly spent. We do not know the poet's sexual needs or preferences, and even if we did, Western detractors' fascination with the East's supposed attachment to pederasty is beside the point and lacks cultural context.[15]

One should therefore take precautions when trying to reconstruct a historical reality based on such texts. In order to sharpen the image, other sources should be studied to supplement those that are purely literary, and another perspective should be sought that takes into consideration the contextual aspects of cultural production.

Several scholars have begun to make use of such a methodology, or at least to examine other types of sources. As described earlier, Rowson's source is an important shadow play written in Egypt in the early fourteenth century. Although it is part of a wider literary discussion of homoeroticism, a play is a different form of art, and since it is intended to be presented in public, it should be seen as part of a different discursive field, with another set of conventions and a different relation to the context (a point that Rowson does not elaborate). In the same volume, Steven M. Oberhelman discusses dream interpretation literature.[16] Considered scientific knowledge in many parts of the premodern world, these texts evolved from ancient Greek origins and continued to proliferate through translations and original contributions in many Islamicate societies. Representing an important layer of sexual consciousness, it is also a source largely untapped for the study of sexuality.

In an earlier book, Basim Musallam made an important contribution to the array of sources at the disposal of researchers and suggested another path for the study of sexuality.[17] Musallam showed that medieval Muslim scholars debated the permissibility of contraception in the form of coitus interruptus. The debate had its foundations both in the science of medicine/biology, where issues of procreation and fetus formation were deliberated, and in the science of legal jurisprudence *(fiqh)*. In the absence of a clear ruling on contraception in the Koran and the *ḥadīth,* scholars resorted to the teachings of medicine and chose to adopt a medical theory that saw fetus formation as a joint man-woman venture, in contrast to another theory, which assumed that males contributed much more to the creation of the fetus. Combined with a belief in predestination, this enabled most jurists to rule in favor of contraception. Musallam is more controversial when he moves from these intellectual debates favoring contraception to social history. In later chapters, in a clear attempt to address issues on the agenda of many modern third-world states, he discusses the effect such a policy of contraception might have had on demography. His contention is that it limited population growth to some extent. Although this point remains moot, his book demonstrates the importance of the study of fields such as jurisprudence, medicine, and philosophy for understanding sexuality.

Musallam's is one of very few attempts to discuss medical, philosophical, or even legal sources dealing with sexuality and gender problems. One important study written in this vein was an article by Paula Sanders, titled "Gendering the Ungendered Body."[18] Focusing on the status of hermaphrodites in Islam, Sanders too combines medical and legal knowledge. For Islamic orthodoxy of the first centuries, with its clear demarcation of male and female spheres at home, in prayer, and even in death, hermaphrodites presented an almost insurmountable difficulty. Religion designated no social space for an ungendered human. By describing the combination of medical efforts to determine the primary sex and of juristic measures to create social venues for the undetermined hermaphrodite, Sanders convincingly shows us how questions of sex and gender were dealt with in medieval Islamic jurisprudence.

As Rowson's, Oberhelman's, Musallam's, and Sanders's use of theater, dream interpretation literature, medicine, and legal texts illustrates, a new store of sources may be at our disposal to enrich the study of sexuality and gender. Given this wealth of material, how can we best utilize it to understand sexual relations and transformations in attitudes and practices? One possibility is a microhistorical study of sources. Systematic microstudies may teach us about the specific sexual ventures, temptations, and tribulations of a sultan, a poet (bearing in mind the reservations stated earlier), or, in rare cases, someone who left a candid diary—provided, of course, that the researcher is able to cut through the many layers of righteousness, deceit, false rumor, or even libel that often accompany discussions of sex. Yet especially when it comes to these always sensitive issues, it would require a leap of faith to assume that such case studies could somehow represent the mores, attractions, or beliefs of larger segments of society. We must look for an approach that, while focused and attuned to nuance, also allows us to look beyond the individual case and see the entire discursive world of sexuality in a given society.

Taking these examples and methodological considerations as its point of departure, this book presents several sets of discourse on sex that were prevalent in Ottoman Muslim society from its earliest days to the modern period. Among the texts it examines are those of the legal system, the flourishing literature on morality, medicine and its ancillary disciplines, the subversive and anarchic shadow theater, and dream interpretation literature in its many variations. Another vantage point, external, critical, and yet influential, may be found in travel literature written by outsiders visiting the Ottoman Empire. All these genres, including travelogues, were interrelated and may be conceived of as parts of one sexual meta-discourse. Yet each also had its own internal logic, which did not always correspond fully to that of other clusters.

The basic concept guiding this book resembles in many ways the idea of "scripts" put forward by John Gagnon and applied by Jeffrey Weeks to historical research.[19] Scripts, as Gagnon suggests, are a metaphor for the internal and external blueprints in our minds for sexual quest and sexual actions. We all have in our minds, like scripts for movies or plays, these outlines that suggest the "right" kind of sexual attraction, the expected course of action, and the anticipated outcome of our actions. These scripts offer us a set of guidelines, which we do not necessarily follow but which allows us to recognize the parameters, the borders, within which we act and the points at which we transgress prescribed boundaries. Weeks points out that "there is another value to the metaphor. It suggests that there are a variety of possible sexual meanings coexisting at any one time."[20] In the modern world, we are constantly exposed to rival scripts: in church, in court, at the cinema and on television, in medical texts, and in popular knowledge. It would be reasonable to expect that in earlier periods a similar proliferation of scripts existed. There was never a completely unified view of sexuality, no single coherent internal or external voice to guide people through the socio-sexual maze. The choice of scripts may have been more restricted, and the power of some obviously stronger than that of others. But there is no doubt that Karagöz, the rude and outspoken hero of the Ottoman shadow play, suggested to his audience a totally different script than the one offered by the quarter's preacher at Friday prayers, and neither would fully correspond to the one upheld by state law. Yet just as gay movements and conservative authorities today may be divided on the issue of the permissibility of same-sex marriage while accepting the basic division into heterosexual and homosexual, underlying all these different subdiscourses in the premodern period was a basic understanding of the human body and its sexuality. One of the aims of this book is to show how this set of assumptions was broken down in the nineteenth century and hardly ever replaced with a new set of scripts and discussions.

## THE OTTOMAN MIDDLE EAST

Spatially, the focus of this book is the Ottoman Middle East. *Ottoman* here does not necessarily mean Turkish-speaking, or even always under Ottoman political control. I propose to see it as a discursive world at the center of which stood the Ottoman dynasty, which had governed most of it politically and culturally since the early sixteenth century. It is my contention that this world, stretching from North Africa through the Arabic-speaking lands of the Fertile Crescent and into Anatolia, united to some extent by religion and culture, shared the same text-based sexual outlook. Some of these textual products, such as Karagöz or state law, originated in the imperial center. Others, such as dream interpretation, had a more pronounced presence in the Arab world. Yet here too there was an underlying unity, strengthened by the constant translation of texts (mainly from Arabic to Ottoman Turkish, but also in the opposite direction) and by the free movement of the intellectual elite among urban centers. No doubt there were differences among such centers and their outlooks, but there was also a great deal of similarity, and it is this fundamental similarity that I would like to pursue.

I also believe that in discussing discourses of sex, a long-durée historical method is required, which may sometimes be mistaken for an essentialist approach. Just as in Europe the one-sex model persisted for almost two millennia with only minute changes, so in the Ottoman Middle East medical, religious, and legal concepts held sway for long periods of time, with slow, sometimes imperceptible changes. In order to see these developments and to understand the significance of change, at some points our discussion will take us away from the Ottoman period to the early centuries of Islam or even to Greek antiquity.

Yet clearly even at the center there was never a single, consistent, and fully coherent culture to the exclusion of all others. Hegemonic views, which occupied the core, were constantly at odds with other views at the margin. Heterodox groups, religious and ethnic minorities, and the socially unprivileged developed contending discourses. These were sometimes very different from prevalent ones. Although this book is mainly concerned with the unifying components and therefore with prevailing views, it attempts not to lose sight of the cultural margins and the discourses they produced.

## THE SCRIPTS AND THEIR SOURCES

Our starting point, in chapter 1, will be the script of the body. Equally distant from divine and human law, from the "juridico-discursive mechanisms" and from the longing of Sufi poets, medicine and its conception of the human body were ostensibly governed by the laws of nature. In the tradition of Galen and Ibn Sina, physicians in the Ottoman Middle East operated until well into the nineteenth century under the ancient axiomatic idea that four elements represented in the human body by four humors governed and balanced our physical and emotional constitution. Their anatomy offered a different and, from our point of view, outrageous model of human bodies and their reproductive organs. These medical concepts and theories had an important bearing on questions of sexuality and provided explanations for problems such as gender formation and sexual inclinations, prowess, impotence, deviation, and procreation. As a result of the high esteem in which medicine was held throughout most of the period, popularized traces of medical theory were used by many other discursive sets to substantiate their own sexual scripts.

Influenced by *ulema* and their conceptual world, though more attuned to the changing mores of the period, state law, discussed in chapter 2, was strictly applied in courts for a short period of time, mainly in the sixteenth century, but had an impact on lawmaking for a much longer span of time. Imperial *kanunnāme*s, collections of laws and directives sent to courts throughout the empire, included sections on proper and improper sexual conduct, recommended sanctions for certain acts, and even suggested a pecuniary scale of fines according to the gravity of the felony. *Kanunnāme* compilations indicate the emergence of a different legal perspective on sex in the Ottoman elite. Formulated by the sultan and his leading servants, they represented ruling-class attitudes about sexual morality perhaps more than any other script available to the public. Yet the two main systems, *şeriat* and *kanun,* also created a kind of synergy to produce a manifestation of power, which, as Foucault rightly observes, did not merely repress sex, but through its various mechanisms—courts, legal formulas, judges, punishments—also produced and constituted desire. In other words, by creating the binary oppositions of right and wrong, licit and illicit, law had a major influence on definitions of sexual mores. This influence is evident, explicitly or implicitly, in all other discourses.[21]

Chapter 3 examines the devotional script in its two major representations: Sufi and orthodox. Since well into the nineteenth century a secular outlook had no legitimacy or cultural content in the Muslim Middle East, religiosity was ubiquitous and all discussions of sex were, in a certain sense, religious. The word *devotional* here is therefore convenient shorthand to describe the texts of *ulema* and initiated Sufis that relate to sexual concerns of faith, ritual, and performance. Perhaps contrary to our expectations, of all the scripts presented in this work, the devotional one was the most ambivalent and the least coherent. Religious texts are not limited to the sacred law and are not a uniform body of literature. Rather, within defined boundaries, they were a constantly changing discursive world. Throughout the centuries, *ulema* and Sufis wrote copiously on questions of sexuality. Their writings ranged from legal tracts on marriage and divorce, sodomy, and fornication, to collections of the Prophet's sayings *(ḥadīth)* and legal opinions *(fatwa),* to poems of devotion, and even to tracts extolling the beauty of young boys as a way to imagine the magnificence of the divine. Never easy to define, constantly shifting, and often merging at the seams to blur clear definitions, Sufi writings and their orthodox counterparts still present at their core two very different attitudes toward sex. For most of the period under discussion, the two waged a sometimes violent battle for primacy.

In fact, one could say that orthodox treatises and the more radical kind of Sufi literature should be discussed as two separate scripts. Indeed, in most modern scholarship they are seen as two distinct bodies of thought and are seldom discussed together. But although this separation has certain advantages from an analytical point of view, it also has a number of drawbacks. This is where al-Shaʿbi's story, with which we began our discussion, would fit. Although the seventeenth-century author who retells the story was an adherent of a Sufi brotherhood and a scion of a well-known Sufi family in Jerusalem, in its outward appearance this is an orthodox text. The treatise he wrote is a concentrated assault on Sufi adoration of beardless boys. It contains quotations of the Prophet and the four righteous caliphs, legal considerations, and reasoned explanations. But, as we could see in the ʿAbd al-Qays story, it also conveys the author's own understanding of human sexuality, which shares many basic assumptions with that of the Sufis he attacks so vehemently. The terms he uses are similar, and in many cases, so are the questions and the sources. In their debates, radical Sufis and the *ulema* who opposed them produced the same sexual script. Another point we should keep in mind is that from outside the world of *ulema* and initiates, from a layman's point of view, it was probably harder to understand the subtleties of the discussion. Both parties were revered and respected by most for their erudition and devotion. The message transmitted to society at large must have been a single, albeit equivocal, one.

Psychology and psychiatry were not established medical disciplines in the early modern Middle Eastern world, of course, but interesting discussions regarding the human psyche are to be found in the very rich literature on dream interpretation, explored in chapter 4. Since dreams were believed to manifest special prophetic powers, their interpretation was recognized as a science even by the *ulema*. A voluminous oneiric literature developed in which sexual dreams and their meanings figure prominently. It is here that the most blatant and overt connections between sex and power were often made. There is another difference between dream interpretations and the scripts previously discussed. Whereas knowledge of the law and of religious discourse was generally the domain of the elite and in many ways also represented elite values, dream interpretation books allow us at least a superficial glimpse of the lives of more popular classes. In the introduction to dream interpretation books, authors often emphasize the importance of gathering information from a variety of people from different social strata.

A more vivid description of popular views on sexuality is presented by the actual scripts of plays, mainly from the shadow theater known as Karagöz, discussed in chapter 5. This popular form of entertainment, employing translucent puppets against a backlit screen, was always very bold, even rude, as European travelers frequently described it. The sexual world it depicted was uninhibited, its social space teeming with sexual activity, its women powerful, and its manner of discussing sex and sexual morality often shameless and unrelenting. The theatrical sphere calls for an investigation of the relationship between popular and elite culture and between theater and reality. Could these shadows have represented for society a sexual alternative, one more promiscuous and uninhibited? Did they serve as a warning against the disintegration of public morality, or did they represent a potentially viable social reality?

All these textual and nontextual manifestations of sexuality were reflected, refracted, interpreted, and distorted through the writings of European travelers and researchers. For centuries this literature evolved as a special kind of discourse, separated from all others. Based on constant comparisons with their own changing sexual world, European authors created in the minds of their readers fascinating, if skewed, displays of "Islamic" sexuality, traces of which are still apparent in modern research on the topic. But European travel literature should not be examined exclusively from the point of view of its impact on Western images of the Orient. Translations of popular travelogues into Arabic and Turkish, as well as the rapidly spreading use of French and other European languages, introduced travelers' conceptions and misconceptions to local elites, with shattering results, as we shall see in chapter 6.

Premodern sexuality was not static. Most of the scripts mentioned here were in constant flux in the premodern period, with the Ottoman era representing but one phase in a dynamic process of transformation. In the nineteenth century, however, the pace of change quickened: new legal codes of Western origin replaced the *şeriat* and the *kanun;* Sufi practices and doctrines were sometimes banned by centralizing governments, while the importance of their more orthodox counterparts diminished as a result of growing secularism; modern medical theory and practice replaced the older theoretical construction and brought with it a new attitude to sexual matters; dreams no longer appeared to have the same magical power of foresight, and their traditional interpretations were felt to be inadequate; a public introduced to modern theater and the movies neglected shadow theater and replaced it with new forms of visual entertainment; new media—the modern novel, magazine, advertisement, and recorded song and music—appeared on the scene.

Strangely, the disintegration of old sexual scripts and the availability of new ones, mostly from the West, did not give rise to a different set of local scripts or to a different sexual discourse. Instead, as the nineteenth century progressed, the Ottoman Middle East seemed to shirk almost all prevalent forms of text-based sexual discourse and to retreat into embarrassed silence. The last part of the book is an attempt to provide a partial explanation for this phenomenon.

CHAPTER I

# The Body Sexual

## *Medicine and Physiognomy*

Medicine, its conceptions of the human body, and the sexual script it produced provided the scientific basis for most sex-oriented discourses in Muslim Middle Eastern societies. Its injunctions and prohibitions, believed to originate in scientific knowledge, were subsumed by other discursive arenas, from literature to sacred law, almost intuitively, as part of their basic assumptions about the world.[1] This was true as long as these discourses could maintain a common coherent basis, but the changes brought about by new medical knowledge at the end of the eighteenth and throughout the nineteenth centuries created a rift between this and other arenas in which sexual matters were discussed.

This chapter traces the basic theories and concepts of traditional Ottoman Middle Eastern medicine as they relate to male and female sexuality, to the sexual and asexual body, and to the mechanics of sex. Medical developments throughout the period, culminating in major changes in the nineteenth century, brought about a crisis of discourse. As I hope to demonstrate, the discrepancy between changes in medical knowledge and in other discourses created an unresolved tension in the array of sexual scripts, which resulted in confusion and a sense of foreboding.

### MEDICINE'S AUTHORITATIVE VOICE

Medicine's image as a set of cosmologically anchored, almost divine scientific facts gave its texts, specifically those based on the Galenic tradition, a unique standing in society before the modern period. While other disciplines, such as dream interpretation lore, were believed to be inferior manifestations of the word of God as interpreted by the *ulema,* medicine had become a powerful discourse with an autonomous status. The period's authors recognized this status in their classifications of the sciences.[2] In some respects, we can even say that medicine's standing rivaled that of religion. God's message was given in many different and contradictory voices. Orthodox *sunna* may have been the officially sanctioned norm in many cases, but Sufi sects of all hues, and other Islamic groups, proposed different, sometimes conflicting interpretations of religion, thus posing a constant challenge to orthodoxy's claim of axiomatic truth. Medicine, in contrast, seemed to the lay public almost unequivocal, despite outside challenges and arguments among physicians about medical methods. Tensions between common medicine and prophetic traditions, which never assumed center stage, were already resolved to a large extent by the fifteenth century.[3] Thanks to the efforts of Ibn Qayyim al-Jawzīyya, Jalāl al-Dīn al-Suyūṭī, and their contemporaries in the fourteenth and fifteenth centuries, few voices of dissent or doubt disrupted medicine's authoritative voice.[4] Its message, seemingly unconcerned with relative morality, commanded special authority, almost reverence. When looked at as a sexual script, pre-nineteenth-century medicine became a major voice in the discursive world of educated social groups.

Furthermore, since the dominant medical system throughout most of the period espoused a holistic view that created interdependence among the cosmos, the elements, the soul, the body, and its constituent parts, it was fully compatible with a religious view of the universe and man's place within it. While elements and humors were the prevalent theoretical currency, medical discourse also allocated limited space to divine intervention, through the several souls that animated the body and made it function. Thus it did not appear to counter religious knowledge or to threaten its standing, and over the years a clear modus vivendi was established to safeguard the boundaries between manmade science and God's absolute truth.

## OTTOMAN MEDICINE AND ITS TRANSFORMATIONS

Throughout the centuries, incremental changes in the Islamicate world, notably by famous physicians such as al-Rāzi, Ibn Sina, and Ibn al-Nafīs, along with many others, largely transformed the basic corpus of ancient

Greek and Roman medical knowledge, changing practical aspects of diagnosis and treatment and making invaluable contributions to the development of medical sciences.[5] With time, Galen's revised concepts became much more than a medical theory. In the manner of a paradigm in the Kuhnian sense, Galenic medicine had become a set of basic assumptions, ideologies and cosmologies, tools and methods, as well as a set of queries and a specific terminology, all of which created an enclosed medical world.

This is not to say that the theory was unchallenged. In the Ottoman world, curative knowledge was multifaceted and eclectic. Practitioners of medical systems prevalent in the Byzantine world and in Safavid Iran shared the stage with those specializing in Indian and Far Eastern methods. A place of honor was reserved for a set of vague medical ideas based on the Koran and the *ḥadīth* (known in Arabic as *al-ṭibb al-nabawī,* prophetic medicine) alongside popular medical practices performed by Sufis and other mystics believed to be endowed with healing powers. Yet only humoral medicine enjoyed official support and privilege, as well as the endorsement of the intellectual elite. Such popular medical concepts may have held sway in the minds of many people or may have been preferred as methods for treating disease, but intellectually (and therefore textually) they remained on the cultural fringes, vying for right of entry but never quite achieving it. Only physicians proficient in Galenic medicine attended to the sultans' health, practiced their craft in major city hospitals, formed important guilds, and compiled most of the medical treatises.

We know little about the origins of the Ottoman medical tradition. The first Ottoman authors of medical texts were residents of Anatolia who found their way to other cultural centers in the Middle East, such as Cairo and Tabriz, and returned home as physicians. One of the earliest medical texts in Turkish was a pharmaceutical treatise, *Khawāṣ al-adwiya,* composed by a little-known author, Murād Ibn Isḥāq. A later author, Celaleddin Hızır, known as Haci Paşa (d. 1412), began his religious studies in Egypt, switched to medicine after an illness, and was later appointed head physician in Cairo's hospital *(maristān).* He wrote several books, including an original one on disease and cure *(Shifa al-asqām wa-dawā' al-ālām)* around 1380. In addition to the basic tenets of Galenic medicine, this book contains many observations from the author's own experience, including a detailed study of pneumonia and its symptoms. Later, Haci Paşa wrote a few books in Turkish, including *Teshilü'ṣ-ṣifa,* an abridged and simplified adaptation of Ibn Sina's *Qānūn,* which became quite popular in the Ottoman Empire and was later translated into German.[6] Ibn al-Nafis's great work, *Al-mūjiz* (on which more later), was translated into Turkish around the same time as *Ḥall al-shifa*, by Cemalüddin Aksarayı (d. 1388).[7] These works placed Ottoman medicine squarely in the great ancient Roman-Islamicate tradition and set the stage for this scientific paradigm in following centuries. Even later works, such as Şerefeddin Sabuncuoğlu's famous treatise on surgery, *Cerrāhiyyetü'l-haniyye,* are in fact translations or adaptations of earlier famous works in that tradition.[8]

In Western Europe the paradigm had been gradually eroded in the sixteenth and seventeenth centuries, giving rise to the basic precepts of modern medicine in the eighteenth. But while such transformations occurred in Europe, the Ottoman world felt secure in its knowledge, and the paradigm was not deeply shaken. Humoral medicine remained paramount well into the nineteenth century.

Yet physicians and theorists in the Ottoman world never ceased to discuss, develop, and advance medical theories and empiric studies. True, their forays outside classical humoral medicine were few, short, and far between, but the period's physicians wrote sophisticated experimental tractates based on accumulated experience and knowledge gathered from other medical cultures both within and outside the borders of the Islamic world. Quite a few books of medicine were written in the Middle East from the fifteenth to the nineteenth centuries. They ranged from medical encyclopedias based on Ibn Sina's famous *Qānūn* to special treatises on topics such as eye treatment, surgical operations, contraception, and sexology.

In the sixteenth century new medical knowledge was introduced, mainly in relation to the treatment of New World diseases such as syphilis, but these treatments were integrated with relative ease into the old system. A few decades later, several local physicians were influenced by the Swiss physician Paracelsus's ideas about experimentation in medicine, as well as by his critique of humoral concepts. Paracelsus (1493–1541) opposed humoral medicine and noted hereditary patterns. He also believed that the body was reducible to minerals (sulfur, salt, and mercury) and therefore curable by using chemical-based drugs. Another emphasis of Paracelsian medicine, perhaps more crucial to our investigation, was the study of bodily tissues that connect and separate body parts. At the time this did not amount to much as far as medical praxis was concerned, but it certainly gave physicians a new and challenging theory to debate. One such physician is Sāliḥ Ibn Naṣrallah Ibn Sallūm (d. 1670), a native of Aleppo who was the head physician *(hekimbaşı)* of the empire at the time of Sultan Mehmet IV (r. 1648–1687).[9] His treatise *Ghāyat al-Itqān fī Tadbīr Badan al-Insān,* in which he devotes a chapter to the medical ideas of Paracelsus, gained some fame in the empire during the second half of the seventeenth century. A few years later, Ömer Şifai of Bursa (d. 1742), a devout Sufi and one of the greatest physicians of his time, wrote several innovative books. Most notably, he translated some of the writings of Paracelsus and wrote an eight-volume book titled *Jawāhir al-farīd fī al-ṭibb al-jadīd* (Unique Gems of the New Medicine) describing some of the new discoveries of European medicine.[10]

The outcome of these scholarly forays appears to have been a rejection of Paracelsian medicine, as is evident from the fact that Ibn Sallum's chapter on Paracelsus was not translated into Turkish and that few others developed the new concepts and practices described in Şifai's books. Further attempts to investigate the Paracelsian approach and other budding European medical ideas, such as translations into Turkish of treatises written by the Dutchman Herman Boerhaave (d. 1738), met with a similar fate. In his book on Ottoman science, Adnan Adıvar suggests that while Galenic medicine was still officially supported and sanctioned, presumably by court officials, there was an awareness of new medical approaches in external medical circles. Later, in the eighteenth century, advances were made in the study of disease, mainly in Vesim Abbas's *Düstūr-ı Vesim fi tibbi'l cedīd ve'l-kadīm,* in which he reached the conclusion that certain diseases were infectious through contact.[11] In another field, that of anatomy, Al-ʿItāqi's *Tashrīḥ al-abdān,* written around 1632, seems to have been modeled on the work of Andrea Vesalius (1514–1562) and his famous book, *Fabrica.* Indeed, several figures in copies of al-ʿItāqi's *Tashrīḥ* seem to have been adapted from Vesalius, and some of the material on human anatomy is clearly the result of new Renaissance knowledge.[12]

But by and large Ottoman medicine remained unconvinced of such new ideas and attached to its Galenic roots. Until well into the nineteenth century, most physicians theorized on this basis.[13] Perhaps the clearest demonstration of this adherence is the fact that Ibn Sina's *Qānūn* was fully translated into Ottoman Turkish only in the late eighteenth century, albeit with comments and several additions. If early modern European ideas influenced local medical knowledge, it had to do with breaking the holistic view of the body and its parts as a reflection of the cosmos and its elements. One of the possible outcomes of such a change may have been a stronger emphasis on the body, as opposed to the earlier emphasis on its constituent parts. Discoveries in anatomy and Paracelsian discussions about the attributes of common tissue and membrane, rather than singular organs such as the lungs, the heart, and the liver, may have assisted in transforming the view of the body from an assembly of organs into an integrated whole.

Real paradigmatic change began to appear only with the upheavals of nineteenth-century reforms, when translations and adaptations of new European knowledge made their way to the core of the medical profession. One of the first books to spark this revolution was Ataullah Şanizade's compendium *Hamse-i şanizade,* a series of five books published in Ottoman Turkish from 1820 onward, incorporating new medical knowledge from Europe. Şanizade (d. 1826) was a brilliant and innovative physician and theorist (as well as musician, astronomer, and historian) who did much to integrate new medical knowledge with the old. His views on medicine encountered much opposition, mainly because of his support for surgery-based study of anatomy. As a result his request to dedicate his chef d'oeuvre to Sultan Mahmud II was denied. In time, however, the compendium came to replace the earlier canonic texts, and was fondly named *kanun-i şanizade* (Şanizade's canon), referring, of course, to the old master's *Qānūn.*[14]

Although the compendium formally adhered to the humoral system and other concepts of ancient medicine, it was here that blood circulation was mentioned for the first time as a scientific concept and as part of a different medical theory. Some of the terminology included in this book formed the basis for a new medical profession that was beginning to take shape.[15] At the same time (1827), the first school of medicine was established by Mahmud II in Istanbul, and it was reorganized several years later by a group of Viennese physicians invited to the Ottoman court. In Egypt, Clot Bey, Mehmet Ali's French chief physician, published books similar to those of Şanizade and brought modern medicine to readers of Arabic. Here too, a medical school was founded in 1828 under the tutelage of European physicians, to be followed a few years later by a similar school in Tehran.

In the 1840s, Charles White reported: "The Ottomans have now overcome their prejudices in other matters connected with the therapeutic and pathological sciences. Subjects are now freely furnished to the school of anatomy. . . . Abdullah Efendi proposed, and Tahir Pacha readily directed, that the bodies of all convicts, dying in the bagnio, should be sent to Galata Serai for the purposes of dissection, and this without distinction of creed."[16] By the late nineteenth century, with most medical studies being undertaken in European languages (mainly French), the transformation, at least in the main centers, seemed to be well advanced.[17]

## UNDERSTANDING THE BODY

In certain cultures the body is understood to be simply the sum total of all its parts: eyes, hair, heart, limbs, and so on. In others, it is seen as a more complex entity, of which the soul or mind is an essential element. Assuming the existence of a sensual or "desiring soul" (Arabic *al-nafs al-shahwaniyya,* Turkish *nefs-i şehevi*), Islamicate medical tracts written in the Roman-Islamicate tradition assigned sexual attributes and libidinal urges not to a soul divorced from body, but to one that springs from the body's elemental composition (fire, air, water, and earth) and reflects its humoral balance.[18] Thus the body, by virtue of its composing substances rather than any divinely appointed soul, would have a strong or weak sexual urge, a feminine or masculine, active or passive, penetrating or penetrated type of sexuality.

Such a mode of thinking shuns the role of the body as an autonomous unit that stands apart from the world around it and that is also distinguished from its constituent elements. The body is a relatively minor link in the great chain of being, an integral part of a larger system encompassing the cosmos, its elements, the humors that represent them, human limbs and organs orchestrated by these humors, the blood and semen formed by them, and so on. Originating in this all-inclusive cosmological theory, classical Ottoman medical tracts were concerned with relations among cosmic elements, body parts, and sexual drive. Physical motivating forces of sexual desire, the interrelated operation of sexual organs, and the organic differences between male and female sexualities were manifestations of an all-encompassing nature.

This view also envisioned man and woman as part of a continuum of perfection, leading from the basest creatures to the celestial. Man in this scheme of things was the crowning achievement of terrestrial creatures, whereas woman was regarded as a less-developed version of man, physically and mentally. This perception of the man-woman nexus was manifest, first and foremost, in sexual comparisons. Female sex organs and the mechanical functioning of female sex were believed to be flawed versions of the male.

Describing a similar conception in premodern Europe, Thomas Laqueur defines it as a "one-sex" model and proceeds to prove that men and women were believed to have different versions of the same sexual organs until well into the eighteenth century. Laqueur was criticized for his claim that this was the only mode of understanding the relationship between men's and women's genitalia in European medical discourse. Cadden and others have shown that alongside this conception there were other, more nuanced ones. It appears that a similar idea of sexual resemblance was also prevalent in Ottoman period medicine. Yet the term *one-sex* is a misnomer that, at least in the Middle Eastern context, obfuscates the main point: women, though of the same sex, were seen as biologically inferior. As will be demonstrated later, in medical treatises women's sexual organs were indeed understood to resemble those of men, but they were also believed to be an inherently flawed version, manifesting, as it were, woman's lower place in the chain of being. Rather than "one-sex," this set of ideas should be defined as the "woman as imperfect man" model, or, for short, the "imperfect-man" model.[19]

This model presents itself in descriptions of the operation of sex, in graphic illustrations of the sexual organs, and even in terminology. Terms such as semen (Arabic *mani,* Turkish *meni*), testicles *(khisi, khāya),* and semen ducts *(sharāyīn mani)* were used to describe male and female organs and secretions alike. The boundaries between them, as far as biology was concerned, were blurred and could sometimes be traversed, as when, for example, a woman would grow a penislike clitoris and turn into a quasi-man.

Imperfect-man conceptions also meant that if women were almost men, and if sexual organs were liable to change under certain circumstances, then the difference between men and women was one of quantity rather than total opposition. It follows (though it was never actually stated) that sex between men and women may have been conceived of, mentally, in a very different manner than our modern discourse conceives it. In other words, the absence of a distinct two-sex model implied that there was no deep, inherent difference between homo- and heterosexuality. It also followed that having what we would now view as same-sex relations need not be a travesty, at least as far as "nature" was concerned.

Yet there was one difference, it seems, between Western European attitudes and Ottoman Middle Eastern ones. For most Islamicate societies, such sexual transformations from feminine to masculine were to be avoided at all costs. Precisely because corporeal boundaries are so unstable, because the world can so easily slide into anarchy, women (by gender) were to be kept women (by sex) even when such transformations took place. Men were to remain men even if surgery was called for to remove their femaleness. Much of the legal discourse was therefore devoted to the erection of boundaries and to defining maleness and femaleness in indistinct cases.[20]

In Western Europe, mainly during the eighteenth century, these perceptions changed radically, and the two-sex model that we are familiar with today became the paramount paradigm. But even when these modern medical practices and theories were introduced to the Middle East a century later and incorporated into medical treatises in Arabic and Ottoman, the texts remained ambiguous, clinging to earlier imperfect-man interpretations. This, as we shall see, created a discrepancy between the medical theory of sex, on the one hand, and the growing discomfort with same-sex relations on the other.

## ELEMENTS, HUMORS, AND SEX

Male and female sex, sexual behavior, and the spectrum of sexual attraction and rejection were based primarily on the humoral makeup of each human being. We must therefore begin with a short description of the humoral system as it was understood and practiced in the Ottoman era.

Until the nineteenth century, the basic tenets of traditional medicine as presented in Ibn Sina's compendium were the baseline of medical knowledge. For practical purposes, doctors mostly referred to the Qānūn's famous abridgement and complement, *Kitāb al-Mūjiz,* written by Ibn al-Nafīs in the thirteenth century and translated into Ottoman Turkish by the physician Ahi Çelebi in the sixteenth.[21] The theory still held sway as late as the early nineteenth century in the main medical centers of the Ottoman and Iranian Qajar empires.[22] According to the tenets of humoral medicine, human bodies were composed of four elements (*arkān* in Arabic)—earth, water, air, and fire—represented by four humors flowing in the body *(akhlāṭ, amzija)*—black bile, phlegm, blood, and yellow bile, respectively, to which several human attributes corresponded (see table 1).[23] Over the years physicians improved on the theory and the praxis, often incorporating findings from medical literature in Europe and India, and certainly expanding the rudimentary elemental system to account for the many variations of the human condition. Table 1 demonstrates how wide-reaching and omnipresent assumptions about the humoral balance of the body had become.

Early Hippocratic and Galenic theory assumed the need for a precise balance among the humors (*iʿtidāl* in Arabic) to enable the human body to function properly. Whenever this single balance was upset *(khurūj ʿan al-iʿtidāl),* the person would develop symptoms of illness, and only restor-

TABLE 1. ELEMENTS, HUMORS, AND THEIR ATTRIBUTES

| Element | Humor | Attributes | Gender | Age (Masculine) | Social Group | Sexuality (in Males) |
|---|---|---|---|---|---|---|
| Fire | Yellow bile | Hot and dry | Male | Adolescence | Rulers/ soldiers | Sexual |
| Air | Blood | Hot and humid | N/A | Adulthood | Clerics | Sexual |
| Earth | Black bile | Cold and dry | N/A | Old age | Peasants | Nonsexual |
| Water | Phlegm | Cold and humid | Female | | | Nonsexual |

NOTE: In all tables, empty cells indicate that the *şeriat* and *kanun* law did not address the relevant categories.

ing the balance of the elements and the humors could restore complete health. Leeches were used to draw a dangerous excess of blood, and suction cups applied to rid the body of harmful excess air. Innumerable simple and complex drugs were devised to increase the level of a certain element or to decrease that of another.[24]

Later developments of this paradigm, mainly those elaborated in the Islamicate world, introduced the concept of numerous personality types based on different "normal" equilibriums among humors to account for the many types of personality traits within the normal range. Such was the choleric type, who, with an increased quantity of air-as-blood in the body, would have an easily enraged personality and a volatile sexuality, and the phlegmatic type, who, with a surplus of water-as-phlegm in his veins, would be cool-headed and slightly lethargic even under pressure. Although not equitably balanced, and tilted toward one of the elements, these types were not seen as unfit. One of the physician's main tasks, according to the tenets of late humoral medicine, was to define the right equilibrium for the specific patient and to restore that particular personal stability, rather than a perfect balance of the humors.

Humoral balance was assumed not only to differ from one individual to another, but also to vary in keeping with a person's sex, age, class, and ethnicity. A male's basic disposition—hot and dry—was expected to be different from a female's; that of Turks to be different from that of Jews or Arabs; and a young woman's humoral balance to be unlike that of an old one. All these categories are, naturally, very relevant to the understanding of sexuality. It seems that sexual difference was at the base of many such distinctions and characterizations and became one of the mainstays of the division into categories. The difference in humoral balance between men and women, for example, was developed mainly to account for their different sociosexual outlooks and gender definitions. Differences between old and young were in large part meant to account for variations in sexual prowess. So, apparently, were discussions of ethnic and racial differences.[25]

Gender, race, age, class, and disposition can all be seen as placed on a single elemental continuum in which the male is always hotter and dryer (or, in other words, contains more fire and air) than the female.[26] Heat, being the main motivating force of creation, gave men the advantage. Woman's imperfection was in essence caused by an inferior blend of humors, and that imperfection could be greater or lesser depending on how far removed it was from the perfect male composition.[27] Prepubescent boys, like women, were imperfect men, the only difference being that a boy had the potential for change whereas a woman was trapped in her imperfection. Likewise, someone could be nominally an adult male but possess many female attributes, which would place him in a different point on the scale, closer to women. A person's place on the scale also served as indication of his or her sexual prowess, appetite, and fertility. Various ethnic origins were positioned on a similar scale, to be judged and condemned according to their preordained humoral balance. Books were written to explain ethnic character through assumptions about ethnic and racial makeup. These naturally had to do with climatic considerations, so that people originating in Northern Europe, for instance, were believed to have a colder and wetter (therefore feminine) phlegmatic disposition, while desert dwellers in warmer climes were expected to have a choleric or bilious one.

## READING THE BODY'S SURFACE

The elements composing the body and its character also had a hand in shaping its external form. Heat, to take just one example, would cause hairiness, as could be observed in the tendency of birds (whose disposition was known to be hot and dry) to grow feathers. Such obvious connections between the constitution of the body and its shape led scholars to two conclusions. The first was that there are ways to learn about one's humoral makeup, and therefore character, from one's outward appearance. The second is actually the opposite: since people belonging to the same ethnic group often have similar features, one must conclude that different races or ethnicities share common humoral balances and therefore common sexual character traits.

These assumptions stood at the base of the science of physiognomy (Arabic *qiyāfa,* Turkish *kiyafet*), or, more popular in the later centuries, *firāsa/fıraset,* which was regarded as a subdiscipline of medicine. Following Ibn Sina's classification, two Ottoman bibliographic compendia, by Hajji Khalifa and Taşköprüzade, describe it as one of medicine's ancillary sciences, alongside disciplines such as chiromancy. It was held in high esteem until the nineteenth century.[28] In the classical period, books of physiognomy were used by janissary recruitment crews touring the villages of Anatolia and the Balkans in search of candidates for military service, and by palace officials buying slave girls for the harem. Such books were particularly handy when trying to assess the promise of sexual gratification.

One of physiognomy's basic assumptions was that sexual tendencies, potency, and libidinal appetites were reflected in the features of one's face and body. In the words of the *Kiyafet Name,* a famous Ottoman manual of physiognomy: "Know that it is a way to learn inner states from outer appearances."[29] Thus, social operations of differentiation, classification, stigmatization, and even, to some extent, political and social privilege were based on quasi-medical assumptions about people's appearance. *Fıraset* manuals provided the buyer of a slave and the man in search of a bride with a detailed guide to sexual potential. Each and every characteristic of a body part formed part of the puzzle. Some indicated sexual prowess, while their opposites demonstrated frigidity or weakness. All these can be located on a chart that describes the sexual and asexual personalities. Table 2 is based on an accumulation of Arabic and Turkish texts of the sixteenth and seventeenth centuries.

These attributes, common to many books in the pre-Ottoman and Ottoman periods, relate masculinity above all to a hot disposition, which means a preponderance of yellow bile and blood. As they age, men lose heat and therefore also sexual power. The highly sexed man is relatively short and heavyset. His head is large in relation to his body, his neck wide, his voice low and sonorous, his body hairy, his arms fleshy, his fingers short and chubby, and his testicles big. The size of the penis does not indicate either sexual prowess or fertility. A disposition tilted toward the cold elements and a physique that is delicate and hairless are signs of femininity in a man. Such a man's head is small in relation to his body, his limbs delicate and hairless, his hips narrow, and his testicles small. In general, feminine attributes such as wide hips or a high-pitched voice indicate a tendency to be effeminate and thus possessed of a woman's sexual tendencies.[30]

Women tend to have a cold and humid disposition, although it is interesting to note the tension in several manuscripts between the common tendency to ascribe to all women a greater sexual appetite and the attempt to suggest that women with an excess of blood (which makes them,

TABLE 2. SEXUAL AND ASEXUAL CHARACTERISTICS OF MEN AND WOMEN AS DESCRIBED IN FOUR TEXTS

| | Sexual Characteristic | | Asexual Characteristic | |
|---|---|---|---|---|
| *Organ or Property* | *Men* | *Women* | *Men* | *Women* |
| Height | (1) Short<br>(2) Short | (1) Tall | | (2) Taller or shorter than average |
| Weight | Heavyset | Thin | | |
| Voice | (1) Low (+)<br>(2) Low (+) | | High-pitched | |
| Disposition (humoral balance) | (3) *Hot*<br>Dry = prowess, but little seminal fluid<br>Humid = great genital power | (2) *Safravi* (bilious); a woman with a "fire" disposition is sexually active | (3) *Cold*<br>Dry = little developed prowess<br>Humid = weakness after intercourse | |
| Head | | | (2) Small | |
| Face | (4) Long = shamelessness | | | |
| Forehead and brows | (2) Blemishes near forehead | | | |
| Eyes and lids | (2) Languid, half closed<br>Blemish (+)<br>(3) Trembling = perverse and desirous<br>(4) Light blue = shamelessness<br>Bilious red = desire | (2) Languid, half closed<br>(3) Twinkling = beauty | (3) Twinkling = effeminate | |
| Nose | (1) (4) Flat and broad<br>(2) Flat and broad; blemish near nostrils sign of sexuality (+)<br>(3) Curved = lascivious | (1) Flat and broad<br>(2) Flat and broad | | |

| | | | |
|---|---|---|---|
| Cheeks | (2) Puffy close to eyes | | (2) Puffy = sexual frigidity |
| Mouth | (4) Wide | | (4) Thin = weakness in intercourse |
| Chin | (2) Blemish = sexual nature | | |
| Beard | Copious beard = sexuality | | (2) Lack of beard = sexual incapacity |
| Neck | (2) Fat (+) | (3) Thin = weak character | |
| Shoulders | | | (2) Narrow |
| Arms and hands | | Headline ends at fourth finger<br>(2) Fleshy Venus mound | (2) Hairless |
| Fingers | (2) Short and fat (+)<br>Big third section of thumb = homosexuals, whores, drunks | (2) Short and fat (+)<br>Big third section of thumb = homosexuals, whores, drunks | |
| Chest | (1) (4) Hairy (+) | | (4) Hairless |
| Breasts | | (1) Medium sized = love and affection | |
| Belly and navel | (3) Fat | | |
| Waist | | | (3) Fat |
| Penis | (1) Average sized | | (1) Bigger or smaller than average indicates other things (small = knowledge; big = blameworthiness; long = stupidity) |
| Testicles | (1) Big = courage and power | | (1) Small = cowardice |
| Hips | | | (2) Narrow |
| Legs and feet | | | (3) Small and delicate |

+ = Clear sign of sexual prowess/desire

NOTE: In all tables, empty cells indicate that the *şeriat* and *kanun* law did not address the relevant categories.

SOURCES: Information in this table was collected from the following books and manuscripts, as indicated by parenthetical numbers:

1 = *Kenzü'l-Havass*
2 = *Gizli Ilimler Hazinesi*
3 = *La physiognomonie arabe* (late twelfth to early thirteenth centuries)
4 = *Kiyafet Name*

by default, hotter and therefore closer to men) are sexually more voracious. In the case of women, writers also devote more attention to external, mainly facial, clues to the shape and size of sexual organs. Thus the width of a woman's lips could be a sign of the width of her vagina, and their thickness a sign of the size of the labia. The color of her face and eyes, the shape of her nose, and the size of her thighs indicate a woman's sexual appetites and tendencies. Heavy thighs are an indication of an oversexed woman. A red face and blue eyes (commensurate with colder climes) suggest that the woman is sexually frigid.[31]

This shift of focus in describing the physiognomy of both genders, in which the man's bodily traits are used to indicate his general character while the woman's traits are used mainly to ascertain more about her sexual parts, can be explained by the fact that this literature was written by men for men, and much of it was indeed meant to help men find sexual partners. Authors devote more attention to similar male attributes only when they are intended to be sexual partners, as in the following set of instructions for choosing slaves at the slave market:

> If you need a slave to be with you for friendship purposes, someone who will serve you for companionship and love games, he must be a man of medium height, and also medium build. He should not be too fat *[semiz]* or too thin *[zayıf]*, nor should his waist be thick. Rather tall than short. His hair should be soft, not stiff, but its color may be black or yellow as you wish. His palms should be round and soft. His skin should be delicate, his bones straight and his lips the color of wine. His hair should be black [?] his eyes hazel colored and his brows and eyelids black, but not connected. He should have a double chin *[çift gerdanlı]*. His chin should be white spotted red like the fuzz on a quince. His teeth should be white and straight and his members of the right proportion. Any slave that matches these descriptions will be gentle, of good temperament, loyal, and docile.[32]

Although we know that Mamluks and Ottomans made use of *firaset* wisdom in everyday life, to purchase military slaves and to recruit boys for the *devşirme* palace service as well as to buy slave girls in the market, it is hard to say to what extent such physiognomic descriptions were taken at face value. One can find quite a few descriptions of young, tall, and slender male beauties who do not fit the textbook description of the sexualized male but who are possessed of remarkable sexual skills and power. Yet such physiognomic descriptions persisted throughout the period and had an influence on popular imagination. Under such "scientific" pressure, it is no wonder that men held their beards in such high regard, and did their best to present themselves as heavyset and sturdy.

Being slim-waisted and close-shaven certainly was not à la mode for serious men in the Ottoman Middle East.

## ERECTION, EJACULATION, EXCESS, AND MODERATION

Another theme recurring in premodern medicine was descriptions of the sexual mechanism and the way it operates. Several basic questions were posed. The first was the reason for intercourse: why do men and women desire to copulate, and what purpose does copulation serve? The answer given by most physicians in the pre-Ottoman and Ottoman periods was that while it was God's will to perpetuate the human race, His vehicle for creating the actual desire for sex was the desiring soul. This force pervades both men and women and drives them to seek sexual intercourse. It should be noted that from the medical point of view, and in line with the one-sex paradigm, there is no differentiation between the sexual drives of men and women, and there is certainly no assumption that women cannot or do not enjoy intercourse as much as men do.

One bodily reason for desiring intercourse was the need to discharge accumulated semen, conceived of as refined and "whitewashed" blood that the body manufactures constantly in order to reproduce. As Basim Musallam has shown, in antiquity there were two opposing theories. One (Aristotle) held that only males had semen, and the other (Hippocrates and Galen) that both sexes produced it. Ibn Sina, though siding with Aristotle on most matters, conceded that women also had semen, but that this semen was soulless and therefore inferior to male semen, serving mainly as "matter" to be shaped and formed by male semen. The final claims for the equal nature of male and female semen and the insistence that female semen was also soul-containing come from the writings of Ibn Qayyim al-Jawzīyya in the fifteenth century, taking his cue from Islamic prophetic traditions and jurisprudence.[33] In the Ottoman period this became a basic tenet of sexual discourse.

Since women were believed to produce an analogous kind of semen in their bodies, albeit of lesser quality, the need to dispel the substance affected men and women alike, strengthening the resemblance between the sexes. As we shall see, even when the guiding principles of medicine began to change in the nineteenth century, the idea of a desiring soul remained prevalent in Middle Eastern medical circles and lodged itself in medical texts adapted from Western Europe.

Early authors of medical texts were aware of the need to awaken the desiring soul and to produce desire as a precondition for successful intercourse. Foreplay is discussed often and takes into consideration the needs of both partners to the sexual act. But authors often go beyond simple discussion of foreplay and suggest other measures. Reading stories that instill lust; watching others, including animals, perform intercourse; and bathing or even shaving one another are some of the measures proposed in several texts.

A second set of discussions questioned the relationship between abstinence and sexual urge. Young people were said to be like waterskins. Their seminal fluids were believed to accumulate in the testicles or ovaries with no outlet. When too much semen collected, body heat rose and intercourse was sought. "If one abandons intercourse *[cimaı terk ise],*" says Eşref bin Muhammed, an early Ottoman physician, in his book *Hazā'inü's-sa'ādāt,* "little by little pains begin. In a kind of escalating motion, the body begins to fail. Eyesight might weaken; tumors might form in the testicles or in the ureter." Kemal Paşa Zade (also known as Ibn Kamāl Pasha), a famous physician who was also a statesman, *'ālim,* and author, writing in Arabic, gives a rather more sophisticated and detailed description of the process. His explanation, perhaps translated from an earlier Arabic manuscript, is based on humoral imbalance caused by incomplete transfer of essence from other organs to the testicles and the penis. According to Kemal Paşa Zade, disease and health in connection with intercourse are always a function of particular humoral balance. Thus, people who are hot and wet (with an excess of blood and white bile) may indulge in intercourse as much as they please, while those with cold and dry dispositions are liable to be harmed by an excess of intercourse.[34]

A person who wishes to avoid these illnesses must have regular intercourse in adulthood, and in certain cases, in the absence of intercourse, masturbation should be used.[35] The only exceptions to this medical recommendation are sworn celibates, such as nuns, monks, and certain Sufis, who never indulge in intercourse, thus conditioning their bodies to maintain a low level of semen production, and old people whose semen production declines and whose bodies find other outlets for it.

Yet abstinence is not the only dangerous habit that lurks in the world of sex. The result of overindulgence in intercourse may be similar or worse. Overworking the semen-producing mechanism endangers health in a different way, producing even more perilous results: "Strength decreases, the light of the eyes becomes weaker, the nerves/sinews become powerless, the heart weakens, and phenomena such as trembling, shivering, spasms, paralysis, forgetfulness, bad habits, heaviness of the mind, insolence, or cowardice occur, each one of them a serious problem. Those who practice too much intercourse will encounter these problems one by one, so it is necessary to protect the body."[36] Thus, one of the first sexual lessons a fifteenth- or sixteenth-century intellectual reading medical texts, or a patient listening to his doctor's advice, may have learned is the ancient rule of moderation and temperance, harking back to Greek antiquity. One must not abstain from sexual activity because lack of intercourse may lead to disease. Indeed, one should seek and encourage it in order to stay healthy, but care should be taken to avoid excess and loss of vital heat lest the same consequences, or even worse, occur.

Since periodic discharge of all semen is crucial to keeping one's health, partial evacuation can also cause trouble and bring about ailments. Incomplete discharge occurs when the male fails to rid himself of all the semen held in the testicles or, to be more precise, when his partner fails to extract it all. Only a young, healthy woman's womb has the power to absorb every drop of semen, drawing it out, as it were, from the testicles. Al-ʿItāqi describes the way in which a woman's uterus attracts semen: "During intercourse, the uterus comes nearer the mouth of the vulva and naturally, the passage of the uterus descends to the level of the mouth of the vulva to attract semen. It becomes as narrow as a canal through which not even a single hair can enter so that it can attract semen and protect the fetus."[37]

Any sexual partner who cannot perform this complex task is therefore inadequate. Thus, having intercourse with old, weak, or ugly women may be dangerous for men, presumably because their powers of suction are diminished. This is also true of sex with women who are menstruating, those who have just recovered from illness, and those deprived of sex for a long time. Sex with minors, young boys in particular, may have similar dire consequences.[38] Although it was assumed that women too need to evacuate accumulated semen, their predicament is seldom mentioned. Some believed that the menstrual cycle was the mechanism by which they accomplished this.[39]

The dangers of excess intercourse, abstinence, and partial evacuation had a bearing not only on the choice of sexual partner but also on positions during intercourse. This aspect of medical discourse seems to have benefited from, or at least engaged with, Indian medical discourse, alongside the more conservative Galenic teachings. In order to attain complete discharge, the preference was for positions in which the woman serves as a vessel for the semen to be poured or drawn into. Doctors recommended the missionary position. Having intercourse lying on one's side was not recommended because in this position it is harder for the man to unburden himself. Nothing was worse, it seems, than for the woman to be on top. Here another danger compounded the one of nonevacuation. The woman's liquids, including her semen, were liable to penetrate the man's penis and cause disease: "It is also claimed that being underneath means that the man is weak *[erün aşağı yani zaif olur]*. [The position in which] the man is on his back and the woman gets on top of him may cause many kinds of damage. It is claimed that the woman's water might enter the man's penis. If this happens the man's semen does not vacate completely, and many kinds of ailments await him. But this intercourse in which the woman is on top is considered safer for a pregnant woman."[40]

Medical tracts reiterate and reproduce some common views about the nature of intercourse and mainly those that place the male partner "on top," in a position of power in relation to the sexual partner. Yet while these suggestions may have had their roots in common thought, it was more than just cultural preference couched in medical terminology. It is interesting to note that at this early stage, before syphilis was recognized and diagnosed, there is hardly any mention of the danger of contracting disease by infection during intercourse. These attempts to restrict positions and the warning against contamination by the woman's fluids are perhaps an early indication of awareness of such dangers.[41]

Being faced with so many dangers in intercourse, men may opt for masturbation as a safer sexual practice and as a solution to the problem of discharge, but medical treatises warn against too frequent relief through such practices. Masturbation *(zeker tutmak, ele oynamak)*, they claimed, may cause anxiety, make one forgetful, weaken the penis, and blunt the mind. Furthermore, it destroys the natural propensity for intercourse:

> It is like a person who, by being greedy, takes out his money and buys any food that appears before his eyes, even when it is not tasty, then leaves it and tries another. Having bought it, he leaves it with regret because his greed forces him to. Until one day, his purse is empty. When he is hungry he sees many good foods, but when he comes to take the first, there is nothing in his purse. This time he unfortunately stays hungry. He cannot fill up the greed in his eyes. Having spent his property, nothing is left in his purse of strength. Because when the load of weakness falls on a person, no one can save him at any time. The road is long. It is necessary not to waste the provisions of power, and God knows best.[42]

This discourse, widespread in Arab and Turkish-speaking areas of the Ottoman world, offered a sexual script that went hand in hand with orthodox sexual taboos, such as having sex during menstruation or having sex with minors or boys, and gave them scientific sanction. In some cases, the script limited the choice even further, to young healthy women, stigmatizing all other sexual choices as unhealthy and even dangerous from a medical point of view. In this respect, medicine is an orthodox discourse. Yet by accepting and promoting the imperfect-man model, it was also compatible to a large extent with other sexual scripts, in which homoeroticism and same-sex relations were more common.

The message driven home was not one of sin or shame, nor was it an attempt to instill a new puritan sexuality. It was a call for moderation and continence. As in Galen's Rome, sexual energy is described here as a resource that men have in limited quantity and, if squandered, may lead to impotence and disease.[43] Although not couched in the same terms, the Hippocratic idea of *calor genitalis,* or vital heat that preserves the virility of the male body, still dominated local medical thinking and the sexual script that it heralded. It was far more important to preserve the body's supplies of sexual energy and not squander them than to pick a sexual partner of the right sex.

The critical change introduced by early Christianity, the attempt to reshape the body, to teach it to behave differently, to "prize it from the physical world,"[44] and to deny the reverence owed to the vital sexual heat, did not take place in the medical script of the pre-Ottoman and Ottoman Islamicate world. Here, sexuality still adhered to the same ancient values espoused by the Hippocratic writer.[45] In this respect, the changes wrought by the nineteenth century, as we shall see later, were much more revolutionary in Ottoman than in European culture. Whereas Europe's Victorian tendencies had some roots in the Christian early rejection of the physical body, in the Ottoman Middle East no such rejection of the body and its sexuality was manifest.

## GENETICS, SEMEN, CONCEPTION, AND DEVIATION

Similarity between men and women was not limited to sexual urges and needs. Both sexes were believed to have analogous powers of procreation. This was made clear in discussions of semen production, fetus formation, and the resemblance of a child to its parents. While earlier Islamicate medical discourse, based on Socratic ideas of (male) form and (female) matter assumed an imbalance between the types of semen produced by each of the sexes, now physicians seem to have agreed that both men and women produced semen with productive potential, and therefore both took part in conceiving the fetus, fighting to bequeath to the newborn their gender characteristics.

In describing the production of semen, the metaphor most often used in medical tracts was not a machine or the natural world, but rather the stove and the process of food preparation. As the desiring soul overtakes a person, in other words, when men and women feel lustful, the body becomes a kitchen in which the seminal essence is produced. The body works in perfect concert. The heart becomes a bellows, the testicles an oven, the ovaries cooking pots, and the kidneys grinding machines. A new human is being prepared. Eşref bin Muḥammed encapsulates the process:

> When the heart's movements pick up *[katırak etmeğe başlar]* the nerves heat up, the kidneys are working as if grinding, and the brain extracts a substance. At a certain point in time, as a result of this motion, each member of the male and female body produces a drop of blood *[kan]*. All the blood that assembles from the top of the head to the toes of the foot collects in the groin *[bel]*. From the testicles two veins *[sınır]* emerge. It is there that the blood collects. In the course of this motion the tips of the nerves wash the blood white. Next the male member is pulled, drawn, thrown out by the heart's movement.[46]

Kemal Paşa Zade offers a similar description. In his version, however, the collected semen is not just an essence of the body parts, but also of the qualities represented by them. The heart provides the animal spirit *(al-quwwa al-ḥayawānīya),* which enables sensation and movement, and the brain produces encapsulated forms of the senses themselves and the power of movement. All these collect at the back of the brain and flow down from it, through the hollow of the spine to the kidneys and the testicles. Kemal Paşa Zade also develops the idea of a wind, or *pneuma,* an ethereal and powerful airlike substance that originates in the heart and allows the penis to inflate. This, he says, is the reason for the immense pleasure of intercourse. Since it connects all the organs to the penis, the *pneuma* causes heating and inflammation, and the body is filled with it to bring animal-like satisfaction.[47]

Myriad mini-drops representing limbs, organs, and attributes combine to create a DNA-like substance that reproduces the form and spirit of the creating body. This conflation of semen with blood, which may have found further proof in descriptions of embryology in the Koran, had a bearing on sexual morality that went beyond mere transubstantiation.[48] Blood, semen, and milk were seen as different representations of the same basic substance cooked and concentrated in different ways. Al-ʿItāqi, the seventeenth-century author of *Tashriḥ al-abdān,* a book on human anatomy, describes it as follows: "One section [of the menstrual blood] can be improved by nature. This section has three parts; one nourishes the fetus; another becomes fleshy and fatty to fill the spaces in the fetus, and the third part goes to the breasts to produce milk."[49]

Blood, semen, and milk, therefore, had sexual and reproductive connotations. Breastfeeding was seen as an act akin to intercourse in that it endows the baby with the attributes of its mother or wet nurse. Hence the emphasis placed in *sharīʿa* law on the status of children who were breast-fed by the same woman as blood relatives *(maḥram)* of her biological children. Blood oaths and other acts involving touching or licking blood were also believed to be ways of partaking, albeit in diminished form, of the blood source's attributes, in a quasi-sexual manner.

When intercourse takes place, medical texts went on to say, male combines with female semen to produce a fetus that resembles its parents. This resemblance, as well as the sex of the fetus, depends on the level of intrinsic vitality in each of the two portions of combined semen. The level is not simply a reflection of the person's basic vital power. It also depends, to a large degree, on the pace of intercourse and on the physical and mental state of each of the partners while having sex. When, for instance, there is real passion between a man and a woman during intercourse (and, some say, when they climax together), vital heat increases and the result is bound to be a healthy boy.[50]

Local medical tracts from the sixteenth to the nineteenth centuries insisted on the woman's contribution to procreation even in the face of contending theories, such as monogenesis, favored in Western Europe for some time in the early modern period. When new medical knowledge in the seventeenth century "proved" that male testicles were the only organs capable of producing semen, al-ʿItāqi mentioned this theory but made it clear to his readers that he did not accept its premises, by prefacing the discussion with "physicians also claim" and ending it with "only God knows the truth."[51]

Although men and women were believed to possess equal powers of procreation, a female child was still regarded as a deficient version of the male. The birth of a girl may result from incomplete or unsatisfying intercourse. In pre-Ottoman medical tracts, known and utilized in the empire, it was claimed that female sex, or even feminine characteristics in a man, are a sign of dominant female and weaker male semen. In the contest between male and female semen, the more powerful one transforms the weaker and dominates it, or, as al-Rāzi explains, "Femininity or masculinity occurs only in accordance with the prevalence of one of the two semens over the other in quantity and quality, until one of them becomes the one that transforms *(muḥīl)* and the other the one that is transformed *(mustaḥīl).*"[52] In some cases, when neither the male nor the female semen is clearly prevalent, all kinds of intermediate stages are likely to occur. These range from the masculine female to the effeminate male, with hermaphrodites being an extreme case, a pure equilibrium between the father and the mother.[53]

As al-Rāzi develops this idea of a competition between male and female semen, he concludes that *ubnah* (passive male "homosexuality") is a result of the same contest. At times the outcome is such that the man, though having clear visible male traits, is prone to be a *ma'būn,* a male who prefers to be penetrated by another male. In most such cases, he says, the male in question is not a "perfect" male in that his penis and testicles tend to be smaller and closer to the groin than average male organs. As a result, the erogenous zones of such a male would be much closer to the anus than for other males. It may be gathered from al-Rāzi's writings on the subject that the other type of same-sex behavior, what is sometimes described as "active male homosexuality" (but actually refers to men who prefer to penetrate other males), was not considered a medical problem of any kind. Cast in al-Rāzi's terminology, the problem was mainly one of erogenous zones and vital power, not an issue of same-sex intercourse, which he ignores altogether.

In al-Rāzi's world, *ubnah* is clearly a biological defect, not a deviation or a sin. It is genetic rather than psychological or cultural, and people in such a predicament should be treated to heal the disease as far as possible. Yet as Rosenthal points out, al-Rāzi's choice of title for the treatise, "the hidden illness," indicates that this type of homosexual behavior was frowned on and considered shameful in the Abbasid period. The treatment he recommends for *ubnah,* in line with Galenic concepts of humoral effect, consists of heating the penis and cooling the anus, or, in more precise terms, warming up the area of the penis and testicles, rubbing ointments on them, and bathing the genitals, preferably by maids and slaves trained as surrogate sexual partners. At the same time the patient's lower back and anus should be cooled down by placing wet rags on his backside, enemas of rose water and vinegar, and encouraging him to practice "active" intercourse.[54]

Several authors, including Ibn Sina and Ibn Hubal, contested al-Rāzi's views. They pointed out that some persons affected by *ubnah* may be physically better endowed than other males. Their disease cannot, therefore, be genetic and cannot be caused by weaker male semen. They concluded that *ubnah* is a cultural disease, or one spurred by the imagination. These are people who have accustomed themselves to nonvirtuous ways and to feminine behavior.[55] Instead of receiving medical attention, they should be punished for their sinful behavior and made to see the error of their ways. Here, again, the emphasis is on the "passive" form of intercourse, not on homosexuality in general. What the two approaches had in common was the understanding that *ubnah* was bad and that whether caused genetically or psychologically, it should be made to go away.

A century or two later, medical texts did little to determine which of the two outlooks was correct. In fact, most texts of the pre-Ottoman and Ottoman periods do not deal with this issue at all. Although sixteenth- and seventeenth-century medical tracts do not shy away from discussing same-sex intercourse, *ubnah* is not part of the discussion in any way. We may offer two contradictory explanations for this fact. One is that this subject was so shameful that physicians preferred not to deal with it at all. Another explanation, perhaps more plausible, is that contemporary physicians had a hard time putting their finger on the problem. "Passive" male intercourse was seen as weakness, perhaps, but not as a disease that needed treatment or punishment. It is difficult to argue from silence, but taking into consideration other discourses, such as dream interpretation and erotic literature, it seems that the early Ottoman attitude to male "passive" intercourse was one of indifference. This was some people's preference, it was part of the spectrum of normal sexual behavior, and it was not to be considered deviant in any way.[56]

## PERSISTENCE OF THE IMPERFECT-MAN MODEL

Premodern medicine in the Middle East, like its European counterpart, adhered to the imperfect-man model. Rather than a dichotomy, in this discourse men and women inhabited a sexual continuum. If anything, Middle Eastern medical tradition was more adamant on this subject and more resistant to opposing ideas. This manifested itself in the assumption that both men and women create semen, in the idea that both sexes have similar sexual prowess and appetite, in the claim that procreation was in effect a collision between male and female semen that formed the fetus, and in the assumption that the female vagina and uterus were an undeveloped version of the male penis and scrotum (see figures 1 and 2). Al-ʿItāqi, in the seventeenth century, basing his discussion on Vesalius's sixteenth-century book, describes this last assumption in no uncertain terms:

> The Uterus is the organ which produces the baby. Its shape is like the penis and the testis of a man. But the penis has grown outwards and is complete.

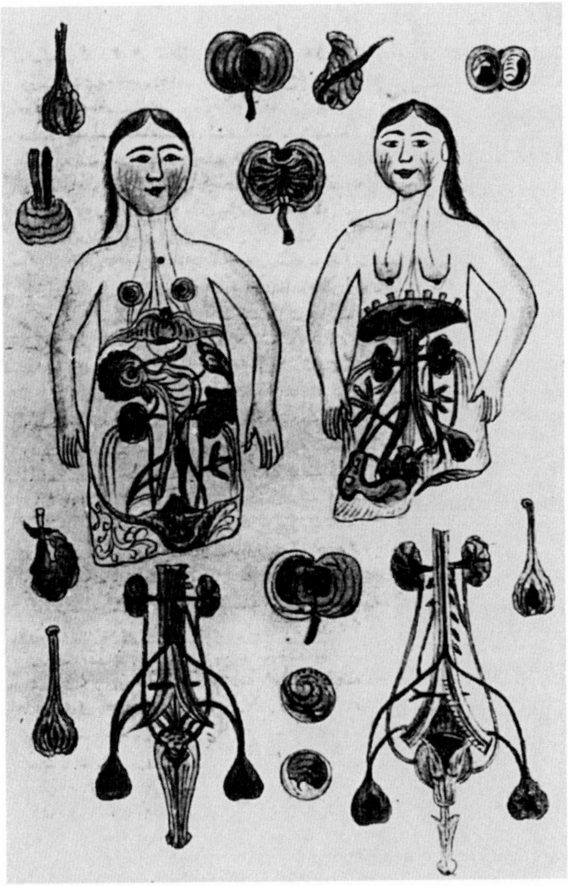

Figure 1. Urogenital system in the female, probably adapted by the author from Vesalius. This is perhaps meant as a male *(left)* and female *(right)* description. Note the penislike urethra and vulva and the androgynous form of the figures. Shams al-Dīn al-ʿItāqi, *The Treatise on Anatomy of Human Body and Interpretation of Philosophers (Tashrīḥ al-abdān)*, p. 166.

The uterus is incomplete. It is inside the woman. However its shape is nearly the same as that of the penis. Some physicians say that it resembles a frozen penis. Its neck is like a penis. For this reason, the penis is a mold of the uterus and the uterus is like a tunic of the penis. The female testis is like the male testis, but the male testis is larger and round; it is slightly ellipsoid, and is placed outside. The female testis is smaller and slightly oval; it is placed on both sides of the vulva.[57]

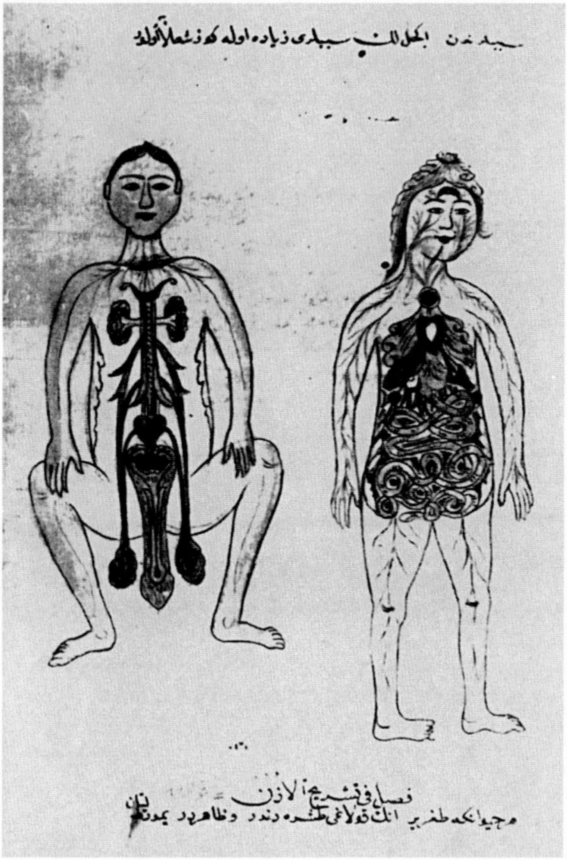

Figure 2. Urogenital system in the male and visceral system in the female. Al-ʿItāqi, *The Treatise on Anatomy of Human Body . . .*, p. 165.

This inherent similarity in particular was cause for alarm. Since in Ottoman Middle Eastern societies gender roles were so clearly divided, and since the precise definition of a person as man or woman was essential in all walks of life, the possibility of transgression was frowned on.[58] Thus, the fifteenth-century surgery manual *Cerrāhiyyetü'l-haniyye* describes in detail cases such as those of women with enlarged clitorises and penis-like protrusions and of men with women's breasts, and the surgical procedures needed to remove them (see figures 3 and 4).[59] Here is what the author, Sabuncuoğlu, has to say about the female penis and the operations necessary to cut it off:

Figure 3. Operation to remove penislike clitoris. Şerefeddin Sabuncuoğlu, *Cerrāhiyyetü'l-haniyye,* Bibliothèque Nationale de France.

> There is a part of the female vulva that is called *tılak* (clitoris) in Turkish. In some women it is so big that it may be ugly to look at *[şöyle büyük kim nazarda kabih olur]* and in some women it is as big as the male member and they have intercourse like men. In Arab lands *[diyar-ı Arabda]* they cut it. The way to do it is to hold the redundant part that should be cut in your hand, or to hold it with an implement, and to pull it upwards, but do not cut off the skin so as not to create a blood flow *[ta'kim kan boşanmaya].* Afterwards treat it for infection. As for the redundant flesh *[lahm-ı zayid yaʿni artuk et]* that grows inside the womb and is attached inside the womb, perhaps like the tail of a beast *[canavar kuyruğı gibi]* and protrudes out of the womb, and that is why the ancient doctors called it *maraz-i zenebi;* its treatment is also cutting.

Such examples of graphic description are relatively rare in late premodern Middle Eastern medical tracts. But the fear of indeterminate sexuality, the danger of moving from one sex to the other (particularly from female to male), persisted even as these ideas changed in European med-

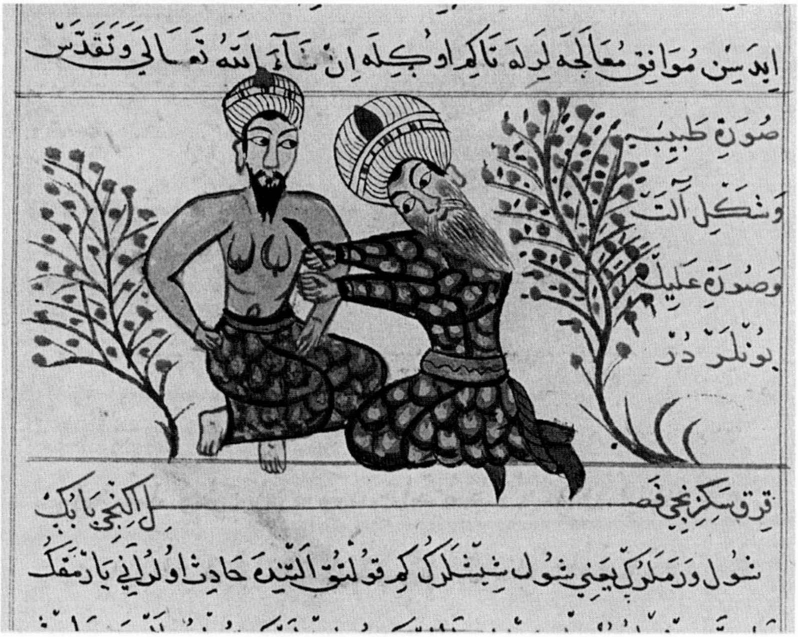

Figure 4. Operation to remove womanlike breasts. Sabuncuoğlu, *Cerrāhiyyetü'l-haniyye,* Bibliothèque Nationale de France.

icine. When the first European-style medical tracts were written in Istanbul and Cairo, authors were acquainted mainly with eighteenth-century medical work and even older tractates. Such old-style work is often quoted, translated, or mined for illustrations. Thus, in Şanizade's *Hamse,* first published in 1826, both drawings and their interpretations hang on to the imagery typical of the older paradigm, in which female sexual organs were drawn and described as similar to males'. Figures 5 and 6 are a set of drawings from the *Hamse.*

In his descriptions of female reproductive organs, the ambiguous transfer of new medical knowledge is even more pronounced. "The testicles of women are called *mahzanateyin* [ovaries, 'bird's nests']," explains Şanizade. And he goes on: "The tendons tying these ovaries to the uterus [he sometimes uses the term *mecari fālubiye,* fallopian tubes][60] are said by surgeons to be the female version of males' semen conduits." Speaking of the recent discovery that eggs are produced in the ovaries, Şanizade's description becomes even vaguer. He loosely describes vessels

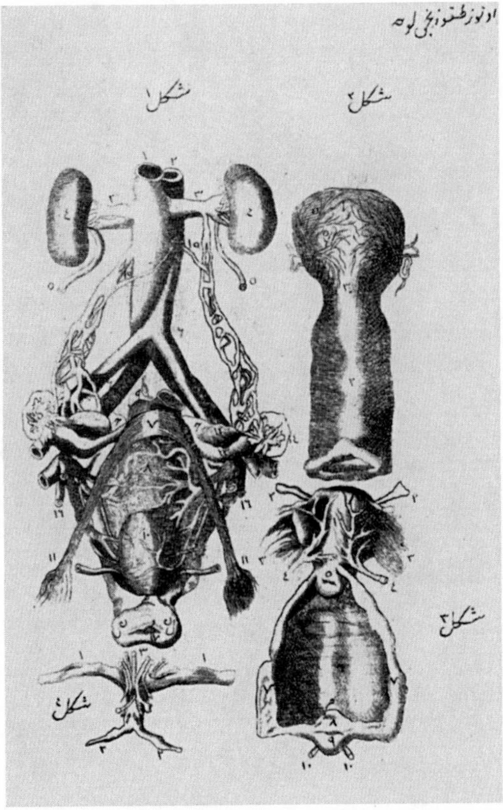

Figure 5. The vagina and uterus *(upper right)* depicted as malelike penis and scrotum. Mehmet Ataullah Şanizade, *Hamse-i şanizade,* book 1, p. 39, drawing 39.

intended to collect and dispense the "cooked food essence"[61] by means of certain eggs, thus incorporating the newly discovered female egg into the old medical discourse. "These eggs," he continues, "are also said to be means of reproduction."[62]

This sense of ambiguity may also explain the almost total disappearance of older descriptions of the reproductive mechanism. All those descriptions, produced and reproduced endlessly by premodern physicians, about the production of semen, the role of the internal *pneuma,* the mixing of male and female semen, and the dangers and benefits of coitus, had to be discarded in the face of new empirical evidence. Yet, for a long time the new two-sex model failed to register. The belief that men and

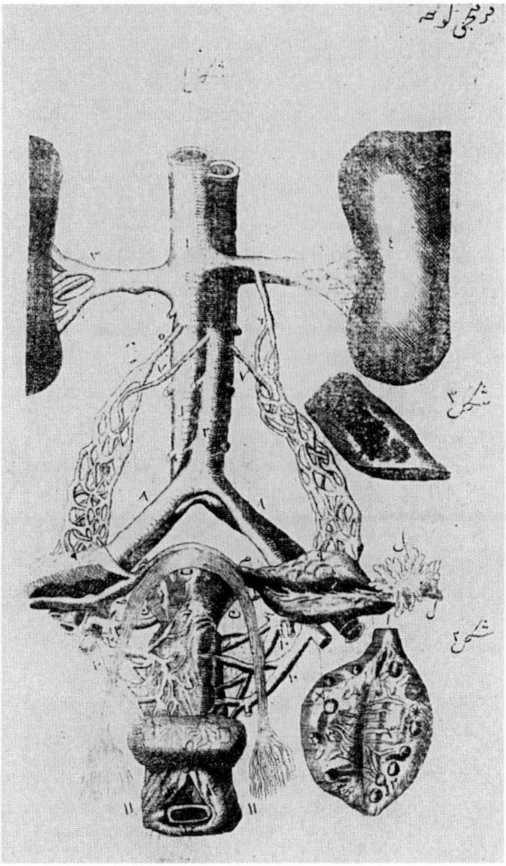

Figure 6. The vagina and ovaries. Şanizade, *Hamse-i şanizade,* book 1, p. 39, drawing 40.

women were of the same sex was retained, but the medical underpinnings and logic of the imperfect-man model slowly dissipated.

## FEAR OF THE SEXUAL

As the nineteenth century unfolded, the focus changed. Humoral balance was no longer mentioned, and the terminology of the old paradigm—ancient terms such as *the desiring soul, elements, humors, pneuma, chyle*—gradually disappeared. These terms were replaced by a description of anatomy based mainly on French, German, and Italian pathological surveys, and by literature on diseases, symptoms, and cures.[63]

These new texts seem much closer to what we recognize as modern medicine, although in many cases they contain remnants of the "old" medicine interspersed with the new. In this radical change of discourse, the work of Clot Bey, Muhammad Ali's French chief physician in Egypt, was probably critical.[64]

With a new emphasis on hygiene and disease symptoms, with chapters devoted to nascent psychological discourse and an emphasis on children's health and disease, the new outlook should have been concerned with sexuality, but one looks in vain for a new perspective on sexual matters in nineteenth-century medical tracts. New books on medicine seem to deny the existence of a sexual drive and ignore the possible implications of sexual intercourse. This denial of sex is felt more acutely precisely because the older books discuss sex and sexuality so openly and unreservedly. It is as if sex vanished altogether from medical discourse.

There are several reasons for this denial. Around this time—the end of the eighteenth century—Western medicine developed a careful morality that required distance from (mainly female) patients and had pronounced reservations about bodily contact.[65] In European clinics and medical literature, sex was discussed gingerly, using codes and euphemisms. In translation this oblique terminology may have been completely lost, leaving Arabic and Turkish texts silent on the matter.

But this silence was also based on internal developments. As we have seen, in the course of the nineteenth century Ottoman medical discourse did not relinquish the imperfect-man model, and it continued to uphold its basic assumptions about sex and sexuality. Thus a discrepancy emerged between the contents of new medical texts and the underlying assumptions of older ones. The sexual act could no longer be explained in the ancient manner, by recourse to a desiring soul, to the accumulation of semen in the male and female body, to the need for humoral balance, and to all the scientific baggage that such explanations entailed. The kitchen metaphor was replaced by a mechanical one; the decrepit humoral theory was exchanged for a more sophisticated outlook involving newly discovered cells and tissues. But since the new ideas as yet carried no conviction, the mechanism they offered instead was rejected.

We may contemplate another possible reason. In Europe the two-sex model evolved gradually, and its basis was not necessarily, or even primarily, in medicine. Its roots, as Laqueur shows, were to be found in political and social changes that preceded medicine, were in constant dialogue with it, and gave the new paradigm its main impetus. They emerged from the struggle over public space and the place that women should occupy in it. Those arguing for giving women a right to full participation in politics and public life were required to move away from the one-sex paradigm and to seek another way of arguing for the rights of women. Describing them as a totally different sex, rather than a flawed version of the same sex, was one way to build a case for complementarity. Such discussions, from Jean-Jacques Rousseau to Mary Wollstonecraft, set the background against which the new medical discourse emerged and anchored itself. In the Middle East no such change took place prior to the modern period, and thus one further anchor for the new two-sex model was absent.

Furthermore, throughout the centuries, the antiquated imperfect-man model gradually came to a symbiosis with Islamic orthodoxy and koranic teachings about the body, about the relationship between men and women, and about social space as these were interpreted by the *ulema* in the Ottoman era. We can even assume that Islamic orthodoxy's sexual script was shaped, to some extent at least, by Galenic concepts of the body. The new paradigm, however, was more difficult to align with what, by the nineteenth century, had become an ossified and entrenched religious view. It was much more difficult to argue for the inferior place of women in society when they were no longer regarded as incomplete variations of men. If men and women were to be understood as parallel but unconnected creatures, religion's entire cosmological scheme would collapse.

The result was in the first instance an inability to accept and internalize the new model. Within the pages of new books of medicine, the old paradigm still held sway. Later in the nineteenth century, when the overwhelming pressure of evidence forced physicians in the Middle East to succumb and truly incorporate the new message, a growing discrepancy emerged between the discourse of medicine and other cultural and political spheres. While society at large continued to adhere to the old values, continued to see men and women as part of one continuum, and resisted women's entry into the public sphere in the tacit understanding that they were biologically inferior to men, medicine taught a different lesson. A basic premise had been removed from the discursive world of sex. As we shall see in later chapters, the process of adaptation and alignment of other sexual scripts was also long and arduous.

CHAPTER 2

# Regulating Desire

## Sharīʿa *and* Kanun

The law is above all an instrument for control and regulation, both in its application and in the standards it upholds. As such it could tell us a great deal about definitions of right and wrong, about what ought not to be done. But as Foucault rightly notes, law does much more than regulate and repress sex. Through its various mechanisms—written codes, courts, judges, and lawyers—it also constitutes desire. In other words, by creating and enforcing the boundaries between licit and illicit, punished and unpunished, law is a major influence shaping the sexual world.[1]

Laws are also cultural artifacts produced by people, and therefore they are capable of revealing their discursive and cultural context. This, however, presents a problem for the cultural historian. A body of law may be a reflection of the ruling elite that produced it, conveying its values, its norms, and its worldviews, and presenting the hierarchies inherent in its thought. But it may also be a treacherous mirror, displaying values that were meant for others, ethics that promulgators never believed in, regulations they never adhered to, and rules they never intended to keep. In other cases, laws may have their origins in divine commandments and stay unchanged for long periods of time, reflecting the norms and ideas of a past era (or, for believers, of a perfect heavenly society). Our search for cultural content in legal systems should therefore proceed with care and a critical eye.

Sex, a divisive practice and a potential source of anarchy and rebellion, is one of the first things that societies attempt to control, and the decisions of lawmakers backed by the power of the state often have the greatest impact on the formation and regulation of sex. Middle Eastern societies were no exception. They developed a considerable body of law to regulate sexual relations. But in order to discuss Ottoman-era legal sexual discourse and its relation to society, we must first understand the complex legal system of the empire, its evolution, and its relation to Islamic law.

In Islamic cultures, law emerged from the beginning as a primary pillar of the faith system. Especially during his period at Medina, when he added the burden of leadership to his role as prophet, Muhammad's teachings included a substantial body of law and regulation of social matters. These were expanded and elaborated by later generations. The ground rules for the promulgation of laws in Sunni Islam were determined mainly in the ninth century by the founders of the four major schools of law. These ground rules, or *uṣūl al-fiqh* (the roots of jurisprudence), as they came to be known, established that lawmaking should be restricted to several specific sources or mechanisms. The first was accepting laws verbatim from the Koran or from the valid corpus of *ḥadīth,* also known as *sunna*—the sayings and deeds of the Prophet. In all cases where the Koran laid down a clear law, it was not to be abrogated or replaced by any other law. When no such koranic formula existed, the *sunna* of the Prophet, as recorded by trustworthy transmitters, was to be admitted as law. When no clear indication could be found in the scriptures, another mechanism was sought—an analogy *(qiyās)* between laws decreed by the *ḥadīth* or the Koran and the case at hand. Finally, a fourth tool, widening the scope of legislative mechanisms, was consensus *(ijmā')* among religious authorities on the validity of a custom or ritual.

A long campaign was waged during the ninth century for and against the validity of a fifth principle, human reason *('aql, ra'y),* but eventually the validity of reason as a source for the promulgation of law was curtailed, and, for reasons that are beyond the scope of this discussion, it was officially rejected and denied recognition. In various schools of law, other sources, such as local custom *('urf, 'āda),* the good of the people *(istiḥsān, istiṣlāḥ),* and the needs of the state *(siyāsa),* were recognized instead as valid sources for jurisprudence but were always considered secondary, and their application was restricted.[2]

In light of these strict principles of jurisprudence, Islamic states faced a problem from the earliest stages. Some of the laws, especially those that had their origins in the Koran or the *sunna,* did not allow for efficient state control or for the economic viability of the state. Manslaughter, for example, was one offense that the *sharī'a* left to the parties involved to negotiate, limiting the state's right to interfere. Taxes were set at a minimum, making it difficult for the ruler to maintain his army and bureaucracy. As a result, most premodern Islamic states maintained two or more parallel legal systems. One implemented the sacred law, and the others were created to fill in what was perceived as lacunae in the legal system or to provide legal alternatives more in tune with the social and political preferences of the ruling elite.[3] In most cases, separate law codes were written, often called *Qānūn* (*kanun* in Turkish), a term borrowed from the Greek. Usually special cadres of judges and other functionaries were prepared and separate court systems were established to provide these alternatives.[4]

It is often assumed that the Ottoman *kanun-sharīʿa* system is a simple extension of the dual-code principle just described.[5] But a close examination of the process and a careful reading of the texts demonstrate that Ottoman legislators chose another path. In the fifteenth century, defying established practices in surrounding medieval Islamic states, they adopted a judicial system in which kadis—officers of the sacred law—were to be trained in government-funded religious schools *(medreses)* under a strict study program sanctioned by the state. Having graduated, their positions secured, they were required to comply and adjudicate in accordance with both systems of law at the same time.[6]

Moreover, beginning with the reign of Mehmed the Conqueror in the second half of the fifteenth century, the jurists kneaded the sacred law (which from now on I shall refer to as *şeriat,* using the Turkish spelling to differentiate the system prevalent in Ottoman times from other manifestations of the *sharīʿa*) and the central elements of "secular" state law into one compounded system. The guiding principles that enabled this unification were *siyaset* (Arabic *siyāsa*) and *örf* (Arabic *ʿurf*).[7] These provisions in the sacred law, officially sanctioned as secondary mechanisms of lawmaking, recognized the need of states and rulers to legislate their own laws for their subjects' welfare. In the fifteenth and sixteenth centuries, following a series of developments in Islamic jurisprudence, the principle of *siyaset* afforded jurists the leeway to combine *şeriat* with the ruler's legislation.[8] This was not always easy. Unlike in other areas, such as civil and commercial law, in personal and criminal law the *şeriat* had a vast body of jurisprudence.

Sultanic promulgation and the *şeriat* were sometimes at odds about questions such as punishments for crimes (sexual offenses are a good example of this, as we shall see later), fiscal laws, and the guiding principles of slave ownership. But conscious of their state's image as upholder of eternal justice, heads of the judiciary in the fifteenth and sixteenth centuries found ingenious ways to resolve the differences. Most notable among them were the seal bearer *(nişancı)* Celalzade Mustafa Paşa,[9] the *ʿālim* Kemal Paşa Zade (who was also a physician, as we saw in the first chapter), and the famous jurist Şeyhülislam Ebüssuud Efendi,[10] Sultan Süleyman's legal counselor and his chief mufti. In his *Balance of Truth,* Katib Çelebi, an Ottoman official of the next generation, described the process thus: "[Ebüssuud] and Kemal Pasha Zade harmonized most of the man-made legislation of the Ottoman State with the sacred law, and remedied the defects in both the civil and the religious administration. Thus they put the state in order."[11] Not all the problems were solved. Some issues were in perpetual contention, indicating structural differences in basic outlook, as well as in matters of procedure such as laws of evidence and witness testimonies. Still, sixteenth-century *kanun*s are a masterpiece of equilibrium between the needs of state and the demands of sacred law.[12]

Although in *kanunnāme*s[13] sent to courts of law throughout the empire the reverse was clearly stated, whenever sultanic law and the *şeriat* were in disagreement, the sultan's law was the overriding system. Judges were expected to uphold this principle, sometimes against their better judgment.[14] As a result, for several centuries a symbiosis existed between the two systems, such that makes it difficult to discern, when reading the records of Middle Eastern courts, which parts of the judicial process were dictated by the *şeriat* and which by the *kanun.* State officials upheld this symbiotic coexistence as one of the pillars of the empire, a marvel of wisdom and statecraft.[15] Perhaps at low ebb during the later seventeenth and eighteenth centuries, it never disappeared completely. From the inception of the *Tanzimat* reforms at the beginning of the nineteenth century we find a resurgence of the *kanun-şeriat* system, which went on to influence legislation during the formation of the late Ottoman legal code known as the *Mecelle* in the 1870s and 1880s. Even though there was no longer consensus as to the *şeriat*'s preeminence, such conceptions of a combined legal system can be traced even to the present day. Thus, one may argue that legal systems in former provinces such as today's Egypt and Tunisia, where the *sharīʿa* is formally considered a major source of law promulgation, follow the same pattern.

We may say with some certainty, therefore, that wherever tensions or discrepancies arose, there was a conscious and persistent effort to harmonize the *kanun* with the *şeriat.* While in matters such as violent crimes and revenues the state would do its utmost to preserve its power and affect legislation, even at the expense of upsetting this careful balance, in sexual matters this was obviously not the case. Given their desire to maintain the empire's appearance as guardian of the sacred law, lawmakers could have left regulation of sex to the *şeriat,* with minor amendments, such as in rules of evidence and testimony. The fact that they chose to enter this minefield and to insert fundamental changes in laws concerning sexual behavior, as we shall see in the following sections, attests, I believe, to the importance of these changes. If we accept this premise, another conclusion to be drawn is that in examining state laws we have to pay special attention to nuance. Treading cautiously in an effort to keep friction to a minimum, legislators were careful in their choice of words and definitions. Considered in this light, variations in emphasis or wording may serve as indications of shifts in legal and social emphases, of enhanced social control, and perhaps even of the way the whole amalgam of extramarital sex was perceived.

What follows is an examination of the treatment of criminal law and, more specifically, sexual transgression as they figure in both flanks of this symbiosis: *şeriat* injunctions, sometimes harking back to the first centuries of Islam, and *kanun* legislation of the sixteenth century. The purpose of the examination is to unravel the way in which the promulgation of the *kanun* changed the emphases of the *şeriat,* and to suggest reasons for these changes in emphasis.

## SEXUAL TRANSGRESSION IN THE *ŞERIAT*

A comparison between the *kanun* and the *şeriat* in the field of sexual conduct should begin with an examination of the boundaries of transgression in each code (which may be seen inversely as the sexual boundaries of the household, or of legal sex). These boundaries may be described in the form of a grid pattern or a table enumerating violations of proper sexual conduct and the punishments these entailed.[16]

The first thing to notice is that the *şeriat* was never fully codified and that a great deal of ambiguity remains as to its exact rulings in many matters. Indeed, there is no single code that claims to represent its rulings until the nineteenth century. In our world of clear-cut legal codes, the tendency of Islamic jurists to present an open-ended discussion, albeit making their views clear, might seem impractical. But this practice had its roots in the surrounding cultures of the Middle East in late antiquity where such a mode of presentation was considered more polite, fair, and reasonable, and where, to quote Daniel Boyarin, "ideologies are always in dialogue with their others within the culture."[17] It also had to do with the idea of *ijmāʿ* (consensus), as if the author were saying, "I present my views on the matter along with contrasting opinions, and I leave it to my peers to reach consensus on the matter at hand."

In any case, by comparing several compilations of discussion from the thirteenth to the sixteenth century, we may arrive at a more or less accurate description of mainstream Sunni legal concepts regarding sexual offenses.[18] Within these there is an emphasis on the Ḥanafi (Hanefi) school of law *(madhhab, mezhep)*, regarded by the ruling elite as the leading school, but consideration is also given to other schools: the Shāfiʿi, the Māliki, and the Ḥanbali were known and their teachings followed in other regions of the empire. These various schools should be viewed as a law-making pool from which the creators of Ottoman law could draw. More important, in their discussions they sometimes present the opposition Ḥanafi view more clearly than the Ḥanafis themselves. The sources used here represent several major legal authorities that were known and often used by jurisconsults.[19] Although they differ in some ways from one another and sometimes prescribe different punishments or solutions, their basic outlook is very similar and is shared by most other legal sources.

The *şeriat* is not an egalitarian law system. It assumes that there are basic differences between categories of people and that the law should thus treat them differently. In discussions of sexual offenses there are several basic lines of demarcation. The first differentiates between men and women. In almost every case, even when punishments are similar, the *şeriat* makes a point of referring separately to males and females. Further important distinctions are between married and unmarried, adult and minor, Muslim and non-Muslim, free and slave. In the realm of judicial process, the *şeriat* stresses the koranic differentiation between "regular" crimes *(jināyāt)* and those transgressing limits set by God *(ḥudūd*, sing. *ḥadd)*. These latter include crimes and misdemeanors such as fornication *(zinā')*, false accusation of fornication, theft, and drunkenness. While *ḥudūd* crimes violating specific divine principles are to be harshly and decisively punished, *jināyāt*, including manslaughter and assault, are often left to be resolved by the negotiating parties. Islamic legal thought did much to attenuate the differences, to prescribe punishments for *jināyāt*, and to allow the kadi some discretion in punishing *ḥudūd* crimes when the strict demands for evidence were not met. Yet this basic distinction was prevalent in *sharʿi* thought, and remains unchanged to our day.

These opposites—man-woman, adult-minor, married-unmarried, free-slave, as well as the pair *ḥudūd* and *jināyāt*—can be traced in most law books and in every treatise about sexual crime. They may be seen as the basic grid lines along which the *şeriat* considers any subject relating to sexual transgression. Other dynamic contrasts, which we know existed in Islamic history and in other premodern societies, such as between upper and lower classes, race or ethnicity, citizen/subject and noncitizen, and violent and nonviolent crimes, are seldom referred to.[20] Neither is there serious reference to questions of male and female position in intercourse. The absence of these categories, which were so important in late antiquity, is evidence of the great revolution that Islamic legal thought heralded in its outlook on sexuality in the first centuries.[21]

Within these categories, the law lays emphasis on several themes. First and foremost is *zinā'*, which can be translated as both fornication and adultery and refers to almost any act of illicit "straight" sex.[22] For women this includes any full sexual coitus barring intercourse with the legal husband or master. Intercourse is defined here as the insertion of the male penis into the female vulva. For males, *zinā'* is interpreted to mean sexual intercourse with any but the four legal wives and an unlimited number of female slaves (or, in the words of Islamic jurists, where there is no claim to ownership of the vulva by the man).[23] This basic difference between men and women, allowing men the privilege of sex with many partners, runs through all *şeriat* sex laws and accounts for distinctions in punishment for male and female.

If convicted of *zinā'*, both men and women are liable to be punished by death or severe beating, but conviction is rendered almost impossible by two mechanisms. The first is the need for four trustworthy male eyewitnesses to the act; the second is the notion of quasi-ownership *(shubhat al-milk)*, which affords men a series of claims to ownership in many cases (such as sex with a female slave who does not belong to him, but can be shown to have been received as a pledge).[24]

Deliberations of same-sex intercourse in *şeriat* literature closely follow these grid lines. Same-sex anal intercourse practices are usually referred to in legal texts as *liwāṭ* or *'amal qawm lūṭ* (the deeds of Lot's people), harking back to the biblical story of Sodom. The Koran recounts this story in considerably more detail, accusing "Lot's people" of "approaching men lustfully instead of women."[25] One of the first problems the *ulema* had to deal with in this respect is whether such practices are equivalent to *zinā'*, and should be punished as *ḥudūd* offenses defying God's commandments. There was no doubt in any jurist's mind that these were serious sexual transgressions, but the Koran does not explicitly discuss homoerotic sex in the framework of the punishment for *zinā'*. In the formative texts of the *sharī'a*, a long debate ensued on crime and punishment for same-sex intercourse. According to most of the jurists, only acts mentioned explicitly by the Koran as crimes committed against God can be punished as *ḥudūd*, and the principle of *qiyas*, analogy between two comparable cases, cannot apply here.

Abu Ḥanīfa, the eponymous founder of the Ḥanafi School, drew an analogy between homoerotic anal intercourse and similar intercourse with women, coming to the conclusion that since the male organ is not inserted into the vulva, neither falls into the category of *ḥadd*. So even though intercourse between males is an abominable crime, for which they will surely receive divine punishment, it is not a *ḥadd* offense.[26] Many jurists declared that in principle perpetrators should be executed, but even the strict Ḥanbali jurist Ibn Taymiyya, who insists on the death penalty for both perpetrators, concedes that repentance should obviate punishment.[27] The question of punishment for sex between males remained moot and subject to heated debate in all schools of law.[28] The reader is left with a sense of ambiguity concerning such crimes. They are described in the most derogatory terms and are often accompanied by warnings of doom for those who indulge in them, but the question of punishment is in most cases left undetermined.

Female homoerotic practices *(siḥāq, musāḥaqa)* add another dimension to these deliberations. Since the basic requirement for a sexual offense to be declared *zinā'*—the insertion of a male organ—is absent, it is even more removed from the basic concept of fornication and the punishment of *ḥudūd*. Some jurists, notably the Ḥanbalis, demand a discretionary punishment *(taʿ zīr)* by the kadi for such acts. Yet again, most sources are in agreement that although the act should be condemned, no legal punishment is required.[29]

Further questions are raised about the age, freedom of choice, and religious belief of perpetrators of sexual offenses. Ḥanbali texts see no reason to differentiate between slaves and freeborn in this respect, but other schools operate on the basic premise that slaves, not having full jurisdiction over their own bodies, should also have diminished legal responsibility, and that free men and women should be punished more severely.[30] Most sources prescribe harsher punishments for married people engaging in homoerotic sex, and most concede that a minor's responsibility is more limited than that of an adult. There is very little discussion in Islamic legal texts of the period about the sexual positions of parties to the sex act (penetrator/penetrated, sometimes described as active/passive).[31] Finally, here and there questions are raised concerning sexual relations between people of different religions. Views on this issue are also divided: Ḥanafis and Mālikis consider it permissible under certain conditions, whereas the Ḥanbalis ardently oppose it.[32] The general tendency is to prohibit and punish sexual intercourse between non-Muslim men and Muslim women. Tables 3 and 4 describe the most common views about punishment for sexual offenses in Islamic law up to the sixteenth century.

TABLE 3. COMMON PUNISHMENTS FOR MALE SEXUAL OFFENSES IN THE *SHARĪʿA*

| | Status | | | |
|---|---|---|---|---|
| *Offense* | *Minor Male* | *Unmarried Male* | *Married Male* | *Other Male* |
| Heterosexual *zinā'* | If sexually active and participated in *zinā'*: *ḥadd*, lashes | *Ḥadd*, lashes | *Ḥadd:* death penalty | Slave: reduced punishment (50 lashes) |
| Homosexual *zinā'* | *Aḥdāth*, *murd*, usually considered unpunishable | Debated: *ḥadd* or none<br>Even if no *ḥadd*, lashes and "suffering" *(taʿzīb)*<br>Some insist on stoning | Debated: *ḥadd* or none<br>If *ḥadd:* stoning or beheading<br>Abu Hanifa suggests imprisonment<br>Some suggest no punishment | |
| Sodomy with legal spouse | Debated: some say forbidden, but no punishment | Debated: some say forbidden, but no punishment | Debated: some say forbidden, but no punishment | |
| Sex with slaves | | Forbidden with father's or wife's or mother's female slave | Forbidden with father's or wife's or mother's female slave | *Dhimmis* cannot have sex with Muslims |
| Minors in sex | No such category | | | |
| Procuring and prostitution | | Procuring of slave girls is prohibited | Procuring of slave girls is prohibited | |

| | | | |
|---|---|---|---|
| Abduction and marriage | | | |
| Abduction; no marriage/rape | | | |
| Sexual harassment | | Forbidden, but no punishment unless intercourse took place | Forbidden, but no punishment unless intercourse took place |
| Severe harassment | No such category | | |
| Rape | Debated: some say no *ḥadd* punishment for raped minor male, although minor's erection is proof of lust | | Husband may divorce raped wife, but should not detract from *ṣadāq* |
| Perjury and hearsay evidence | | *Ḥadd:* same punishment as for *zinā'* | *Ḥadd:* same punishment as for *zinā'* |

TRANSLATION OF TERMS: *aḥdāth* and *murd* = beardless boys; *dhimmi*s = non-Muslim subjects under Islamic rule; *ḥadd* = a crime against God; *ṣadāq* = dowry; *ta'zīb* = shaming or causing to suffer; *zinā'* = fornication/adultery

NOTE: In all tables, empty cells indicate that the *șeriat* or *kanun* law did not address the relevant categories.

TABLE 4. COMMON PUNISHMENTS FOR FEMALE SEXUAL OFFENSES IN THE *SHARĪʿA*

| | Status | | | |
|---|---|---|---|---|
| *Offense* | *Minor Female* | *Unmarried Female* | *Married Female* | *Other Female* |
| Heterosexual *zinā'* | *Ḥadd* punishment: lashes | *Ḥadd* punishment: lashes | *Ḥadd* punishment: stoning, unless raped | Divorced and widowed wives are not considered *muḥṣan;* therefore no death penalty |
| Homosexual *zinā'* | | Debated: most agree on discretionary punishment. No *ḥadd* because no insertion | Debated: most agree on discretionary punishment. No *ḥadd* because no insertion | |
| Sodomy with legal spouse | | | No punishment for wife | |
| Sex with slaves | | | | |
| Minors in sex | | | | |
| Procuring and prostitution | | Procuring of slave girls is prohibited | Procuring of slave girls is prohibited | |
| Abduction and marriage | | | | |
| Abduction; no marriage/rape | | | | |
| Sexual harassment | | | | |
| Severe harassment | | | | |
| Rape | | | Husband may divorce raped wife, but she keeps her rights | |
| Perjury and hearsay evidence | | *Ḥadd,* same punishment as for *zinā'* | *Ḥadd,* same punishment as for *zinā'* | |

NOTE: In all tables, empty cells indicate that the *şeriat* and *kanun* law did not address the relevant categories.

## SEXUAL TRANSGRESSION IN THE *KANUN*

It is sometimes claimed that the *kanun*'s origin is local custom, or older Turkish or Mongol legal systems, and therefore it is based on principles completely different from those of the *şeriat.*[33] There may be some truth in these assumptions about origins, but when we compare the basic premises of both systems, we can say with certainty that at least where criminal law is concerned, the legal mind that created the imperial *kanun* was greatly influenced by the underlying structure of the *şeriat.* This is true also of pre-Ottoman *kanun* systems and contemporary ones such as that of Dulgadir, which Uriel Heyd translated and studied.[34] Yet though there are visible similarities between the *şeriat* and the *kanun,* there are also meaningful differences. The different attitude of the *kanun* can be clearly discerned in the legal codes promulgated in the mid-sixteenth century under Kanuni Sultan Süleyman ("the Law-Giver" or "the Magnificent" as he was known in Western Europe), who ruled from 1520 to 1566. As his moniker suggests, one of Süleyman's most important attributes in the eyes of his subjects was his immersion in questions of law and legislation.

For several centuries following its promulgation, Süleyman's series of codes, known as *Kanun-i Osmani,* were considered the most important body of sultanic law in the empire, and subsequent sultans were given new copies as they came to the throne.[35] Attaching great importance to sexual offenses, it opens with a chapter on *zinā' (zinaya muteallik curmi beyan eyler).* The first regulation in the code concerns a married Muslim male who commits fornication:

> If a Muslim commits *zinā',* if it is proven by the *şeriat* and the perpetrator is a married man, and if the perpetrator has a property of over a thousand *akçe,* he should pay a fine of 300 *akçe.* If he is of medium sized property of up to six hundred *akçe* he should pay 200 *akçe.* Below this, up to 400, a fine of 100 [will be demanded]. If his property is smaller, a fine of 50 *akçe,* and if his situation is strict poverty *[gayet fakir olsa],* 40 *akçe* will be taken.[36]

The *kanunnāme* then goes on to detail the punishments for *zinā'* committed by unmarried men, married women, widows, slaves, and others, with a list of fines attached to each. Other crimes in this chapter include solicitation, entering a house with intent to commit sexual intercourse, sexual harassment, and false accusation. Other chapters mention crimes such as pederasty, solicitation and prostitution, prohibition of male-female gatherings near the public bathhouse or near a water source, and false accusations of *zinā'*.[37]

The *kanun* accepts the basic *şeriat* distinctions between men and women, adults and minors, free and slave, Muslim and non-Muslim. As in the *şeriat*, these categories run the gamut of *kanun* legislation relating to sexual transgression and eclipse all other categories. If we try to construct a table of crimes and their punishments (see tables 5 and 6), the basic grid lines will be almost the same as those of the *şeriat*.[38] However, the *kanun* adds several other instruments to its socio-legal toolbox. These include punishments that do not exist in the *şeriat* such as fines, banishment, or forced labor; a progressive scale of pecuniary fines; and a differentiation between violent and nonviolent crimes of passion. On the other hand, presenting, as it were, only the human aspects of the law, it dispenses with the *şeriat*'s division of *ḥudūd/jināyāt,* while paying lip service to the principle. Another distinction is that the *kanun* identifies as legal bodies entities such as villages, town quarters, and households or extended family structures. These bodies are responsible for morality, for driving out criminals, for locating family members who are runaway criminals, and for handing them over to the police. Perhaps more important for our purposes is the legal outcome, which, based on the same basic distinctions and on the same basic legal reasoning, reflects very different concerns and values.

To begin with, penalties prescribed in the *kanun* are much more lenient than those prescribed by the *şeriat*. Thus, for fornication *(zinā'),* the perpetrator will only be fined according to his or her status. Flogging is prescribed as punishment for a few crimes, such as recurrent procuring. In cases of rape or abduction, where serious violence is involved, the perpetrator is to be punished by castration. No sex crimes are punishable by death. *Kanun* regulations sometimes emphasize that punishments should "kick in" only if and when the perpetrators are not punished by the *şeriat*. This is often perceived as mere lip service to the sacred law, but it is a necessary element in combining the two systems. What the *kanun* seems to imply is that there are "perfect" cases where the *şeriat*'s strict demands for proof and intention could be met. In these cases, the punishment sanctioned by sacred law is required. In "imperfect" cases, however, which make up the great majority of cases, and where guilt can be proven only by more flexible standards, the sultan's law should be allowed to take its course.[39] This may be seen as an extension of the principle of discretionary punishment allowed by the *şeriat* in such cases.

As mentioned earlier, the punishment for most offenses committed by consenting adults is a fine, a type of punishment nonexistent in the *şeriat*. The range of fines is determined by five factors: wealth, personal

TABLE 5. PUNISHMENTS FOR MALE SEXUAL OFFENSES IN THE *KANUN*

| | Status | | | |
|---|---|---|---|---|
| *Offense* | *Minor Male* | *Unmarried Male* | *Married Male* | *Other Male* |
| Heterosexual *zinā'* | | Progressive fine (100; 50; 30) | Progressive fine (300; 200; 100; 50; 40) | Slave: half the fine of a free man in same category |
| Homosexual *zinā'* | With other minors: punishment and fine | Progressive fine (100; 50; 30) | Progressive fine (300; 200; 100; 50; 40) | |
| Sodomy with legal spouse | | | Chastisement and fine | |
| Sex with slaves | | With father's or wife's or mother's female slave: chastisement and fine | With father's or wife's or mother's female slave: chastisement and fine[a] | |
| Minors in sex | If child yields to pederast, chastisement. Also fine for father | If child yields to male assailant, chastisement and fine; face blackened, nose and ears cut | | |
| Procuring and prostitution | | Procuring of slave girls is prohibited | Procuring of slave girls is prohibited | |
| Abduction and marriage | | Divorce and punishment Kadi performing the ceremony shaved and fined | Divorce and punishment Kadi performing the ceremony shaved and chastised | Infidels should pay half the fine |
| Abduction; no marriage/rape | | Even if only intent: castration | Even if only intent: castration | |
| Sexual harassment | | Entering with intent: punished as *zinā'*. Kissing, words (boy or girl): chastised = only fine | Entering with intent: punished as *zinā'*. Kissing, words (boy or girl): chastised = only fine | |

*(continued)*

TABLE 5 *(continued)*

| | Status | | | |
|---|---|---|---|---|
| *Offense* | *Minor Male* | *Unmarried Male* | *Married Male* | *Other Male* |
| Severe harassment | | For stripping, severe indignities, cutting hair: chastisement and prison | For stripping, severe indignities, cutting hair: chastisement and prison | |
| Rape | | | | |
| Perjury and hearsay evidence | | If accused woman swears innocence: chastisement and fine for accuser. If man falsely accuses another: chastisement only | If accused woman swears innocence: chastisement and fine for accuser. If man falsely accuses another: chastisement only | |

[a] If with his son's female slave or his own *mukātaba* (a female slave whom the owner has pledged to manumit at a certain later date), there should be no punishment.

NOTE: In all tables, empty cells indicate that the *şeriat* and *kanun* law did not address the relevant categories.

TABLE 6. PUNISHMENTS FOR FEMALE SEXUAL OFFENSES IN THE *KANUN*

| | Status | | | |
|---|---|---|---|---|
| *Offense* | *Minor Female* | *Unmarried Female* | *Married Female* | *Other Female* |
| Heterosexual *zinā'* | Progressive fine (100; 50; 30) | Progressive fine (100; 50; 30) | Progressive fine (300; 200; 100; 50; 40)[a] | Widow: progressive fine (100; 50; 30)<br>Slave: half the fine |
| Homosexual *zinā'* | | | | |
| Sodomy with legal spouse | | | | |
| Sex with slaves | | | | |
| Minors in sex | | | | |
| Procuring and prostitution | | Chastisement and fine | Chastisement and fine | Infidels: half the fine |
| Abduction and marriage | | If cooperating: her vulva to be branded and fine paid by father | If cooperating: her vulva to be branded and fine paid by father | |
| Abduction; no marriage/rape | | | | |
| Sexual harassment | | | | |
| Severe harassment | | | | |
| Rape | | | | |
| Perjury and hearsay evidence | | If accused man swears innocence and there is no evidence: chastisement and fine for the woman | Rumor of fornication: accused pair cannot marry even if woman is divorced. If accused man swears innocence and there is no evidence: chastisement and fine for the woman | |

[a] If woman's cuckolded husband accepts her, he shall pay the fine.

NOTE: In all tables, empty cells indicate that the *şeriat* and *kanun* law did not address the relevant categories.

status, age, servile status, and religion. We may construct a scale according to which in most cases a wealthy, married, free adult Muslim man or woman would pay the highest sum. For a *zinā'* offense, such a man would have to pay 300 aspers *(akçe)*. A poor male slave would have to pay only 25 aspers for the same offense. A poor, unmarried free woman would pay 30. Others would pay fines relative to their station.[40]

Another point is that penalties for female sexual offenders are in most cases equivalent in form, as well as gravity, to those set down for men. Although the *şeriat* also preaches equal treatment of men and women, it insists on formal distinctions. For committing the same *zinā'* offense, according to the *şeriat*, a man is to be punished by stoning, while a woman is to be beheaded. In the *kanun*, this insistence on different punishments disappears. A free married woman committing adultery is required to pay a fine identical to the one paid by a free married man in the same economic category, and a spinster or a widow has to pay a fine similar to the one paid by men of comparable status. It is worthwhile noting here that *kanun*s from the neighboring state of Dulgadir, which were older and probably served as an example for Ottoman legislators, still differentiate between punishments for men and women. According to the Dulgadir code, a guilty woman should pay only half the fine imposed on a man guilty of the same offense.

A woman who has committed adultery is required by the *şeriat* to divorce her husband (and, of course, there are harsher punishments in store for her). The *kanun*, however, in stark contrast, states that in case the husband is willing to continue marital life with his wife, he may do so: "If [the husband] nevertheless accepts her, and he is rich, he shall pay 100 *akçe* by way of fine [imposed on a consenting] cuckold *[köftehor]*— but it has been customary to collect 300 *akçe* by way of fine [imposed] on a cuckold, if he is in average circumstances he shall pay 50 *akçe*, if he is poor, 40 or 30 *akçe*."[41] Men were indeed expected to divorce their fornicating wives, but if they did not, they were only required to pay another fine, as "cuckolds," in addition to paying their wives' fines. The legal logic appears to be that by staying married, the husband in effect participates in his wife's crime or at least condones it, and is therefore culpable. In practice this may have been a rare case, but nevertheless it admits the possibility of continued marriage following a wife's infidelity. No similar injunction is set for truant husbands.

Last but not least, regulations that apply to heterosexual adultery and those that apply to homosexual offenses are similar. Persons engaging in homosexual acts (which were not always strictly demarcated from having anal intercourse with women) are demanded to pay exactly the same fines as men and women caught in an act of adultery.[42] There is one case where this rule does not apply—young men offering their sexual services to older men. These are to be punished by flogging and a fine. If the offender in this case is a minor, his father or guardian has to pay in his place. It is interesting to note that female homoerotic intercourse is not considered a felony, and there is no law pertaining to it.

The *kanun* of the sixteenth century, at least in matters of sexual morality, may appear to be relatively permissive. In anachronistic terms it may even be viewed as liberal. But, as Heyd and Imber have shown, a closer look reveals that this is not necessarily so. The *şeriat,* prescribing harsh punishments for sexual offenses, made it almost impossible to indict and condemn people for such offenses. Its strict demand for several qualified eyewitnesses who saw the act itself and can attest to the actual insertion of the organ, as well as the threat of harsh punishment for false accusations, made these laws all but inapplicable.[43] In the *kanun,* although punishments are less severe, a person could be tortured in order to elicit a confession of guilt, or, if no confession is obtained, convicted and punished on very flimsy circumstantial grounds. In sum, therefore, each of the two systems strikes a different balance between evidence and punishment. Evidential gaps between crimes and punitive sentences in the *şeriat* proved to be too difficult to bridge, and in this sense the *kanun* should be seen as a corrective. The differences between the *şeriat* and the *kanun* should be sought not in the degree of overall leniency, but rather in the different premises, aims, and priorities of each system.

For one thing, these differences reflect the need of a ruling government to impose law and order on its subjects. While the *şeriat* was mostly formed outside the ruling institutions, the *kanun* is the product of a strong state, with a tendency to centralize and bureaucratize. This tendency is evident first and foremost in the realm of law enactment and bureaucratization of the courts. Since sexual offenses were always considered a source of unrest, and since the religious code left many problems unresolved, the state bureaucracy realized that it needed a more efficient mechanism to regulate and control sexuality.

Yet the sultanic codes (and in this case Süleyman's *kanunnāme* is just one among several) recast adultery and fornication as relatively minor offenses for which, instead of the death penalty, a fine would be paid. The change encompassed all possible perpetrators, men and women alike, and all forms of sex, including same-sex intercourse. Exceptions were violent sex crimes, kidnapping, procuring, prostitution and pederasty, in short, sexual offenses that contained an element of violence or solicitation. Even admitting the rarity of executions for adultery under *şeriat* law and the fact that most people in this society were strict believers, this set of rules sent out an entirely new message and formulated an entirely new legal-sexual script. At least from the ruling class's vantage point, adultery and fornication were not grave crimes or sins against the creator. They were regarded as what in later codes of law became known as felonies or misdemeanors. One could pay an admittedly heavy fine and go on with life. A fornicating woman could return to her husband and her home and be forgiven, at least by the state.

European travelers to the Middle East prior to the nineteenth century often recounted harrowing tales of adulterous wives drowned in the Bosphorus and of men slashing the throats of their wives and daughters on such suspicions. Although clearly exaggerated, their stories may have had some foundation in truth. In seventeenth-century Jerusalem, for instance, a relatively high number of cases were reported to the *sharīʿa* court in which women were found dead, ostensibly by accident. This may imply that at least in rural societies, some men took the law into their own hands and the court turned a blind eye. Still, the fact that such cases were not brought to court and that during the same period very few cases dealt with adultery shows that this leniency was also carried into social praxis.[44]

But how can we explain the very detailed and progressive system of fines? Is it an egalitarian approach? Could it be an indication of the state's recognition of the social values of equality? In trying to explain this phenomenon we should bear in mind the fiscal structure of the empire. Based on a clear division between those who paid taxes (usually referred to as the *reaya*) and those who received the economic surplus (the *askeri*), with a much smaller group in between who neither paid nor received, the Ottoman empire was not a progressive modern state. Furthermore, the bureaucracy did not often regard any single person as an independent socioeconomic entity. People were always considered part of a larger group—a village, a household, or a tribe—and thus consideration of a person's economic status should not have been the norm for legislators. A better explanation involves the concept of accountability. The *şeriat* already recognizes the reduced responsibility of slaves, youths, and non-Muslims. Ottoman-era lawmakers seem to have developed and perfected the principle to suit their needs. According to the new hierarchy, adult members of the wealthier *askeri* ruling aristocracy always had full responsibility for their actions. Others were less accountable, on a descending scale in relation to the aforementioned categories. One could not expect a poor young slave woman to be as accountable for her actions as her mistress.[45] Nor, for that matter, could one expect an immensely wealthy and powerful slave, such as the grand vizier, to be less accountable than a journeyman.

The implications of this new legal order for sexual culture are far-reaching. In effect, this Ottoman hierarchy stands the concepts of sexuality common in late antiquity on their head. Choice of sexual partner is not a unique privilege of "mature free (Muslim) males," as it supposedly was in ancient Greece and in the *şeriat.* On the contrary, by laying down a progressive scale of fines, the system favors the socially underprivileged. At least as a script available to the public, a guide for sexual behavior, the *kanun,* with its codified orderly laws, declared that while the ruling elite was bound by moral responsibility, the lower classes were allowed a wider margin for illicit conduct. The *kanun* does not curtail slaves' sexual freedom any more than it does that of free people; nor is there mention of any gender-defined restrictions on sex. In male homoerotic sex, the question of who penetrates whom is seldom discussed. It seems to be taken for granted that unless the crime in this case is pederasty, that is, older men having sex with minors, it is not a serious crime.

Equality between men and women in the same economic bracket where fines are concerned suggests an underlying social system where men and women possess property and are regarded as economically equal. This may be highlighted by a comparison with the code of Dulgadir, from around the same time, in which women were supposed to pay half the fine demanded of men. Such a comparison demonstrates once more that the Ottomans made conscious changes to the law, in accordance with social practice and worldview.

One explanation for this new sexual outlook has to do with the emergence and development of households. The household was the basic building block of the state and the elite from the sixteenth century on. Heads of such households, most of them the sultan's slaves, became grand viziers, ministers, governors of provinces, and commanders of the army, and many served in rotation as *nişancı*s (bearers of the seal), *reisülküttab*s (chancellors), and high-level functionaries of the imperial palace. Indeed, the sultan himself, often the son of a slave girl and growing up in the harem, was part of this group. These men, perhaps more than any other social group, had a hand in the shaping and promulgation of the *kanun.*

Yet these people were not born into the aristocracy. Their origins were often humble and obscure. Service in the palace in the sixteenth and seventeenth centuries was based mainly on meritocratic values, and economic or social status did not always hold value for one's place in the political hierarchy. Many of the officials were recruited as slaves from lowly Christian village families and retained memories of their origins and of their childhood days. We know that many in the Ottoman slave elite re-established contact with their original families. Although they were never reintegrated into their old biological family (one of the reasons being that they became part of a Muslim aristocracy), they created *vakıf*s (*waqf*s) and built public institutions for their villages, sent their children back to their regions of origin to be raised, and in general reclaimed their own pasts. This must have influenced the way they conceived of social and economic differences. The concept of reduced responsibility for the lower classes may have emerged from that background.[46]

From another perspective, a new household came into being each time a *kul,* a state's servant, was granted permission to form one, usually accompanied by marriage to an aristocratic wife (without necessarily being manumitted beforehand). The new house functioned as a surrogate family for its founder. Brought into the empire's service as slaves, members of the governing elite regarded their own retinue, slaves, and concubines as a circle of support and familial warmth. This perpetual creation of families, in which the founder himself was partially detached from homeland and social roots and often married to a woman of superior status, was not favorable to a strict patriarchal structure. The lady of the house was the man's equal or even his superior. This situation may have led to a different sexual-hierarchical conception of society.

Yet another layer of explanation, not entirely independent of the previous one, and admittedly more tentative, has to do with the first glimpses of women's power at court. Although the period referred to as "the Sultanate of Women" only began a few decades after the promulgation of these codes, by the mid-sixteenth century the sultan's mothers, wives, and concubines already resided in the palace and had considerable power in court and state. We may assume that they also exerted an indirect influence on law enactment. Their position in the royal court (and in its many corollaries in smaller households) probably suggested a more egalitarian approach to questions of gender, especially since the sultan himself was often involved in legislation.

Finally, there was also the possibility of influence from below. In the towns and villages of Anatolia, marital and sexual affairs were often adjudicated in accordance with local custom. Kadis working in these areas were sometimes more lenient when it came to questions of fornication and extramarital sex. In some cases, more liberal pre-Islamic customs retained their power long after the advent of the Ottoman state. The authorities were familiar with local customs, and the promulgation of the *kanun* may have taken some of these customs into consideration.[47]

To recap, from the sixteenth century onward, the *şeriat* and the *kanun* were amalgamated, or came very close to amalgamation, into one legal system in the empire. Most *kanun* experts describe the effort to make the two systems compatible, but their basic assumption is that they remained too distant from each other to form one whole. Our new understanding of the dynamic nature of lawmaking in the Muslim world, coupled with a better comprehension of the *şeriat* as a set of premises rather than a legal code, have supplied us with sufficient contradictory evidence to doubt the veracity of the old "dual-system" view. I suggest a different concept here, according to which the sultanic law and the *şeriat* did, in fact, come to form one compatible system. The *kanun* was interwoven with the *şeriat* with painstaking care within the sphere that legal experts of the time could have accepted as Islamic, inside the boundaries of *örf* and *siyaset*.

This merger has important implications for our discussion of the relationship between law and society as it relates to sexual transgression. If we can regard the *kanun* and the *şeriat* as parts of one almost integrated system, the common basis for comparison becomes much wider. There was an important element of self-awareness in legislation. On the basis of this assumption, we can describe discrepancies between the two systems not as two different conceptions of law, but rather as evolution within the same legal and cultural sphere. Thus we may assume that those loci where the *kanun* insists on parting with the *şeriat* and promulgating a different set of laws are not accidental, but rather replicate the cultural and political dynamics of the period, and that even small changes were premeditated and meaningful.

The period's legal codes reflect the emergence of a new household pattern, with different emphases and restrictions. A new type of ruling elite came into being and acquired political and economic power. This elite group contributed to the shaping of Ottoman legal practices, and the *kanun* carries significant traces of their social outlook and their cultural world.

Describing the nature of these practices and the definition of areas in which differences were systematically maintained and those in which the *kanun* preferred not to challenge the *şeriat*'s reasoning constitutes the second part of the argument. *Kanun* injunctions did not change the basic categories of right and wrong suggested by the *şeriat*. There was no attempt to introduce new social categories or ethnic and racial divisions. On the whole the elite seem to have accepted the Islamic ideal of an *umma*, an Islamic "nation," that is not divided by race, class, or ethnicity. Yet the *kanun* offers a sociosexual script very different from previous legal systems. It seeks to improve the status of women vis-à-vis sexual morality, to enhance equality in heteroerotic and homoerotic sex, and to prescribe more lenient punishment for nonviolent sexual offenses. A parallel attempt was made to punish violent sex crimes more harshly than those that did not involve violence.

## BREAKING WITH TRADITION

In the late-seventeenth-century Middle East, *kanun* legislation was allowed to fade away and kadis returned to *şeriat* literature for adjudication of sexual crimes. This is usually attributed to a period of intense religiosity generally seen as part of the process of decline within the state.[48] The argument presented earlier may, however, provide a better explanation. Rather than attributing the tribulations of the *kanun* and the reemergence of the *şeriat* to a never-ending decline and growing religious zeal, we may suggest that *kanun* legislation represented the outlook of specific elites at a particular historical juncture at the center of the empire. In later centuries major changes occurred, including a localization of Ottoman elites in the provinces, an entrenchment of old households as a quasi-aristocracy, and the reestablishment of orthodox *ulema* households that took over the craft of legislation and rearranged it to fit their own different legal (and hence sexual) outlook. The active promulgation of laws was never neglected altogether. In this respect there may be more than just a casual connection between the laws of sixteenth-century *kanunnāmes* and those enacted two hundred and fifty years later, in the Reform (Tanzimat) era. Alongside the infusion of external legal thought, underpinning the new codes were internal developments of previous centuries.

New impetus was given to the production of laws in the nineteenth century. The state's attempts to redefine itself, centralize, and cohere, both at the center and in some of the provinces (mainly in Egypt and Tunisia), brought with it a surge of legislation in civil law, commercial and naval affairs, contracts, and criminal law. Unlike attempts made in former centuries, this round of legislation was characterized by a conscious separation from the *şeriat* and was measured against the highlighted backdrop of European legal systems. Mention was made of the *şeriat*'s sacred status, and the old tradition of *kanun* was invoked, not least by using the name *kanunnāme* for the new legislation, but this time legislators chose a different path, which marked a deep breach with the previous attempt to harmonize both systems.

Legislation efforts began with the establishment of new armies in Egypt and at the center of the empire in the first three decades, but the bulk of new legislation work began in the late 1830s, following the establishment, in 1837, of the Meclis-i Valayı Ahkam-ı Adliye, or the Council of Justice, as it came to be known, under Sultan Mahmud II. The famous Gülhane Rescript of 1839, which launched the Reforms, gave these efforts royal sanction and formal endorsement. A first collection of regulations, titled *Ceza Kanunname-i Hümayun,* or Royal Criminal Code, was promulgated by a committee headed by Hüsrev Paşa, a veteran palace slave and former grand vizier, in 1840. Copies of it were sent to all province governors and courts with directions to apply them in courts. This was little more than an elaboration of the principles discussed in the Gülhane Rescript, with an emphasis on questions relating to the conduct of state officials, eradication of bribery, equality in adjudication, and other laws associated with a growing bureaucratic state. Deliberations of principle and punishment were cursory and issues of sexual conduct were not brought up.[49]

A few years later, in 1858, under Sultan Abdülmecid, another code of criminal law was promulgated by a committee in which Ahmed Cevdet Paşa, who was to lead legislation efforts for the next three decades, played a leading role. Trained as a traditional *ʿālim* who attained the prestigious rank of Mecca kadi, Cevdet embraced the Reform movement and was a zealous promulgator of new "Western-style" laws. His committee's code of law, titled *Kanunname-i Ceza* (Criminal Code), is more detailed than the previous one, and the principles of legislation are spelled out in the preamble. Some thought was given to the relationship with the *şeriat,* and the guiding concept offered is that the criminal code is situated in the gray area where the *şeriat* has no say. Whenever the *şeriat* decrees that criminal matters be returned to the concerned parties for arbitration, the new code explains, it confers on the state the right to punish criminals under the principle of *taʿzīr.* In practice, though, the new code allows itself a much broader margin of jurisdiction, sometimes in clear contravention of the sacred law.

Clearly emulating contemporary Western codes, *Kanunname-i Ceza* divides crimes into three categories: *cinayet* (crime), defined as deserving of exemplary punishment, including life imprisonment, hard labor *(kürek),* and prolonged exile; *cunha* (offense, felony), defined as one in which a disciplinary punishment is needed, such as one week in prison; and *kabahat* (fault, misdemeanor), which is characterized as a deed to be reprimanded and punished by fines or by imprisonment of up to one week. There is also a stipulation that allows courts to reduce the sentence by a third of the period for good behavior.[50]

This code, emerging in a tumultuous era of change, deals with an array of new problems. Some of these problems have to do with new technology-related crimes, accelerated urbanization, and a burgeoning bureaucracy. There are punishments for tampering with telegraph lines and messages, for counterfeiting money, and for illegally printing forged documents. Other worries are the growing occurrence of urban violence and white-collar crime. The reader gets a sense that these new laws are concerned to a great extent with the need to control and manage the populace. The new state apparatus needed to know where its subjects were at all times and to be able to locate them if and when the need arose. One series of laws, for instance, threatens to severely punish those who falsify transit documents *(murur tezkeresi)* and those who fail to report the names of people who rent rooms on a daily basis at inns, restaurants, or coffee shops.

Laws concerning sex and sexuality are mostly subsumed under the heading "About Crimes Concerning Violation of Honor" *(hetk irz edenlerin mecazati beyanında)*. This title hints in many ways at the contents of the code. One general peculiarity of these new laws is their "purged" language. Sex crimes are rarely declared for what they are. Instead, very often, some other euphemism, such as *indecent act,* is used, which allows the reader or the jurist to guess at the exact meaning. Many of the new laws under this heading involve sexual relations with minors, either by force or by consent. Anyone who commits an indecent act *(fiʿl ṣanīʿ*—the regulation does not specify) for a fee with a minor (which, under this law, is surprisingly defined as age twenty-one or younger) will be imprisoned for at least six months.[51] If a parent or legal guardian forces a minor to commit such an act, the parent or guardian is liable to be sentenced to at least five years of hard labor.[52] If an indecent act is committed with a girl who is not yet married, in addition to a sentence of hard labor the perpetrator will be forced to pay damages.[53] Those who commit indecent acts in public will be imprisoned for three months to one year and fined.[54]

If we compare these laws to the older *kanun* legislation, they emerge as another turning point in terms of basic principles applied to the discourse of sexuality. Sultan Süleyman's *kanunnāme* retained most of the *şeriat*'s basic distinctions: men and women, married and unmarried, adult and minor, Muslim and non-Muslim, free and slave. It also developed the *şeriat*'s principle of reduced responsibility for those who are not free, married adult Muslims, especially in crimes involving women and non-Muslims. In addition, it developed the mechanisms of progressive fines and punishments, and a hesitant distinction emerged between violent and nonviolent crimes. The new set of laws carries some of these principles and mechanisms much farther, while dispensing with quite a few others.

In the reformed legal system, free/slave and Muslim/non-Muslim distinctions are not even mentioned. Three divisions are now clearly emphasized: adults/minors, violent/nonviolent, and public/private. As shown earlier, there was now a clear legal definition of what constitutes a minor. While in previous codes adulthood was equal to sexual puberty, in the new code the age of majority is twenty-one. A number of laws refer to minors and to the need for parents and caretakers to watch over them. Sex-related violence is referred to in detail and punished more harshly than in previous codes of law. There is a new marked difference between indecent acts performed in the privacy of one's home and crimes perpetrated in the public domain.

On the other hand, differences between men and women are attenuated even further in the 1858 code. In fact, the gender difference is mentioned only rarely on the victim's side, when women or young girls are abducted or raped or lose their virginity. In most cases, the sexes of the perpetrator and the victim are not mentioned, and there is never any mention of different punishments, or even separate but equal ones for men and women. It does not seem that this tendency to blur gender differences emerged from a sudden surge of feminism on the part of Ottoman legislators. If we are allowed to speculate in light of similar developments in other sexual scripts, I would assume that this silence was meant to obfuscate, as far as possible, questions relating to gender and sexuality, mainly in order to avoid the mention of same-sex relations.

We cannot at this point demonstrate a conscious elaboration of the system from older *kanun*s to this one. The process described earlier—the amalgamation of *şeriat* and *kanun*—did not repeat itself here, either with the *şeriat* or with the older *kanun*s. The new judicial elite did not, as far as we know, consciously attempt a parallel harmonization of their code with earlier ones. It is therefore much more difficult to prove that the members of the Council of Justice were consciously making changes and carefully elaborating the differences between their outlook and that of older systems. Yet being well versed in the *kanun* tradition and in the *şeriat* and faced with the sometimes vocal opposition of more conservative *ulema,* Cevdet and his colleagues must have been aware of differences and similarities between their modern *Kanunname-i Ceza* and previous systems.

Some of the differences can be attributed to Western European influences, which gradually increased during the 1850s and 1860s. Slavery's disappearance from the code, for example, owes a great deal to British pressures, and a similar process was at work leading to the practical disappearance of the Muslim/non-Muslim legal divide.[55] Indeed, the form and legal apparatus of Tanzimat codifications are known to have been derived from French, Swiss, and Belgian systems. But a careful comparison between the new *kanun*s and the older ones also makes it clear that there was a conscious effort to sift and compare choices. In a way, the directions the new *kanun* has taken and its choice of regulations are an extension of the old *kanun*'s principles. *Zinā'*, for example, which in the sixteenth century version was transformed from a crime against God to a mere felony or indecency, is all but gone in this version. We may venture to say that one could draw, if not a clear linear progression, then a hesitant one between the old legal principles and the new ones.

Yet once again the differences and additions should interest us more than the similarities. These lie in the abandonment of *zinā'* as a legal concept; in an emphasis on personal responsibility; in the emergence of children and minors as a distinct sexual category; in the complete abandonment of religion and slavery as personal attributes that should have a bearing on legal status; in an abandonment of the sixteenth-century concept of diminished responsibility and progressive fines; and, finally, in the "newspeak" adopted by the legislators to discuss sexual crimes without actually saying the sordid words.

It seems that the moving force behind many of these phenomena was internal and had to do with the appearance of the quasi-nation state. The new elite in the second half of the nineteenth century saw its task as one of creating a modern state. In many cases, unaware of the purport of their actions, its members were in fact trying to create a multi-ethnic nation. Their wish to forge a monolithic populace united in its allegiance to the sultan, providing a modern workforce and a modern conscription army with generic education in language, the sciences, and cultural heritage, became in fact an all-embracing nationalizing campaign. In our case—

in legislation concerning sex and gender—this tendency manifested itself in the attempt to destroy the old social boundaries between non-Muslims and Muslims, and between free and slave. All were subjects of the sublime dynasty, all shared responsibility for its welfare, and all deserved to be treated equally.

Perhaps to a lesser degree this unifying tendency may also be seen in the further attenuation of differences between men and women as far as legal status and punishment are concerned.[56] Here, however, we should also assume that external pressure played an important part. Charges of pederasty, homosexuality, or effeminate character were for many years leveled at the Turks and Arabs of the Middle East in travel literature and in Western media (as we shall see in chapter 6). Such allegations, which lawmakers were familiar with, made them very conscious of their image as reflected in legal practice. Silencing the sexual discourse of the law was the end result.

Another outcome of this process, which later became one of its main motivators, is the emergence of the family. Older generations in the elite conceived of their world in terms of households. These hierarchical independent units were very much a part of the old patrimonial state, where vertical walls between segments of the population were the norm. They were built along the same lines as tribes, guilds, and Sufi brotherhoods. Households typically had a hierarchy determined by proximity to the leader and an internal division of labor and responsibility. Family, by contrast, was an indistinct category. Even the terms used for "family" were ambiguous, as the words *usra (üsre)* and *ʿāʾila (aile)* demonstrate, with their vast semantic fields ranging from poverty to clan to relatives. At least in the elite, to which our law-enacting protagonists belonged, the concept of a nuclear family was almost meaningless in terms of social, cultural, or political function.

As a direct consequence of the centralizing and state-building efforts of the elite, however, the clanlike structures comprising the Ottoman state began a long, drawn-out process of disintegration. And as the tendency to define people primarily according to religion, servile status, tribe, guild, or household slowly retracted, the blurred outlines of the nuclear family began to solidify. In this new structure, relations connecting guardians and minors, parents and children, and the family to the exterior became ever more prominent. Children assumed a more distinct role and a personality of their own. Responsibility for their welfare became a state affair, and a new terminology evolved around them. Familial structures also necessitated a new division between public and private, inside and outside. Hence the child as sexual victim, and the renewed emphasis in the criminal code of Sultan Abdülmecid on abuse of guardian power, on sexual abuse of minors, and on compromise of public morality.

It would be a mistake to see the discursive trends discussed here as completely substituting each other over time. *Ulema* continued throughout the period to elaborate *şeriat* law, and the works of the famous nineteenth-century jurist Ibn ʿAbidīn (1784–1836) attest to a lively and fruitful consideration of matters pertaining to personal status laws and sexual offenses.[57] Households were still very powerful even in the second half of the nineteenth century, and in many regions and social spaces in the empire the new laws of the *Tanzimat* era were not well understood or wholeheartedly embraced. New nineteenth-century legislation existed side by side with a revered and sometimes dynamic *şeriat,* and with residues of older versions of the *kanun.* This time, however, there was no symbiosis or strategic alliance between the legal systems, such as the one attempted in Süleyman's time. *Şeriat* and state law were now rivals vying for authority and power.

The discursive world of nineteenth-century law and the sexual script it presented to society could therefore be seen as disjointed. Two—and, with the emergence of mixed courts in some provinces, sometimes three—legal systems, with disparate conceptions of sexuality, formally existed side by side, each offering its own vantage point on morality and sexual conduct. On the other hand, it could be perceived as an expanding discourse. While problems of fornication, same-sex relations, and sex with slaves were still part and parcel of the way older legal scripts referred to sexual matters, a new set of themes was now introduced, with an emphasis on sexual violence, abuse of minors, and equality of minorities.

Yet as this new legal paradigm introduced new themes, over the long term it also narrowed the spectrum of sexual discourse. Replacing the detailed description of older codes with euphemisms and avoiding discussion of pederasty and same-sex relations had a cumulative silencing effect on the sexual-legal script.

CHAPTER 3

# Morality Wars

## *Orthodoxy, Sufism, and Beardless Youths*

In the pre-nineteenth-century Ottoman Empire, there was no Islamic religious discourse. This may sound surprising, but it becomes obvious if we take into account the near-absence of any secular worldview. This meant that religion was omnipresent, although definitely not omnipotent. Everything that men and women did was outwardly imprinted with the stamp of faith and religiosity. Every book, from sacred law to outright pornography, required the necessary formulas giving thanks to God and His Prophet and asking for their blessing. Discourse in fields as diverse (at least to our minds) as science, medicine, art, and politics assumed the existence of an all-pervading divinity. In a cluster of societies such as that of the Middle East, especially in urban centers where Sufi doctrine was popular and spiritual life vibrant, God was everywhere. Indeed, it would hardly be possible to point to a specific boundary that separated the religious sphere from all others. The category "religious discourse" thus becomes too broad to be analytically useful.

In reconstructing Ottoman orthodox and Sufi conceptions of sexuality, it is therefore not religious discourse in general that we must look for, but a discourse that attempts to connect sexuality and spirituality, that embodies a social script. To be more specific, we should discuss texts written by those who participated in intellectual discussions about the role that sex fulfills in the life of faith and about religious obligations concerning sex, texts intended primarily for *ulema* or initiates in Sufi paths and for the educated elite.

Law, discussed in the previous chapter, is but one aspect of this discourse. Regulations and injunctions often express the outcome of a long juridico-philosophic debate and therefore can be seen as its summary. But a system of laws is limited in scope. Its formulations convey only one side of the debate, the winning side, and law is after all only one possible formulation even of these victorious ideas. It is conformist by nature, and often, as is the case with Ottoman *şeriat* law, it crystallizes norms of an earlier age. Furthermore, as we shall see, many aspects of the debate that contribute to the shaping of laws do not find expression in legal outcomes. In a society split by deliberations about the nature of love, attraction, and temptation and their relation to divinity, codified regulations expose only a small part of the picture. In the Ottoman case, the Sufis and their views were underrepresented in the legal framework, as were marginal views within the orthodox milieu.

A description of early Islamic legal debates on sexuality in intellectual circles is not our aim here. This has been attempted in the past and should perhaps be considered once again, but it would involve a time and a place remote from the subject of this study.[1] The questions we should ask ourselves pertain to what scholars in later centuries conceived of as the stance of tradition on these issues, and to the way such traditional positions were interpreted and presented in contemporary Ottoman debates. In this context, as we shall see, the devotional sexual script in the first Ottoman centuries focused on a familiar theme: the question of contemplating the beauty of beardless boys, or *maḥabbat al-amrad* in Arabic. Having been the focus of protracted struggles between Sufis and others, this question became one of the main factors in the downfall of Sufism in later times.

## THE DISCURSIVE FRAMEWORK

The boundaries of spiritual discourse on sexual matters were determined through a series of debates beginning in the first Islamic centuries. Its precursor was the ancient debate about the Koran's ontological status, sometimes referred to as "the question of the Koran's createdness" *(khalq al-qur'ān)*, which was resolved in the Abbasid period following long years of inquisition trials. After the tenth century C.E., the whole Islamic community accepted the Koran as an eternal infallible scripture rather than one created at the time of the Prophet (and therefore heuristic). The outcome of the old debate had implications for many issues relevant to the discourse of sexuality. The group known as *Muʿtazila* or *mutakallimūn* (theologians) insisted that since the Koran did not represent an eternal truth but one tailored for people in the seventh-century Arabian peninsula, distinctions between good and evil were subject to change and accessible to human reason. People could make judgments about them based on a developing human moral standpoint. Their rivals, the tradition-bound Sunnis, insisted that the only criterion for good and evil is revelation and that there is nothing outside revelation to guide believers in their choices. From another perspective, questions of anthropomorphy—namely, whether God has form and attributes that could be described and understood in human terms—were also at the center of the debate. If, as the vanquished *mutakallimūn* claimed, humans do not have the capacity to fathom the divine, and all human attributes describing God can only detract from His greatness, one cannot speak of love for God or even of God's love for His creatures. The realm of profane, human love should be seen as completely detached from that of the sacred and therefore as part of the fabric of social relations to be determined by humans.[2] If, on the other hand, divine attributes can be fathomed and understood by humans, then the validity of feelings such as love, sexual attraction, and compassion are not to be assessed merely as part of fallible human frailty. There is a higher standard by which to assess them.

These issues that split the Muslim community in the past were but faint echoes in the fifteenth and sixteenth centuries, but acceptance of the Koran as the basis for all discussions of morality, and the admission that God has attributes that could be understood in human terms, did not put an end to controversies concerning morality. As the lines of debate were drawn anew in the later Middle Ages, the two groups facing each other on the sexual-moral battlefield were some Sufi sects considered heretical by the orthodox, on one side, and Sunni orthodoxy, on the other. The battle that raged between them for several centuries on the contemplation of male beauty was seen by most as a battle for the soul of the Muslim community. But in order to understand why the debate was so crucial, why sexuality played such a role in it, and why its consequences were to shape the community for ages to come, we must first take note of the changes in Sufism up to and during the Ottoman era.

## THE EMERGENCE OF THE *ṬĀ'IFA*

*Sufi* and *orthodox* may be misleading names for the sparring parties, mainly because the label *Sufi* embraced most of the Ottoman population. The appearance of the Ottoman principality as a state in the fourteenth century coincided with a major shift in the constitution of Sufism. The three centuries from the decline of the Abbasid Empire to the emergence of the Ottoman, roughly from 1100 to 1400, witnessed a change in the makeup of Sufi organizations. An older system, based on a master and his circle of pupils, mostly in an aristocratic setting and lacking established doctrine and continuity, gave way to what Trimingham labels "the *ṭarīqa* stage," in which Sufism became largely a bourgeois movement, based on continuous forms of teaching and on regular transmission of doctrine and method. This period also saw a domestication of mystical spirit, and "new types of collectivistic methods for inducing ecstasy," mostly involving invocation, dance, and prayer.[3]

A century later, at about the time the Ottomans launched their world empire, the Sufis became a widespread *popular* movement, in which allegiance to a leader or dynasty was transmitted alongside doctrine and rule. Another important feature of this new stage was the integration of Sufi groups with other corporations and orders. From this point on, most corporative bodies in the Ottoman state—households, army units, merchant guilds, ethnic minorities—were connected, in one way or another, to a Sufi *ṭarīqa* (*tarikat* in Turkish, translated here as "path" rather than "brotherhood" or "order") and to a Sufi leader *(shaykh/şeyh)*. Thus, the claim that the great majority of Ottoman Muslims in the sixteenth and seventeenth centuries, city dwellers and villagers alike, were Sufis, would not be an exaggeration. The sultan, the bureaucracy, the army, the clergy, and, of course, many of the subjects, the *reaya,* had Sufi affiliations of various sorts among the numerous groups and subgroups that constituted Sufism at the time.[4] Another feature of Sufi life in this period enabled this major transformation. Formerly one had to be a true seeker of the path, to forsake his (or, more rarely, her) worldly life, and to go through the necessary stages from *murīd* to full member, or even to the lofty position of a guide, a *murshid.* Now, in this latest stage, there were two classes of adherents: adepts, going through the entire process of becoming a Sufi, and lay affiliates, who participated in ceremonies, took classes with their *murshids,* and contributed money but did not go through the entire excruciating ordeal. From this time on, the common designation for Sufi groups would be *ṭā'ifa,* meaning "community."[5]

Sufi *ṭā'ifas* ranged from very orthodox ones, such as the Naqshbandi (Turkish, Nakşibendi), to ones that were poised dangerously on the margins of heterodoxy, such as the Bektashi order, closely affiliated with the Janissary regiments, and even to completely heterodox conglomerations of sects, known collectively as the Malāmāti (Melametiyye or Melamilik), several leaders of which were executed in the sixteenth century. Even within *ṭarīqa*s there were often substrains with different degrees of commitment to orthodoxy and the Sunni path.[6]

While offering their devotees an emotional-spiritual experience, most conservative paths strictly observed the commandments and rituals of Muslim orthodoxy. Many *ulema* joined these paths and observed their rites. Others were merely sympathetic, and maintained close relations with orthodox-Sufi shaykhs. Ebüssuud, the great mufti and *şeyhülislam* of the sixteenth century, whom we encountered in chapter 2, is a good example. As an *ʿālim,* he represented Ḥanafi orthodoxy to the letter and did his best to reconcile the *şeriat* and the *kanun.* He did not hesitate to attack several Sufi tendencies vehemently in his *fatāwa* and authorized the execution of Sufi leaders suspected of heresy. Yet Ebüssuud himself came from a devoted Sufi family and was probably a practicing Sufi.[7] This, I believe, was typical of most *ulema* at the time. They did not see Sufism as inherently bad, but were wary of some of the new ideas and of the threat posed to what they perceived as true Islam. The position of Ebüssuud was shared by most *ulema* of his time, in Istanbul as well as in other areas. A study of Palestinian *ulema* whose biographies appear in al-Muḥibbi's *Tārikh Khulāṣat al-āthār,* a biographical dictionary written in Damascus at the end of the seventeenth century, reveals that most of the *ulema* of the period were also members of Sufi groups, and, as al-Muḥibbi often writes, "received their *ṭarīqa*" at some stage of their studies. This was also true for scions of prestigious Sufi families, who in many cases joined the orthodox establishment as local judges or muftis, while maintaining their role as spiritual guides in the *ṭarīqa.*[8]

Rather than between orthodoxy and Sufism, we should therefore draw the line between orthodox Sufis and heterodox ones. The two sides in the debate shared some basic assumptions. Both accepted anthropomorphic descriptions of the divinity, they agreed on the possibility of love between man and creator, and they accepted the likelihood of a beatific vision or of an experience leading to the presence of God. There were, however, a series of issues on which they were divided and kept arguing.

All topics, from positions in intercourse and preferable times of intercourse between a man and woman to bestiality, masturbation, and the sexuality of hermaphrodites, were discussed in depth, usually in clear and unequivocal terms (at least to those who understood the terminology). They were referred to in special treatises, where lines were sometimes blurred between legal discourse and erotic literature. Many of these themes, however, were not new, and their contents were usually not innovative in the Ottoman period. The debate that shook the Ottoman world, with repercussions in politics and culture, was the one dealing with homoerotic love.

At the heart of this debate was the concept of love and its meaning. A hazy distinction between sacred and profane love existed in early Islamic discourse. While essayists recognized the existence and importance of both, orthodox and Sufi writers agreed that in order for it to be considered in the framework of faith, profane love, the love of a person for his earthly beloved, should somehow be an emanation of sacred love. Explanations were usually long and convoluted, but their purport was that love could either be felt toward God (directly) or toward things that God loves (and therefore indirectly toward God). In the Ottoman Sufi context, this idea was often expressed through the concept of *waḥdat al-wujūd,* or the unity of being, thought to have been propounded by the famous mystic Ibn al-ʿArabi (1164–1240).[9] Ibn al-ʿArabi suggested that the entire world was created as God's self-reflection, and that all natural phenomena reflect His essence. The basic tenets of this complex thesis may not have been fully understood by all later proponents of his thought system, but the idea of a world that is at one with God, and of a divine spirit present in all creation, conquered the minds and souls of many.[10]

These tendencies resulted in two opposing views of sex and profane love. One view, held by the more orthodox side, was that since profane love was a path to the almighty and a reflection of divine love, one should beware of defiling it. Orthodox writers, such as the strict Ḥanbali teachers Ibn Taymiyya and Ibn Qayyim al-Jawzīyya, claimed that lovers as a rule are engaged in a sacred task. But since true love of God can be achieved only through love for things loved by God, and since there are certain amorous practices He clearly disapproves of, as stated in the Koran and traditions, sinful love, falling in the category of *zinā',* would lead only to the gates of hell and should be prohibited.

But while the more orthodox sought to tie down heavenly love, radical Sufis chose the opposite route: sanctifying profane love. Some Sufi groups maintained, on the basis of Ibn al-ʿArabi's and Rūmi's works, that God inhabits everything and therefore that love for any object of creation can be the key to beatific vision. In an effort to relate profane to heavenly love, the Sufis developed the idea of gazing at beauty as a path to true love of God. Real understanding of sacred love could be attained, they claimed, through the doorway of worldly love. Just as a father gives his son a wooden sword to practice with before he lets him use a real sword, said Rūmi, seekers of Allah should be given a sight of beauty to admire, through which they will feel the trials and tribulations of love, so that their hearts will learn to emulate the elusive sentiment.[11] In theory there should have been no difference between men and women as subjects for contemplation, but since men were viewed as the more perfect creatures (see chapter 1), and since the presence of women in a Sufi lodge would have caused more of an uproar in society, Sufis often chose pretty young male slaves or initiates, the ideal of beauty at the time, as their objects of loving contemplation. In principle no sexual relations were to take place, and the focus of admiration was to be left intact, as an unreachable shore of yearning.

But things took an expected turn. The idea of gazing at the beauty of young beardless boys, *al-naẓar ila al-amrad,* coupled with the *samāʿ* (Turkish *sema*), a part of the Sufi ritual known as *dhikr* (Turkish *zıkır*), which consisted of music, song, dance, and often sitting close together, produced an irresistible erotic mixture. According to Sufi authors, *samāʿ* "can induce intense emotional transports *[tawajjud]*, states of grace *[aḥwāl]*, of trance or of ecstasy *[wajd, wujūd]*, and even revelations."[12] Suspect from the time of its initial acceptance into Sufi circles in the ninth century, by the eleventh century *samāʿ* had become the main symbol of Sufi heresy. While radical authors described it as an important part of the ritual, resulting from the heightened awareness of the adept and inducing a state of ecstasy, conservative writers denounced the practice as basically pagan, opposed to the spirit of Islam, and inevitably leading to sinful acts. Indeed, the bodily contact occurring so often during the *samāʿ* was sometimes used as an excuse to touch, embrace, fondle, and explore one's beautiful beloved, and the taboo against sexual contact, even if adhered to at some initial stage, soon broke down.[13]

In the sixteenth and seventeenth centuries, *samāʿ* rituals were the subject of many legal discussions and *fatwa*. Ebüssuud devoted several of his responses to these questions, condemning the practice in harsh words:

> Saying that these shameful acts are part of the customs of religious worship, and bringing holy Koran verses as proof of this is also blasphemy, and if they do not repent and denounce these beliefs, they should be executed. As for the dances performed by Sufis of our times, they are in effect pagan dances of the unbelievers, and these performances are similar to those of the infidels. Even the Prophet, peace be upon Him, has declared that support for dance is apostasy, because dance is the practice of the insolent and the shameless.[14]

Several decades later, the Palestinian Ḥanafi jurist Khayr al-Dīn al-Ramli, whose advice was sought far beyond the boundaries of *bilād al-Shām* (greater Syria, the eastern Mediterranean coast), from Anatolia to Egypt, gave two very long responses to questions about *samāʿ* ceremonies in somewhat less definite terms but with the same deprecating tone: "A question from Damascus: about the *samāʿ* and the dancing that goes on during the *samāʿ*. Did our jurists ever discuss this matter and what it entails in terms of permission?" Unlike several other queries in which the applicants made their dislike and disdain for the practice clear, here the question was delivered in a neutral tone. In his answer al-Ramli clearly differentiates between music and singing, on the one hand, which he frowns on but does not condemn altogether, and dance or "motion," on the other hand, which he clearly denounces, particularly in a devotional setting. Chanting is permitted in prayer if it uses verses from the Koran or other sermons; otherwise it should be forbidden. Some Sufi shaykhs, says al-Ramli, claim that performing the *samāʿ* is for some of their initiates, who are in a state of depression, a matter of urgency, "just as a remedy may be needed for a sick person." If that is the case, then it may be performed, but under very strict conditions: First, there should be no beardless youths among them. Second, they should all be of one sex, and there should be no hedonists or nihilists (known euphemisms for pederasts or people who are after homoerotic contact) or women in their midst. Third, the purpose should really be devotional prayer rather than payment of money or service in return for food. Fourth, they should not serve meals or discuss contributions during it. Fifth, they should not rise (to dance) unless their emotions are held in check *(maghlūb)*. And sixth, they should not claim to be in a state of ecstasy *(wajd)* unless it is true. Having given permission to perform *samāʿ* in cases of emergency, al-Ramli returns to his interdiction. Some people claim, he says, that *samāʿ* should be permitted because dancing is common in weddings and banquets, and there is no sanction against this. It is also permitted to sing on special festive occasions, as can be inferred based on a *ḥadīth* attributed to the Prophet. But there is a difference. The occasion of a wedding should be made public knowledge by all means, and singing is one of the means. This is also true for other festivals, but otherwise any public display of music, song, and dance is strictly prohibited.[15]

It is interesting to note Al-Ramli's repeated reference to women here, echoed by other writers in various contexts. This may be an indication that the practice was not purely homoerotic, and in some cases may have involved the contemplation of women as part of the *samāʿ* ceremony.

Another question on the same topic, delivered apparently by an advocate of *samāʿ* practices, came from Shaykh Ibrāhīm al-Samādi of Damascus. The shaykh inquired about the ceremonies that some Sufis practice. This is common among them, he says, and is a tradition passed on from their fathers and grandfathers. They sing verses composed by the masters of orders such as the Qādiriyya, the Saʿdiyya, the Muṭāwiʿiyya, and the like. Reciting these verses creates a sense of heightened ecstasy and a need to move about *(Wa-yaḥṣalu lahum fi athnā' al-dhikr wajd aẓīm wa-ḥāl yuqʿid wa-yuqīm).* They raise their voices and become absorbed in themselves despite the presence of many people around them. They enter the *dhikr* ceremony with pure intentions, their only purpose to mention the names of great people before Allah, but their invocations turn into singing as they are immersed in this passion. Yet there are people who say that these acts amount to apostasy, and that the dance and the raising of voices are a grave failing. They say that all these things are prohibited in the legal schools of Abu Ḥanīfa, al-Shāfiʿi, Aḥmad (Ibn Ḥanbal), and Mālik. They deny the miraculous powers *(karāmāt)* of saints after their deaths and denounce them forcefully in derogatory terms. Are all these claims in accordance with the *sharīʿa*?[16]

Sent by an eminent shaykh in Damascus, probably an acquaintance, and manifesting a clearly positive attitude, al-Samādi's question could not be simply brushed off with a short answer prohibiting *samāʿ*. Here al-Ramli had to tread more carefully and to provide an answer that is polite but firm. Stressing at the beginning that actions can be judged only according to intentions *(Inna al-umūr bi-maqāṣidiha; Innama al-aʿmāl bi-l-niyyāt),* al-Ramli gives an overview of Sufi-orthodox history to show that Islam recognizes only those pious Sufis who have refrained from controversial activities throughout the ages. His long and very detailed answer cannot be quoted here in full, but the tensions and the enmity between supporters of *samāʿ* and its detractors permeate it and indicate that, under the guise of a polite exchange between two religious authorities, passionate verbal clashes erupted between the camps.

Despite al-Ramli's warnings and those of many other muftis of the time, *samāʿ* ceremonies in which adult Sufis and young disciples huddled together were very common. They gave rise to a prolific literature about the dangers of the *samāʿ* and the temptation of young men and women (see discussion later in this chapter). Debates on issues of sexuality inside the Sufi camp focused on the special relations between the tutor, the *murshid,* and his pupil, the *murīd.* Every aspect of this relationship was suspect in the eyes of the conservatives, and the discourse always focused on the dangers of beardless youths. This sense of rampant debauchery was clearly augmented by the special relationship known to exist between a teacher and his pupil.

Describing one such master-disciple unit in early-twentieth-century Morocco, Abdellah Hammoudi paints a vivid picture of this kind of relationship, which may to some extent hark back to earlier periods. Though distant in time and place and therefore with no direct bearing on the subject of discussion, it is brought up here purely as one possible illustration of the adept's position in the relationship.[17] The description of a Moroccan Sufi's process of initiation shifts our attention from the master's perspective to that of the youth. The first task of the master, Hammoudi recounts, was to destroy the young man's former ego and to replace it with a true spirit of devotion. As this was accomplished, another phase began, during which the youth forsook previous ideas of manliness and took on traditional roles of women—grinding flour, preparing meals, and washing clothes. This amounted to a feminization of the disciple and to a clear departure from prevalent social norms. Furthermore, the master's *baraka,* his power of benediction and intercession, was passed on to the disciples through contact with his garments and possessions, or even through bodily contact, including spitting into the disciple's mouth or placing his tongue in it. Sexual intercourse could also be beneficial and endow the young disciple with the coveted *baraka.*[18]

"The disciple," concludes Hammoudi, "is, so to speak, impregnated through a teaching process, which resembles procreation. The master transforms into a saint the young man who rushes to him in a sense-awakening encounter; he basically feminizes his disciple in order to produce charisma: it is a metaphor of insemination, gestation, and birth."[19] At the end of the process the disciple is reborn as a shaykh with a double-gendered identity. He is now an androgenic figure, both male and female.

Assuming a resemblance between this process and the aspects of the social order in contemporary Morocco, Hammoudi contends that the ubiquity of this type of relationship, coupled as it is with the prevalent patriarchal norms of society, produces an inhibiting schema that prevails in modern Moroccan society and perhaps in other Arab-Muslim societies as well. These ultimate conclusions are beyond the scope of this study, but his description of master-disciple relations may be pertinent to the premodern Ottoman context as well and finds an echo in many other texts of the earlier period.[20]

In short, Sufi paths formed the religious backbone of Ottoman society, and most of the Muslim population was somehow affiliated with them. Few were totally committed Sufis, forsaking their personal and family lives, but many, rulers and ruled alike, saw their superficial affiliation with Sufi orders as part of their identity. Some were known to frequent more than one group and to attend *dhikr* ceremonies, which include singing and dancing.[21] Quite a few popular Ottoman Sufi sects integrated into their teaching a unique version of Ibn al-ʿArabi's monistic theology that interpreted the contemplation of beauty, especially the beauty of young beardless youths, as a worldly reflection of divine beauty and, in consequence, encouraged accomplished Sufis to maintain such "spiritual" amorous relations with handsome young boys.[22] In quite a few paths, however, Sufi rituals, and especially the *samāʿ*, involving dance and ecstatic motion, encouraged bodily contact with disciples and initiates and thus facilitated the transition from platonic contemplation of sublime beauty to heavenly sexual intercourse. Such practices enraged the more conservative members of the clerical community, and reactions were swift and furious.

This may seem a minor debate over a marginal sexual issue, but the danger did not lie in sexual debauchery as such, perhaps not even in homoerotic contact. Such illicit sexual practices were known and tolerated from the earliest days of Islam. They were denounced in Islamic moral and legal literature in the strictest terms, but in practice very little was done to curb or inhibit them, provided they were done away from the public eye. For many religious scholars of an orthodox hue, however, and for those in more conservative Sufi paths, the new amalgam of what they perceived as heterodox Sufi ideas and the growing popularity of *ṭāʾifa*s threatened to change the face of Islam. It presented a real and mortal danger to the initial structure of the religion and therefore to the soul of every Muslim. Soon, they feared, these Sufi ideas, so popular and widespread, would find their way to the social and political center. Heresies involving public sexual overtures and staged homoerotic behavior would then be accepted by *ijmāʿ*, the consensus of the community, to become basic tenets of religious dogma. This practice, opposed to all that was held sacred in their view, would lead the whole community to oblivion.[23]

That is why a sense of urgency emanates from so many tractates denouncing the practice. That is also why the seventeenth and eighteenth centuries witnessed a dialectical movement against such practices, the suggestion of antidotes such as strict codes of dress for boys and girls, and warnings against the corrupting power of the gaze. In its implications for the course religion would take in the next centuries, it would not be an exaggeration to compare this campaign over the human body and human sexuality to the impact of the Reformation and Counter-Reformation in Europe.

The doomsday mood that affected many *ulema* of the period finds clear expression in the writings of Sinān al-Dīn al-Amāsi, known as "al-Wāʿiẓ" (the preacher). Al-Amāsi, an Anatolian who moved to Mecca in his later years, wrote a short tractate in Arabic denouncing the practices of certain Sufi sects in the second half of the sixteenth century:[24]

> It has reached such a degree that they brag about it, and blame those who do not possess a beardless youth[, saying]: "You do not practice *liwāṭ* [sodomy] and you do not drink wine, so you are an unrefined Sufi *[ghalīz]*. You are ill-mannered, and we want nothing to do with you." They call themselves refined *[ẓurafā']*, but in truth they are the ill-mannered ones, and they are the sinners. Some of these cursed hedonists give away youths as presents to others and these others show their joy at [having received] the gift, and take pride in holding these youths in their arms. Many of them do not marry women, and instead use boys, saying "we do not have to support them as we do women." They give them names such as "travel wife" *[zawjat al-safar]* or "bed boy" *[ghulām al-firāsh]* or "favorite" *[khāsikiyya]*. . . . You may see many in our times claiming to be learned *ulema*, sitting at the head of a court *[majlis]*, and yet taking pride in their young companions, accompanying them when they go out among people, preceding or following them, and dressing them in the finest clothes until they look their best. Some of them look for the prettiest youths and buy them. In truth they are among the greatest sinners. Not only are they not learned, they are completely ignorant.[25]

This feeling of distress described by al-Amāsi was not at all new. Others in the Islamic world had expressed it in previous eras.[26] It was the popularity of these radical doctrines in the Ottoman period, coupled with the power of *ṭā'ifa*s and their influence over the government and the state, that was such a new and alarming experience. The need to counter this dangerous trend was expressed by many authors of the time, who decided to enter the arena and fight for their views.

## COUNTERING SUFI SEXUAL LIBERTINISM

In the centuries-long battle for the soul of the community and for Islamic public morality, a large number of treatises were written against the dangers of gazing at beardless youths. All available weapons were used—the Koran, the *ḥadīth,* stories about the first caliphs, stories about the founders of legal schools and of Sufi paths, reason, and poetry. The warring parties did not shrink from inventing new traditions or from unearthing old ones discarded long ago.[27]

A typical example of such a treatise against the sexual practices of the time is Muḥammad Abu al-Fatḥ al-Dajjāni's still-unpublished *Al-ʿiqd al-mufrad fi maḥabbat al-amrad* (The Distinct Necklace on Love of Beardless Youth).[28] Al-Dajjāni, a native of Jerusalem, was a well-known scholar in seventeenth-century Palestine. Al-Muḥibbi recounts that he studied in Egypt at al-Azhar, wrote several books and treatises, and died in 1660. He also mentions that Abu al-Fatḥ was an initiated Sufi, following his family's tradition. His treatise is a small one, just twenty-two pages in manuscript form, but it includes most of the necessary ingredients of such tractates.

Al-Dajjāni's preamble is a lament about deteriorating morality, in rhymed prose:

> Nowadays, when Satan plays with us all the way boys play ball, love for beardless boys has spread like a rage, especially among the Sufis of this age. They claim that this association with them is the way of the All Compassionate *[al-Raḥmān]*, but by God, that is the way of Satan *[al-Shayṭān]*, who has overpowered them until he made them forget the one benefactor. What a wonder! How could that which angers God be perceived as his strength and as the path *[ṭarīq]* to Him? Indeed this is a great loss and a grave mistake, which leads to eternal fire. May God protect us from these depths of rebellion. Amen.[29]

Having witnessed this sorry state of affairs for many years, writes Al-Dajjāni, he decided to compile a book containing part of what was already presented in other compositions in the hope that it will help put an end to these vile practices. He goes right to the heart of the matter: "Know, may God grant you success, that sodomy *[liwāṭ]* is forbidden *[ḥarām]* and considered one of the great sins *[kabīra]* by consensus of the Muslims, although there are some disagreements about its punishment."[30]

Starting, as custom dictates, with the opinions of all four schools of law on the issue, he delineates their views on *liwāṭ*, ranging from severe beating and deportation to stoning. Some of the sources he quotes claim that the punishment for sodomy should be harsher than that for fornication *(zinā')*, while others hold that the punishment should be the same. He then deals with the etymology of the word *liwāṭ*, which, he says, comes from Lūṭ, the name of the prophet whose people practiced these terrible deeds in ancient times. God punished them in an unprecedented manner, overturning their houses on their heads and hailing them with stones. It is a sin so grave, he says, that the earth may be unhinged and the angels may flee from all corners of the sky, fearing that the punishment awaiting perpetrators might also befall them, when the earth purifies itself before its master. This description, to which he returns several times in his short book, leads al-Dajjāni to recount a series of stories about Satan (Iblīs) and the way he lured Lot's people to do the abominable deed. In one story, Iblīs disguises himself as a handsome young boy and tempts the people of the city, bringing upon them God's wrath.[31]

Having delineated the stance of the *sharīʿa,* al-Dajjāni goes on to deal with the specific claims of his rivals. The next stage includes proof that even actions not considered *ḥarām* (strictly forbidden) in and of themselves are to be prohibited because they may lead to serious crimes. Kissing one's wife during Ramadān is forbidden, for instance, because it may lead to forbidden intercourse. In the same way, gazing passionately *(al-naẓar bi'l-shahwa)* at a beardless boy, even if he is not handsome, or even at a bearded one or at a woman who is among one's close relations *(maḥārim),* is forbidden. To strengthen his case, al-Dajjāni quotes al-Ghazāli, a paragon of Sufi wisdom, who in his famous treatise *Iḥyā' ʿulūm al-dīn* commented that looking at the beauty of a beardless youth should be forbidden if it reaches the stage where there is a difference of attitude on the part of the onlooker when he looks at him, in comparison to the way he looks at an older bearded man *(multaḥi).*[32]

Now it was time to bring in the *ḥadīth,* and it appears that the war waged was so intense that both sides felt they had to use their creative powers and make use of the many unfounded stories that made their way into *ḥadīth* collections. One reason for this war of traditions was the famous *ḥadīth* that Sufis always quoted as proof of their practices: "I saw my Lord in the form of a youth with his cap awry."[33] To counter it, al-Dajjāni presents a string of stories about the Prophet and his companions, most of which are, even by his standards, false, "weak," or even invented. "It was recounted that God's messenger [Muhammad] once said: 'If one looks at a handsome boy with lust, God shall try him by fire for forty years.' Now imagine [writes al-Dajjāni], if this is the punishment for just looking, how grave a crime it would be to do the abominable deed."[34]

Other *ḥadīth*s attributed to the Prophet include: "My utmost fear for my community is of the deeds of Lūṭ's people" *(akhwaf ma akhāf ʿala ummati ʿamal qawm Lūṭ);* "There are seven which God has cursed and will not pardon in the Day of Judgment. They will be told to enter the fire. [Among them are] the perpetrator, and the one perpetrated upon *[al-fāʿil wa'l-mafʿūl bihi,* by which the Prophet means *liwāṭ,* explains al-

Dajjāni], he who had intercourse with beasts *[nākiḥ al-bahīma]*, and the masturbator *[nākiḥ yaddahu]*"; and "Looking at what is forbidden is an arrow from Iblīs; therefore you should warn the righteous not to sit with beardless youths, nor to speak to them, nor to walk with them, for fear of *fitna* [anarchy]."[35] False or unfounded *ḥadīth*s of this sort, as well as attributions of sayings to the founders of legal schools or to other luminaries, are found in all writing on the subject. The writers themselves sometimes counter the claims of the other party by saying that their rivals' sources are untrue or considered unfounded.[36]

Gradually the emphasis in the treatise is transferred to questions of sight and the sexual gaze. This is where the *ḥadīth* attributed to al-Sha'bi (quoted at the beginning of my introduction) is presented:

> One day the tribe of 'Abd al-Qays [residing on the eastern part of the Arabian Peninsula] sent a delegation to meet the Prophet. As they were being seated in his presence, he observed among them a young boy of radiant beauty. The Prophet motioned for him to be seated behind his back. Then he said, "Dāwūd's rebellion was caused by none other than sight."
>
> And if God's messenger [adds al-Dajjāni], unerring and free of all deformation, guilt or indecency, was concerned by the presence of a beardless boy and sat him behind his back so that he does not have to look at him, what about all those who are not thus immune?[37]

In a sense, this is the climax of the treatise—not just a saying by a revered scholar, but a deed, a physical demonstration of the danger inherent in young boys and of the required caution, by none other than the Prophet, coupled with a saying that compares this sin to the notorious tale of fornication and assassination in the Old Testament and the *ḥadīth*. If nothing else would convince the sinners, if all warnings about hell and fire would not be heeded, then this would be the ultimate weapon to convince those who believe in the one God and his last messenger.

Yet the story imparts an ambivalent message to our sensibilities, attuned as they are to the heteronormalized sexualities of modernity. For one thing, the Prophet in the story, immune and powerful though he may be, acts as if he were attracted to a young beardless boy. Seating him behind his back is not a mere technical precaution; otherwise it would have been the normal practice of the Prophet and his community and would need no further explanation. No, this was true attraction to beauty, in this case young male beauty. Prophet Dāwūd's story adds to our confusion. Why compare the biblical story of David's heterosexual sin with erotic attraction of a male to other males?

Al-Dajjāni, however, is not the least perturbed by this or similar stories he recounts that are attributed to righteous caliphs or to founders of schools of law. It would be as natural for them to be attracted to beardless boys as to women. The underlying assumption here, as in the entire tractate, is that attraction to both men and women is not only normal, but the norm. Nowhere in his treatise or in those of his contemporaries do we find a condemnation of the sentiment. Homoerotic attraction is never described as a deviation or an abnormal attraction, or even as something that defines a minority among men. Indeed, there are some who are more inclined to this type of sexual attraction, but this does not color their sexuality or their gender definition any differently.

If any tone of disapproval for male-to-male sex emerges from this set of treatises, one may find it in attraction of adults to adults. This is not a theme discussed in much detail. Here and there it is mentioned that the prohibitions against love for beardless boys also apply to those whose beards have grown, but most of the stories brought by al-Dajjāni and his peers suggest that if nature takes its expected course, sexual attraction disappears once the boy matures. One such story about the temptation of Suwayd al-Makki, a Sufi shaykh, clearly demonstrates this set of assumptions. It is said that once, when a young boy joined his circle and became his student, al-Makki cautiously sat him behind his back throughout the years of tutoring. His fear of temptation was so great that even when, years later, the pupil's beard grew and was even sprinkled with gray, he did not know this and kept avoiding him. One day the student asked al-Makki to get him a comb. "What will you do with it?" asked the master, and the disciple replied, "I will comb my beard." Only then, realizing that his student was no longer a boy, did al-Makki allow the student to sit facing him.

The boundaries of "normal" sexuality in the devotional script are drawn by this story and its corollaries. As soon as the beard grows, the danger should be gone. Adult homoerotic practice is seldom discussed, and when it is, there are insinuations that this is a "sickness" of some sort.[38] This is true especially for the "passive" partner, the one being penetrated.

The same transformation is expected in the young men. Until fully matured, they were believed to have an untamed sexuality and a natural attraction to older men. The religious discourse is replete with sayings and stories about the active role that beardless youths play in seducing men. It begins with the famous *ḥadīth* "Beware of the sons of the rich, for they are more tempting than women,"[39] and goes on to discuss the many instances where young men dress and make up their faces in order to attract poor, unsuspecting older men.

One conclusion, borne out by most of the texts though never explicitly stated, is that male sexuality manifests two distinct phases across time. In the first, until puberty, the boy's sexuality could best be described as untamed, drawn to older men as well as to boys or women. In the second phase, once they have fully matured, men's sexual behavior changes. From that time on they are expected to be attracted to women or to younger males, but not to men in their own age category. Those who do not complete the transition are somehow flawed.

While the attitude toward sex in many Ottoman discourses was egalitarian, and choice of sexual partner had little to do with class, status, or gender, homoerotic sex was understood as a transgenerational experience. The relatively small space allotted to discussions of adult homoeroticism as opposed to man-boy relations may indicate that homoeroticism within the same age group was not considered a serious problem in the devotional script of the Ottoman period. Yet it would perhaps be more reasonable to assume that although intercourse between two male or two female adults was rejected and denounced just as forcefully, it posed no inherent challenge to the basic tenets of religion. Like many other sexual activities, it was forbidden but expected to occur. Love of and intercourse with boys, on the other hand, were considered a dangerous challenge precisely because they were not understood to be deviations from "normal" sexuality, even by the strictest *ulema,* and because this was rapidly becoming an article of faith for many Sufis and their retinues, challenging orthodox ethical norms.

## THE TAMING OF SUFI LOVE

Reform movements have emerged in Islamic societies since the first generations, but those that appeared in the seventeenth and eighteenth centuries were different. They did not offer messianic salvation in the form of a charismatic leader, nor did they deviate from the teachings of the *sharīʿa.* Their main objective was strict adherence to an orthodox interpretation of the law. In the first part of the seventeenth century, a unique protest movement appeared in Istanbul. Named after its first leader, the popular author and preacher Kadizade Mehmed (d. 1635), and basing its truth on the teachings of a famous sixteenth-century *ʿālim,* Birgivi (d. 1573), the Kadizadeli movement turned its criticism mainly on the most prominent *ṭarīqa*s in the empire—the Khalwatīs/Halvetis and the Mawlawis/Mevlevis.[40] Although adherents of the movement criticized a large array of phenomena, including corruption among the *ulema,* coffee drinking, tobacco smoking, and saint worshipping, the brunt of their attack was against prevalent Sufi norms, especially *dhikr* ceremonies, dances, and music. They were mainly preoccupied with Ibn al-ʿArabi's doctrine of *waḥdat al-wujūd*. Ostensibly they opposed the pantheistic elements of the doctrine and Sufi interpretations of it, which, in their view, amounted to heresy. As Madeline Zilfi writes: "The Kadizadelis made of Ibn al-ʿArabi, dead four hundred years, a test of orthodoxy. Those who used him as an authority, recited his verse or otherwise followed his example, were heretics. While for the Sufis he was 'the First Shaikh' *(şeyh-i ekber)*, the Kadizadelis derided him as 'the Worst Shaikh' *(şeyh-i ekfer)*."[41] Although the sins of the gaze are not always explicitly mentioned, the undercurrents of their criticism, and in some cases clearly expressed opinions, hint at the prevalent fear of the passion for the divine beauty of the beardless.[42]

The critique of the Kadizadelis persisted for several decades in the capital and in other main cities of the empire, and finally initiated a long chain of persecution. By the early 1650s, the new leader of the movement, Üstüvani Mehmed, a Damascene preacher, had captured the imaginations of the anti-Sufi faction. At a time of weakness for the state, during the reign of the sultans Ibrahim and Mehmed IV, he took advantage of the situation to secure, through his ties in the palace, orders for the destruction of great Halveti lodges in Istanbul, and incited his men to attack other lodges. Several Sufi authors and preachers were forced to flee to the provinces in order to avoid persecution. The Kadizadelis further applied censorship to Sufi writings supporting the common practices of the orders, mainly *dhikr* and *samāʿ*. This second wave of protest ended only in 1656, when the new powerful grand vizier, Köprülü Mehmed Paşa, rounded up the Kadizadeli leaders and banished them to Cyprus.

A third cycle began in the 1660s, with the rise to power of Vani Mehmed, a preacher from the city of Van, who became Sultan Mehmed's personal mentor and a spiritual counselor to the grand vizier Fazıl Ahmed, Köprülü's son and successor. Vani also managed to have one Sufi lodge in the capital leveled, "and in 1665, he had the public performances of Sufi music and 'dance' rituals—the *sema, raks* and *devran*—forbidden."[43] That one of the driving forces behind this series of actions was fear of legitimating pederastic activities can be extrapolated from another set of arrests Vani Efendi promoted at the same time, insisting that army commanders dispense with their young male lovers who accompanied them to the battlefield.[44] Vani lost his hold on Ottoman politics and his power over the Sufis of the empire following the defeat at Vienna in 1683, when the disillusioned sultan banished him from the capital. In 1686, the Mevlevis once again received permission to perform the *samāʿ*. It appears that some of the teachings of the Kadizadelis went on reverberating in the Arab *mashriq* until the beginning of the eighteenth century before waning.[45]

Perhaps the ultimate winners in the struggle in the short run were neither the Sufis nor the Kadizadelis. Quietly sympathetic toward Sufi ideals but fearful of their antinomian heresies, moderate orthodox *ulema* succeeded in retaining and even augmenting their power in the early eighteenth century. Their golden-mean path, conservative yet tolerant, appreciative of the merits of Ibn al-ʿArabi's doctrines yet apprehensive of the way they were applied by radical orders, restored a certain balance to the beleaguered Ottoman community in the following decades.

The most important outcome, however, was the reordering of religion in the vast imperial domains. The battle over sexuality restructured orthodoxy and Sufism, not by royal decree or by any carefully thought-out blueprint, but rather as a slow, determined movement on both sides to reconcile their differences and adapt themselves once more to life together in the empire under the rule of sultan and God. In the eighteenth century, the imperial palace contributed its share by minimizing opportunities for conflict, by carefully choosing preachers and other functionaries, and by pre-planning public events and sermons so that this kind of head-on clash between the two warring parties would be kept to a minimum.

Recognizing their part of the bargain, Sufi orders injected new ideas and new concepts into their rituals, minimizing the role of gazing at young beardless youths in their ceremonies to a vague poetic ideal, couching Ibn al-ʿArabi's concepts in carefully worded devotional texts, and tightening control over the *dhikr* ceremony.[46] Although *dhikr* by no means disappeared, in the later eighteenth century its tone was attenuated, the gaze discourse was kept for initiates even in radical Sufi circles, and the open *samāʿ* ceremonies in which Sufis and disciples touched and kissed were performed in semi-secret. Just as the Kadizadeli conflict had spread across the Ottoman universe in the previous century, these corrective measures also found their way to the outlying provinces. As John Voll writes about Egypt and the Arab-speaking world: "During the eighteenth century, the long dialogue between representatives of this type of mystic thought and the more strict Sunni *ulema* gained new momentum. In many areas, scholars worked to reinterpret the Ibn al-ʿArabi tradition in less pantheistic terms, and commentators on his most famous works gave greater emphasis to the transcendence of God. They restated the goal of the Sufi path in terms of the individual being in harmony with the spirit of the Prophet rather than losing individual identity by absorption into the absolute being."[47]

## NO SUFIS, NO DISCOURSE

As we shall see in the next chapters, the nineteenth century brought with it a new set of values and ideas, in which love among men and same-sex relations were frowned on. Now it was no longer just another kind of *zinā'*. Whereas in previous centuries the fear was that heterodox Sufi sexual discourse might challenge the basic values of Islam regardless of the sex of lovers, now this was no longer the case. Sufi ideas were from now on shameful for their homoerotic, not their politically radical, content.

Afsaneh Najmabadi describes a similar process in the Persianate world.[48] When travelers began to visit Europe at the beginning of the century, she says, love and sex were not yet "heteronormalized." One was expected to be attracted to male and female alike, and love for men/boys was seen as more proper and virtuous than love for women. Travelers' first encounters with European elites, where men and women mixed freely, were therefore not interpreted as a display of gender equality. Initially these heterosocial gatherings, steeped in what was perceived as libertine behavior, where pleasures and wine drinking were common, evoked a totally different cultural memory—that of paradise. Women were described as blue-eyed *ḥūri*s (virgin girls), men as the fair *ghilmān* (youths) promised by the Koran: "The spectacle of seeing handsome young men and beautiful young women dancing together was at once the culturally familiar paradisic phantasm of *ḥuri*s and *ghilman* and an unfamiliar spectacle of public heterosociality. The phantasmatic familiarity of the former familiarized the unfamiliarity of the latter."[49] As time passed, however, the allegorical desire for *ghilmān* and *ḥūri*s gave way to an ideal of a heterosocialized society, and at the same time reinforced a heteronormal sense of sex and love, and gender-differentiated notions of beauty became consolidated. The older ideal was now shunned.

The Ottoman world's case may be different. Its encounter with Europe was more gradual and dated back to previous centuries.[50] Yet with the encroachment of European values and norms, Arab and Turkish elites also began to develop a heteronormalized sexual discourse. They too began to feel ashamed of openly declared love for the beauty of beardless boys, even as a spiritual idea, and gradually closed the gates to this kind of talk. From the perspective of the twentieth century, only faint echoes remained of this old idea. Writing about the Sufis in Egypt, Michael Gilsenan describes the recent history of the orders as one of subordination and compliance. "Instead of new forms emerging," he writes, "religious energy was harnessed and turned inward, away from true reformulation or rearticulation. The *'ulema'* thus dominated the relationship more than they knew, by the mere fact that the *ṭarīqa*s were absorbed as the second term in this symbiotic system. The Sufi orders thus became a profoundly conservative social and ideological force."[51]

Needless to say, homoerotic love and sex did not disappear, but now any discussion of such themes became shameful. Wherever possible, new editions of Sufi books were purged of homoerotic material. Books extolling the virtues and beauty of *amrad* (beardless boys) were severely censored, and the discourse on divine love and beauty disappeared from view. In other cases, especially where renowned poets or *ulema* of stature were concerned, homoerotic references in their writings were interpreted as purely transcendental, as a reference to the love between God and man. Sufism's bold challenge to orthodox Islam in the Ottoman empire thus resulted in a complete formal negation of same-sex love.

Whatever was left of Sufi sexual heteronomy was demolished in the following century along with Sufi institutions. Persecuted throughout much of the nineteenth century, they all but disappeared at the beginning of the twentieth. The restriction of the Bektashi order's rites after the decimation of the Janissaries in 1826 and the iron hand with which certain Sufi activities were curbed under Mehmed Ali Paşa and his dynasty in Egypt are well known. In the latter part of the nineteenth century, they experienced short periods of revival and at certain points even continued to exert influence on the government. Abdülhamid II, the last great sultan, for example, was apparently a fervent Sufi and a benefactor of several Sufi groups, including branches of the Shādhilis and the Rifā'is.[52] But while some remained influential, their wings of love were clipped, and they could no longer openly embrace the idea of *naẓar* (the gaze) and of passionate desire for beardless boys. The coup de grâce for the Sufis, along with whatever was left of their sexual discourse, came with the total prohibition of Sufi activity when Mustafa Kemal took power in the 1920s and with the rise of Arab nation-states, in which Sufism was seen as a vestige of the corrupt Ottoman empire.

Although there is no unequivocal evidence, it seems that among the reasons modernizing governments in the Arab and Turkish world had for shutting down Sufi institutions, the Sufis' reputation as sexually perverse loomed large. Although for a long time following the struggle of the seventeenth and eighteenth centuries Sufis played down their heterodox beliefs and kept them under a tight lid, many groups were still considered corrupt and deviant. Rumors about erotic *dhikr* ceremonies and misuse of young boys persisted. The ban on Sufi groups and activities was thus first and foremost an act of silencing born out of fear and shame.

CHAPTER 4

# Dream Interpretation and the Unconscious

Dream interpretation comprises a vast body of literature in the Islamic Middle East. Many such books have been written and compiled, from the first centuries to our day.[1] Most of these treatises are manuals containing lists of symbols and their interpretation, a kind of handbook for the dream interpreter. Although few records describe the way the system functioned in the Ottoman Empire, we have many indications that people who had dreams that seemed meaningful or enigmatic would go to dream interpreters in their towns or villages to inquire about their meaning. As dreams were often considered predictors of the future, their interpretation would have a great influence on the dreamer's conduct and choices in the world.[2] This literature, if its limitations are understood, may offer a glimpse into the Ottoman cultural and sexual unconscious.

## DREAM AS PROPHECY, DREAM AS SOUL

If we are to understand dreams as windows on the soul and therefore on people's sex and gender conceptions, we must first ascertain that dream lore was perceived in those terms. In other words, if dreams were understood to be prophetic implants in people's heads, then the symbols and their meaning need not be closely tied to a culture, place, or time. If a man dreams of intercourse with an unknown woman, and if that dream is to be interpreted solely as an indication that he will vanquish his enemies in the future, then there is no necessary connection between the symbol and the reality of the man's life in seventeenth-century Damascus or Istanbul. The same symbol and the same interpretation can be carried over from one era to the next. If, on the other hand, dreams are an indication of internal emotions and processes, their interpretation should give us a more pertinent description of what people felt and thought about sex.

In June 1962, one of the most distinguished Orientalists, G. E. von Grunebaum, organized a conference in Asnières-sur-Oise in France. The conference, titled "The Dream in Human Societies" and sponsored by the Near Eastern Center at UCLA, was one of the first attempts to look at dreams from an interdisciplinary point of view. Historians, psychologists, philosophers, physicians, and anthropologists attended it and delivered lectures. In his introduction to the proceedings, which were published as a book in 1966, von Grunebaum summed up his impressions of the conference by presenting his views on dream interpretation in Islamic societies. His observations would strike us now as startlingly essentialist. Von Grunebaum makes no attempt to differentiate between periods in Islamic history. In the same narrative, sometimes separated by only a few words, dreams of the Prophet Muhammad and dreams of 1950s Algerian peasants share the same outlook and are presented as evidence for the same "Islamic" mode of thought.[3] But what concerns us more in this context is his view of Islamic dream lore. He does not mince words. Islamic culture, he argues, understands dreams only as messages from the occult, representing an outside, objective reality, never as reflections of the psyche. The West, in contrast, has long ago changed into a rational mode of thinking: "For one thing, we are no longer so deeply concerned with the Hereafter and the supernatural. . . . As a result of our scientific advancement we have become able to afford a renunciation long overdue; we have been able to yield to the idea that the dream is symptomatic of a reality divorced from the psychological reality of the dreamer and his society."[4]

Not all contemporary authorities on dreams would agree wholeheartedly with this observation about the modern West, but this is beside the point. As for Islamic culture(s), it is surprising to see how wide of the mark von Grunebaum was, especially considering the data he presents in his own introduction. Since his own research was based on the dream interpretation guide written by al-Nābulusi in the seventeenth century, von Grunebaum bases his conclusions mainly on this work. In the text he quotes al-Nābulusi's introduction: "For we know for certain that while the humors do dictate some dreams, some dreams are sent by the devil and some originate in the self." In this quotation there is nothing like the outright denial of psychological factors to which von Grunebaum refers. Nor is it ambiguous. Whether these dreams are "true" or "false," whether they are effective as prophecies or not, some dreams originate in the self whereas others are caused by chemical reactions in the brain (the humors). As we shall see, later in the same introduction al-Nābulusi talks about dreams that originate in the aspirations of the self and about dreams that originate in desire, ambition, or confusion.

In the years since von Grunebaum published his introduction, not much has changed. Islamic dream lore is still considered to be unequivocally concerned with the prophetic power of dreams, and not with human psychology, and therefore to hold little value for a retrospective scholarly examination of any premodern psyche.[5] But let us try to make a case for a reexamination of the evidence and the conclusions.

On the solid foundation of Greek and Roman thought, Muslim cultures developed a prolific body of research and literature on dreams. From the earliest centuries, many Islamic philosophers devoted treatises to dream interpretation, known generally as *taʿbīr al-aḥlām* or *taʿbīr al-ru'yā* (or *rüya tabiri* in Turkish).[6] As books on the craft and logic of interpretation were adapted from other cultures and developed in Muslim communities, a special discourse evolved pertaining to the meaning of dreams, their relation to the supernatural, and the way they represented the human psyche. This discourse found expression mainly in an intellectual discussion of the nature of dreams, closely following and enriching a famous debate in Greek philosophy about the abode of the intellect and the origin of the dream. Its basis was the work of Aristotle, famous in Latin as *De divinatione ex insomniis,* developed by some of his students. Muslim scholars, notably the tenth-century philosopher al-Farābi (d. 950), elaborated the ideas suggested by Alexandros, who maintained that intellect is an outer faculty in relation to the human soul, and therefore capable of reaching out of the physical body and actively seeking the divine source to obtain knowledge of the future. Other famous thinkers, among them al-Kindi (ca. 801–866) and later Ibn Rushd (1126–1198), chose to follow the arguments of Philoponus, who, using the same ancient categories of soul, intellect, and imitation, claimed that the intellect has no such powers. It cannot leave the body to seek divine enlightenment, and therefore a dream is merely a continuation of the thought process in waking, divorced from sensual perceptions.[7] The implications of both systems are obvious. If dreams have a divine origin, they can predict the future. If they are merely imaginative thoughts, their divinatory power is substantially reduced but they may be more revealing about the human soul.

Other Muslim thinkers, mainly Sufis such as Al-Ghazzali (1059–1111), Suhrawardi (1155–1191), and Ibn al-ʿArabi (1165–1240), attempted a synthesis. Ibn al-ʿArabi developed his own concept of dreams and their meaning. His passage on dreams is one of the most sophisticated premodern psychological explanations of the phenomenon:

> The instruments [of the soul] are transferred from the manifest side *[ẓāhir]* of sense perception to its non-manifest side *[bāṭin]* in order to see what has become established in the Treasury of Imagination *[khizānat al-khayāl]*—to which the senses have lifted up what they have acquired from sensory objects—and what has been formed by the form-giving faculty, which is one of the assistants of this Treasury. Thus the rational soul, to which God has given ownership of this city [of the human being], looks upon what has been placed in its Treasury, as is the habit of kings, who enter into their treasuries when they are alone to gain knowledge of what is in them.[8]

In this conjunction al-ʿArabi suggested the existence of a third universe, *ʿālam al-mithāl.* This is an imaginal world suspended between the divine world of spirits and our own sensual reality. It seems that some later authors following in Ibn al-ʿArabi's footsteps went so far as to suppose that the direction of the flow of creative power is reversed. It is not divine influence on the mind that creates knowledge of the future and of the hereafter, but rather things imagined or dreamt, at least by people with developed spiritual faculties, that could become incarnated as reality, either in the world of sensual perception or in the netherworld.[9] This theory of *ʿālam al-mithāl,* widely accepted in dream interpretation circles, may serve to emphasize two important points. First, the spiritual world, given shape by our imagination, is intelligible only through our own reality; and second, this seemingly clear differentiation between dream as prophecy and dream as manifestation of the inner self collapses. If the power of imagination is such that it can make things happen in reality, then the dream could be at the same time a reflection of our inner world and a prophecy about the future.

Muslim authors in later centuries were well acquainted with this discourse and it affected their concept of dreams.[10] But most of those who wrote guidebooks to dream interpretation in later years, having incorporated these ideas, did not bother to discuss the philosophical underpinnings of their interpretations. Based on a compromise between the "inner" and the "outer" approaches to the intellect, they developed a practical science of interpretation, assuming, as it were, that dreams represent both messages from the occult and indications of the dreamer's life and circumstances. This implied that any symbol in a dream could represent either an apprehension that comes from within or a veiled notion of a possible future. Although the interpretation of a symbol would most often be presented as a prediction, in a sense it did not even matter whether the result of the dream would be prophecy or a telling account of the dreamer's psyche. Interpreters deciphered dreams by breaking the dreamer's vision into its constituent parts and interpreting each part separately. A dreamer may, for example, see in his/her dream another person drinking from a cup. The identity of that other person, the act of drinking, and the cup itself would all be interpreted separately as symbols, and the interpreter would then try to connect all into one coherent interpretation. The cup in this dream may symbolize a woman. Whether this woman represents something in the dreamer's present life or is part of a prediction about future incidents may be deduced from other evidence gathered by the interpreter, either from the dream itself or by questioning the dreamer.

This pragmatic attitude followed Arab and Persian traditions described earlier, but owed its structure to the *Oneirocritica* of Artemidorus, a second-century interpretation treatise, translated and interpreted by Ḥunayn Ibn Isḥāq (808–873) and Al-Farābi.[11] For many centuries the *Oneirocritica* served as one of the main bases for dream interpretation texts in the Islamic world.[12] As a result of this fusion of indigenous Islamic and Greek-Byzantine traditions, Middle Eastern Islamic notions about the process of dreaming merged with those held in Christian Europe in the early Middle Ages. The practical implications of dream interpretation entertained by both Islamic and Christian interpreters tended to unify the soul and the self.[13] This Greek-Byzantine influence came full circle when, from the late Middle Ages, scholars in Muslim lands translated and adapted Islamic dream interpretation literature to their own needs.[14] These translations found their way to Europe, mainly through Spain, Sicily, and Byzantium, and influenced early modern European dream lore.[15]

## DREAMS IN THE CULTURAL IMAGINATION

It is one thing to say that dreams were believed to originate, at least partially, in the inner self and to represent the dreamer's world, and quite another to prove that these symbols indeed reflect an ever-changing collective human psyche. Having established that dreams were not seen merely as prophesies dawning on the dreamer, the question to address next is the relevance of such texts to Islamic societies. To what extent did writers adapt the original Islamic and Greek texts of earlier centuries to their own lives and times? To what extent do such dream interpretation books represent their cultural values or their symbolic language, rather than the symbols of ancient non-Islamic people? And also, to what extent were dreams central to personal and collective notions of self and society in the Islamic, and, in this specific case, the Ottoman world?

Already at first glance there is evidence that shortly after the first waves of translation from other languages, even as these translations were carried out, some changes were introduced. An adaptation of contents to the religion of Islam, or at least to monotheism, is immediately evident. As he translated the works of Artemidorus from Greek, Ḥunayn Ibn Isḥāq changed some of the content, and in particular deleted or rearranged the parts referring to pagan deities.[16] In later works there are many instances where symbols in dreams were inserted and interpreted in line with such associations from the Koran as they may elicit in the dreamer's mind. Here are several examples taken almost at random. Ibn Sīrīn, one of the earliest compilers of Islamic dream interpretation books, very often uses verses from the Koran for interpretation. It is interesting to note that in some cases Ibn Sīrīn maintains an ancient interpretation, probably translated from Artemidorus, but attributes it to a koranic passage. Whereas Artemidorus interprets a dream of sexual intercourse between a man and his mother, with the mother on top, to be a premonition of death, drawing a parallel between mother and earth, Ibn Sīrīn offers the same interpretation but attributes it to the koranic verse "from her we have borne you, and into her we will return you." Ibn al-Qassār al-Qayrawāni, a tenth-century dream interpreter, attempts to associate as many symbols as possible with the Koran and its exegesis. In his manuscript he suggests, for example, that if a man dreams of having sex with a menstruating woman, he will be drawn away from her company not because it is forbidden, but by reason of the koranic verse "So keep away from women in their courses."[17] And, just as attentive to the power of koranic verse in the minds of his clientele, the seventeenth-century scholar al-Nābulusi, quoting the verse "For we will send the she-camel by way of trial for them,"[18] remarks that dreaming about a she-camel may be a sign of trial or rebellion.[19]

But even in a deeply religious society, many people would not know these verses by heart and did not feel that they were potent enough to infiltrate their every dream. Koranic imagery may appear now and then, but unless they were religious scholars or ascetic monks, most people's habitus—the way they conducted their lives, their local customs, their classificatory schemes—was just as influential, or even more so, than the holy scriptures.[20] While some interpreters held on to the Koran as a primary source of symbolic language, many others had recourse to a variety of other sources for their interpretations. Alongside religious semiotics they posited other cultural experiences drawn from daily life, from non-Islamic neighboring cultures, from profane literature, and from their own accumulated experience as scholars of the psyche.

It is not only through circumstantial evidence that we know of authors' awareness of changing semiotics in dreams, and of changes they made in their interpretations as a consequence. Some of them, following older traditions, openly discussed their perception of the need to adapt interpretations to the changing times. Perhaps the most important among them was the great Damascene scholar al-Nābulusi.

Shaykh ʿAbd al-Ghani al-Nābulusi was born in Damascus in 1641 and died in 1731. His family, originally from the city of Nābulus in Palestine, settled in Damascus a long time before he was born, and joined the local Arab-Ottoman elite. Al-Muḥibbi, the famous biographer of the century, mentions al-Nābulusi's grandfather as *shaykh mashāyikh al-Shām,* a title often referring to the leader of the Sufi brotherhoods in Damascus,[21] and ʿAbd al-Ghani himself was the leading intellectual figure in Syria at the time. He wrote about two hundred books, most of them on poetry, Sufi doctrine, and travel. His book on dream interpretation, *Taʿṭīr al-anām fi taʿbīr al-manām* (Perfuming the Beings with the Interpretation of Dreams), has become the central reference book for dream interpreters, even at the center of the Ottoman Empire. An indication of this status may be found in the very large number of manuscript copies found in the Süleymaniye Library in Istanbul, especially in relation to other compilations.[22] As a towering figure in Sufi literature and Orthodox learning, he stands at a special juncture in the history of dream interpretation, weaving together the threads of earlier dream interpreters to create a unified discourse.

Al-Nābulusi devoted an entire chapter of his *Taʿṭīr al-anām* to the matter of differences between people and their implications for interpretation. Having compiled this book from several previous ones, he tells us, he took the liberty, first, of adding new symbols that were relevant to his time. Second, he based his interpretations of symbols on scientific methods. One should be aware, writes al-Nābulusi, that interpretation is not a matter for astrologers or magicians. It is a complex science based on analogy *(qiyās),* consideration *(iʿtibār),* comparison *(tashbīh),* and doubt *(ẓann)*.[23] Interpretation is to be conducted either by finding the symbolic meaning *(maʿnā)* of things seen in a dream or by association of names in the mind of the dreamer.[24] A good interpreter, he adds, should know the Koran and its metaphors, and should be versed in the *ḥadīth*, but also in poetry, proverbs, and etymology. He should be devoted to his work and observant in order to be able to scrutinize the people who seek his advice. Symbolic meanings may vary according to people's trades and abilities and religions. The interpreter has to ask the dreamer questions about his inner self, his status, his people, his trade and his living conditions (the book is almost exclusively addressed to males). He must do the utmost to clarify all matters that may affect the dream to be interpreted.

The same symbol may portend salvation for one person and suffering for another.[25] Meanings change with the dreamer's use of language. To illustrate, he mentions the classic example of a dream about *safarjal* (quince). For a Persian speaker, the word connotes beauty and repose, because that is part of its semantic field, whereas for the Arab it sounds like an amalgam of two Arabic words, and may mean travel *(safar)* and deportation *(jalā')*.[26] Meanings also change by religion, and there are different interpretations for the believer and the nonbeliever. Eating the carcass of an animal connotes forbidden money for those whose religion forbids eating animals not properly slaughtered, but for others, uninhibited by these religious commands, the same image may indicate benefit and gain. Even different seasons have a crucial bearing on interpretation. Fire, warm clothes, and cold sensations may have different meanings in hot climes or in summer than they do in cold northern countries or in winter.

Al-Nābulusi's work expresses even greater sensitivity to the human psyche when he stretches his imagination to explain that a woman's dream of intercourse in a religious sanctuary in full view of other people might instinctively be interpreted as a manifestation of a sense of shame and an admonition of trouble. But if she were in India, and her religion were different, the same dream would indicate a proclivity to worship and piety because, "according to the commandments of their worthless religion," some of these people worship their gods by fornication in the same manner that the adherents of Mazda *(al-majūs)* worship fire.[27]

These deliberations, echoing in detail other books of earlier periods, demonstrate the relevance of dream interpretations to their times.[28] We may say with certainty that important books on interpretation were not just mindless reproductions or compilations of previous books. They were adapted to their audience, and although tropes and symbols were often similar, some authors made an effort to find the current meanings of the symbolic lexicon for their patients, rather than copy from older books interpretations that might have become irrelevant.[29] Furthermore, interpreters were aware, at least in their explicit introductions, of the fact that different people in the same society would attach different meanings to symbols, and they did their best to offer an abundance of interpretations for each image.

Yet we find that most books on interpretation have much in common and use the same basic repertoire.[30] Rather than substituting new meanings for older ones, most interpreters preferred to add new meanings to the previous layers. Books slowly grew in volume and the art of interpretation became more subtle and rich in content. In books of the Ottoman period we find, side by side, meanings copied verbatim from older books, sometimes representing ancient strata, and new ones, which were probably more in tune with the times. This is especially visible in remnants of Greek attitudes copied from Artemidorus, and in the rich material concerning desert symbols. References to camels and nomads, water holes, tents, and so on were probably not part of the daily experience of most of the people who wished to have their dreams interpreted in sixteenth-century Istanbul or in seventeenth-century Damascus. On the other hand, they may have constituted part of earlier Islamic dream accounts, and may even have been relevant to the cultural imagination of people who encountered nomads regularly and were familiar with stories of the Koran and with the biography of the Prophet and his followers.[31]

Dreams have been associated with the Ottoman state ever since the foundational story of the ruling dynasty asserted itself as a central myth. Osman, the eponymous founder of the dynasty, began his quest to set up a world empire when he reputedly had a vision that his father-in-law interpreted as a prophecy of world fame. The vision, a dream of a tree sprouting from his navel to shade the whole world, became one of the most sweeping legends in Ottoman culture and was used as a powerful device to build and maintain the empire.[32] In fact, Ottoman culture may be described as a "dream culture" in the sense that, true or imaginary, every change in daily life was believed to have had a counterpart in dreams or to possess an otherworldly dimension. People seem to have used dreams for introspection, to interpret the past, to anticipate the future, and to calculate their moves. Dream lore was a unifying discourse, uniting people in a bond of shared experience, knitting together insights from politics, medicine, and religion.[33] This is evident, for example, in the writings of Evliya Çelebi. In his book of travels, *Seyāhatnāme,* dreams prevail over all other methods of interpreting reality. A dream, whether invented or experienced, is always his first choice for making sense of chaos, for giving meaning to an otherwise perplexing existence. Evliya's close relations with his uncle and patron, the minister Melek Ahmed Paşa, were crammed with interpreted visions. Sometimes this world of nocturnal apparitions was so intense that both shared parts of the same dream in their sleep. At other times a clue for the interpretation of the dream that one of them had appeared in the nightly roaming of the other.[34]

One interesting question, which we cannot answer at this point, concerns the effect dream interpretation books themselves had on the evolution of symbolic language. Having achieved great popularity in Middle Eastern Ottoman culture, interpretations became an integral part of life. People's world of associations was influenced by these interpretations to the same extent that it contributed to them. A closed circuit may have been initiated that perpetuated the symbolic values of certain images and allowed for a slow accumulation of meanings. One would thus have dreamt of a cup simply because dream lore, as was well known to everybody, tended to interpret cups as women, and the association would present itself even in a dream. As representations of the unconscious, however, such "recycled" images and symbols are just as valid. A cup may have accumulated other symbolic meanings; for example those brought on by the rapidly growing tradition of coffeehouses as a social arena. But for dreamers, the image of cups perpetuated by interpretation books was just as tangible.

In sum, dreams were central to the Islamic and Ottoman experience. They were understood by interpreters to be much more than just mini-prophecies. They were expressions of both inner and outer voices and, since they were rendered in a symbolic language that was always bound by time and place, of necessity they expressed ideas in the culturally defined language of the psyche. As Lacan would probably suggest, the range of signifiers available to the unconscious was determined by both the daily experience and the knowledge of dream lore. This symbolic language was not static. It flowed and changed constantly, and therefore, for an interpretation to be valid, the interpreter had to be aware of these changes, and insert them into his lexicon of symbols.

## "FREUDIAN" SYMBOLS IN OTTOMAN-ERA DREAMS

What, then, were the images, symbols, and meanings that pertained to sex in Middle Eastern dream lore of the period? In order to examine this question, we may divide the world of sexual imagery into three parts:

1. Images that are nonsexual on the manifest level, such as rings or nails, to which Freudian and post-Freudian dream analyses attach latent-level sexual symbolism.[35]
2. Images that are nonsexual on the manifest level, and do not usually carry sexual symbolism in modern dream analysis, but are often interpreted as sexual or gender-specific in Ottoman-Islamic culture.
3. Explicit images of intercourse and of sexual organs, and the array of meanings attached to them in interpretations.

Even ardent opponents of Freudian dream analysis in modern psychology accept the premise that certain images are most likely to symbolize sexual preoccupations and to veil sexual obsessions. Among those the most prominent are images graphically reminiscent of the male and female sexual organs. Almost any round hollow object may signify the female vulva. Almost any polelike object may signify the male penis. Reduced sometimes ad absurdum, this is still very much part and parcel of modern psychology's dream analysis.[36]

It is immediately obvious to readers of Ottoman dream literature that these objects are very rarely construed as harboring sexual connotations. Rings and bracelets, which in our minds may connote women even without the sexual allusions, do not provoke such immediate associations in the minds of al-Nābulusi or any of his contemporaries.[37] A bracelet is primarily a symbol of a son to be born. A man who sees a golden anklet on his leg in a dream will fall ill, or sin, perhaps because it reminds one of shackles. For a woman it may be a sign of security. A ring, more complicated as a symbol because it sometimes carries gems and inscriptions, indicates authority and rule. It may also portend promise of property, a wife, a child, or slave-girls. If the dreamer is married, a golden ring that appears in his dream indicates that his wife will bear a male boy. A trench *(khandaq)*, another well-known symbol for the female vulva in Freudian interpretation, reminds dream interpreters of moats or fortifications, probably harking back to the famous Battle of the Trench in the Prophet's time. If the dream is about knowledge *(ʿilm)*, then the trench may represent the *ulema*, its ultimate defenders.

The same is true for what modern psychology would construe almost automatically as phallic symbols. Needles, minarets, snakes, tails, canes, nails, or bananas—none indicate a preoccupation with the male organ.[38] Considered able to cure human beings and often represented as an androgynous symbol, the snake is suggestive of an enemy, and paradoxically may also represent a woman or a child. A needle may represent a wife because the wife does most of the needlework in the house. A thread in a needle indicates the completion of a task. An oboe or a flute indicates good news or an announcement of death because of the homophony between *nayy* (flute) and *naʿīy* (announcer of death). A banana signifies many things: property, children, prison, tomb, and books, but nothing reminiscent of the penis, unless we consider male children to be a man's symbolic phallus. Canes or nails, representing weapons and power, were usually considered to be emblems of noble men and fighters. Only where the visual image was particularly suggestive does a slight chink appear in what is otherwise a total denial of Freudian sexual allusions. A person who sees himself hammering a nail into something that is a symbol of woman *(shay' mimma yadullu ʿala al-nisā')* may be thinking of getting married. This is a very hesitant claim to Freudian fame, however, considering the fact that, as we will see later, most interpretation books are very explicit when it comes to sexual imagery.

## SEX IN NONSEXUAL SYMBOLS

Other symbols found within the Ottoman interpretation tradition clearly carry sexual meaning. One set of symbols concerns gendered images. We must bear in mind here that as in most other cases, we are seeing only one side of the gender dialectic. Women did not write, and therefore both male and female imagery in these interpretation books is produced or reproduced by men. Once again, al-Nābulusi sets the basic guidelines. One should understand the principles *(uṣūl)* of interpretation, he says, so that when an unknown image appears the interpreter will be able to identify its category even if it is not found in the book. For instance, all commodities—flour and wheat, honey and wool—stand for property *(amwāl)*. Lions, wolves, mountains, and trees signify men. Pillows, bedding, pots, and pans represent servants and slaves.

Images reserved for women in dream lore, according to al-Nābulusi, are riding implements and saddles, clothes such as wide trousers *(sarāwīl)*, or birds and livestock.[39] Reading Ottoman symbol sets and their interpretation, one may come to the conclusion that this is a precise description. In many instances, clothing represents women, and it seems that woman is imagined as a sort of wrap, or blanket, around the man.[40] Al-Qassār al-Qayrawāni says that the source for equating women with items of cloth is the koranic passage "They are your garments and ye are their garments" (even though the verse itself refers to women and men alike). Household animals—sheep, camels, and cows—also often represent women, perhaps because women were considered part of a man's property *(māl)*, but also because women are connected with household animals as symbols of fertility and riches. Thus a she-camel *(nāqa)* stands for a rich woman, and milking her means partaking of her property or her offspring.[41]

On other matters pertaining to male/female images, however, al-Nābulusi disagrees with Al-Qassār. The latter tends to interpret all birds as symbols for males. Thus a raven is a lying man, and a hoopoe *(hudhud)* is the bearer of news. This, as we have seen in the first chapter, goes along with the assumption that birds, like men, are hot and dry, and that bird feathers, just like male body hair, are a product of this humoral combination. Al-Nābulusi, on the other hand, perhaps influenced by other medical concepts, often attributes feminine qualities to different kinds of fowl. A goose represents a woman with beauty and property. A peacock is a rich and pretty foreign woman.[42] It is also possible that this tension stemmed from the gap between koranic imagery, which Al-Qassār makes intensive use of, and al-Nābulusi's more universal approach to symbols.[43]

It seems, however, that even the great al-Nābulusi was not fully aware of the type of symbolic imagery that women conjured in his unconscious or in that of his contemporaries. Perhaps the most striking set of images representing women pertains to receptacles of all sorts. Here women are often represented as houses; as parts of houses such as porches, arches, beds, and rooms; or as doors through which a man walks.[44] But by far the most potent set of images are enclosed receptacles and objects containing fluids: cisterns, eggs, or cups of glass and china. Artemidorus makes no automatic connection between women and receptacles for fluids. For him a drinking cup is a symbol of life in general, and amphorae represent servants.[45] Aḥmad Mughniyya, however, a twentieth-century author who copied and summed up many of the themes in al-Nābulusi, expands the connection. A cistern, he says, indicates a woman "because of the water that it holds" *(lima yuḍaʿ fihi min al māʾ)*. Cups filled with water are a woman's essence *(Wa-ʾl-aqdāḥ min jawhar al-nisāʾ)*, he reassures us, as if no other explanation were necessary.[46]

An immediate association that comes to mind is that of women's breasts and milk, or of women as receptacles for male seed, but perhaps a better explanation for the enigma may be found in Janice Boddy's work on Hofriyati women.[47] In Hofriyat, a village in northern Sudan, female sexuality is established only when its essence, the womb, is covered and enclosed, literally, by circumcision and infibulation. In the same vein, the male's sexuality is established only by exposure—by removing the prepuce. Cleanliness, purity, and femininity are also linked with certain fluids, notably water and blood.[48] Although female circumcision was not common at the center of the empire, it may be that sixteenth- and seventeenth-century Ottomans shared this view of women as receptacles and made a subliminal connection among women's cold and wet constitution, water (the main purifying substance), and enclosed spaces.

Here it is interesting to note the symbolism attached to the *ḥammām*—the public bath. In Artemidorus's time, the bathhouse evoked no erotic connotations, certainly not female ones. In his mind the bath was related mainly to problems of health and sickness. Tepid water in the bath is good for the body; hot water may indicate health problems.[49] In Ottoman dream discourse, however, the *ḥammām* takes on a different and ominous set of meanings. Rather than being viewed as the abode of purity and cleanliness it was meant to be, it is described almost exclusively as a place of danger, sin, and debauchery with women.[50] "Whoever enters the *ḥammām,*" says al-Nābulusi, "will suffer from worries, for the *ḥammām* is the locus of sins, as its name, derived from the word *ḥamīm* [intimate, even sexual, friend], indicates."[51] In his long discussion of the *ḥammām,* al-Nābulusi clearly equates it with sinful women: "If someone sees [in a dream] an unknown *ḥammām,* there is a woman there whom men visit."[52] This may have been triggered by the fact that the bathhouse was indeed a locus for sexual pursuits, a meeting ground for people where their private parts are exposed in an atmosphere of heat, humidity, and lust.[53] But this raises a question. The public bath in Ottoman society was a rigidly segregated arena. Men and women never mixed there. It would have been more natural for dream interpreters to associate it with homoerotic practices (for which the *ḥammām* was indeed notorious). Perhaps therefore this image had more to do with the unconscious image of women and femininity. The *ḥammām* was a feminine symbol, a warm, enclosed, humid receptacle. Yet men, breaking into this ultimate symbol of femininity, constantly invade and profane it.

## EXPLICIT SEXUAL IMAGERY

The symbolic language of dreams was not limited to veiled, ethereal allusions to sex. Explicit sexual imagery is common in all dream interpretation manuals from Artemidorus and Ibn Sīrīn to al-Nābulusi and Mughniyya. Since discussions of intercourse changed quite a bit from the first centuries of Islam to Ottoman times, we should first survey some of these changes. The older books treat intercourse images as a separate group under several chapter headings. Artemidorus, as rendered by Ḥunayn Ibn Isḥāq, offers the following headings:[54]

- On Intercourse *(fi'l-mujāmaʿa)*
- With Mothers *(fi'l-umahāt)*
- About Acts Too Repulsive to Mention *(fi fiʿl ma la yajūzu dhikruhu min al-qabāyiḥ)*[55]
- About Unnatural Intercourse *(fi'l-mujāmaʿa allati takūnu ʿala al-amr al-khārij ʿan al-ṭabīʿa)*
- About Sexual Relations with Angels *(fi muwāqaʿat al-malā'ika)*[56]
- About Intercourse with the Dead *(fi mujāmaʿat al-mawta)*
- About Intercourse with Animals *(fi mujāmaʿat al-ḥayawān)*

Despite this surprising taxonomy, reminiscent of Borges's famous list of animals, these chapter headings are not whimsical. With careful pruning of pagan beliefs and with substantially altered titles, the translation retains the sexual order implied by Artemidorus. The first chapter, "On Intercourse," discusses sex that is "in accordance with nature, law, and custom," intercourse that takes place between a man and his natural partners: his wife, lovers, or mistresses. Dreaming of such intercourse is usually considered a good omen for business and work, establishing the idea that sexual relations in their proper hierarchies are a good thing.

The same chapter contains a discussion about intercourse with whores and concubines. The dreamlike locus is a whorehouse where having intercourse is an auspicious sign, too, for male dreamers at least. It becomes more ominous if the dreamer feels trapped inside, in which case it might be an indication of death and a premonition of a cemetery because, as Artemidorus explains, there is a certain similarity between male seed (spent in whorehouses) and tears (shed in cemeteries). Next in this first category comes sex between a male dreamer and an older male relative, or even an enemy, who "possesses" him. Apparently, this is not a good sign for the dreamer, as the possessing party may get the upper hand in politics or business. Other images of intercourse follow: with a known woman who is not in the dreamer's possession, or with another man's wife, or, in what seems like an ascending scale of rarity, with a woman who does the penetrating. Finally, the author returns to homoerotic sex with another man, but this time the dreamer is the penetrating party. Being sexually possessed by a woman is not a bad sign for the dreamer, and may also portend good for the woman dreamt about, but dreaming of intercourse with a young poor man as the penetrated party is a bad omen and may mean that the dreamer will lose money or property. All in all, a clear, traditional hierarchy of sex as power is established here, according to which the penetrating party is the giver and the penetrated one is the taker.

All the acts described above—heteroerotic as well as homoerotic—are still within what the Islamized Artemidorus defines as nature, law, and custom *(al-ṭabīʿa, al-nāmūs wa'l-ʿāda)*. From here on, descriptions of coitus seem to escalate rapidly. First are those acts of copulation that are not unnatural but are illegal or against prevailing custom. Among such proscribed acts Artemidorus counts intercourse with a son five years old or under. In a rare occasion of moral preaching, the author adds that those who are wise should refrain from having such intercourse even with children who are not their sons. The same goes for daughters. Where adopted children are concerned, dreaming of intercourse indicates that a great deal of money will have to be spent on their education.

Next on the list is a section on sex with mothers.[57] Dreaming of having sex with one's mother while she is alive and the father is also well indicates hostility toward the father. A mother as a sexual partner also indicates livelihood and involvement with the affairs of the city. Dreaming of sex with one's mother while on a journey is an expression of yearning to be back, and a promise of return to the dreamer's native land. For those with a rich mother it means gifts and inheritance. If the mother is dead and the dreamer himself is ill, a dream of intercourse indicates that he may die quickly and join her.

Discussions of illicit sex with one's mother in Artemidorus develop into a discussion of position during intercourse. If the dreamer has sex standing up *(wahuwa qa'im)*, trouble and sorrow will befall him. People do not use this position, he explains, unless they have no bed. If a man dreams of sex between the thighs of his mother, this is a bad omen because that position is loathsome.[58] It is akin to the mother's labor in childbearing, and predicts poverty and loss. Since "between her thighs" is usually a perfectly normal position in Ottoman discourse, this could be a circumspect way of discussing oral sex, although this is not mentioned in the text. The next position discussed is that in which the woman straddles the man and remains on top. Interpreters have argued about the significance of the mother being on top, says Artemidorus. Some said this forewarns of the death of the dreamer, because a mother is like earth, which is usually heaped on a dead person's grave. Artemidorus discovered, however, that only sick people who had this dream died, while healthy ones continued living a good life. This is because in other positions the man works and tires, while the woman lies back and enjoys it. In this position the man rests and the woman exhausts her strength.

The next heading, "About Acts Too Repulsive to Mention," refers to a kind of intercourse that the translator refrains from describing in detail. In the original Greek text it is obvious that under this heading Artemidorus discusses different kinds of oral-genital contact, but the translator appears to have found no words to describe these acts, or to have chosen not to describe them in a graphic manner.[59] If a man dreams that his wife does these unmentionable things to him, his love for her will abate, for these things cannot possibly indicate love or companionship. If the woman dreamt about is pregnant, she will lose her child, because in this kind of deed the seed is wasted. Performed by the dreamer with an acquaintance, these "repulsive acts" forebode enmity between them, for there is no love in this act. The only ones for whom such acts are a good sign are people whose work is done by mouth—singers, musicians, or sophists. This attitude toward oral sex indicates that in late antiquity fellatio and cunnilingus were acts that incurred shame. But the refusal of the translator into Arabic to even mention them by name demonstrates that subjects of the Abbasid Empire (or at least the Christians among them) found oral sex even more despicable.

Next in line are images of acts that are considered "unnatural," a word that in this context has a different semantic content. Whereas in our modern discourse *unnatural* is almost the equivalent of *immoral,* or the opposite of *normal,* here it implies that such acts cannot be performed in the world of natural phenomena. This category is used to denote acts of copulation with the spirits of the dead or with angels and pagan deities (which were, of course, omitted in the Arabic translation). Dreams of acts that are against nature include having sex with oneself in a variety of ways,[60] for example, kissing one's own penis, which, if the dreamer has no children, may be a promise of male offspring. This section also deals with female homoerotic sex. A woman having sex with another woman will eventually divulge her secrets to that other woman, and if this other woman is the penetrating party and the dreaming woman is married, this may indicate divorce or widowhood. The inclusion of female homoerotic sex in the "unnatural" section probably represents the author's strong aversion to the possibility that a woman would play the role of the penetrating party, the primary adult male symbol, and thus upset the order of the world.

Two brief segments end this discussion of intercourse. The first is a short subsection on sex with the dead. In most cases this is a bad omen and indicates imminent death or illness. It is followed by an even shorter discussion of intercourse with animals.[61]

We can draw several conclusions from this relatively early text. Perhaps most evident is the fact that contrary to Foucauldian claims, it delivers a sense of defined sexuality, albeit different from ours. In this adaptation of a late Greek-Roman text there are clear definitions of normal sexual urges and abnormal ones, there are boundaries of sexual ethics, and there are clear definitions of good and bad sexuality. A basic characteristic of this early dream discourse of sexuality is the noticeable polarities between licit and illicit, natural and unnatural, appropriate and inappropriate. Several things should be noted about the first portion of the text, the one dealing with licit sex. To begin with, homoerotic intercourse was considered just as "natural," "licit," or "pertaining to custom" as heteroerotic relations, at least as long as the penetrating party is an adult male. As we shall see, this aspect changes as we move along Islamic centuries.

Second, the position of the dreamer in the act—as one who penetrates or is penetrated, possesses or is being possessed, engages in oral or anal sex—is crucial for interpreting the dream. And third, the symbolic meaning of these images is never in the realm of sex. The logic is that dreams rarely speak to us in plain language. So whenever sex is dreamt about openly, sexuality is not the issue. Some vestiges of a presumed connection between dreams of sex and real sexual desire may be found only as we approach practices that the author defines as "repulsive" sex. This may be seen as further proof for the existence of a notion of sexuality. People whose sexual urges are repressed as ugly or forbidden may find refuge in dreams. Only in such cases should sexual dreams be interpreted to hold sexual meanings.

What intercourse most often signifies in "Islamicate" Artemidorus's dream interpretation is a mutual relationship of give and take between people, an exchange in which the one who penetrates is the giver and the one who is penetrated is the taker. Being the epitome of the vital human (and divine) spirit as it used to be in pre- and early Christian Greek and Roman societies, male seed was the symbol of a precious commodity. In dreams it became a potent symbol of giving and taking, buying and selling, and other kinds of economic exchange.[62] This was complicated even further by the power relations underlying this exchange. Being penetrated is being given, but penetration usually also signified the upper hand in politics and social relations. The one penetrated was therefore at the same time both a receiver of bounty and a dominated, sometimes abused, inferior party. The interpreter had to take into account all these considerations and weigh the relative social positions of the two partners in order to present a balanced assessment of the dreamt act of coition.

Artemidorus becomes more apprehensive when he discusses certain other kinds of intercourse, mainly oral sex, and anal sex with the male dreamer as a penetrated party. It is clear from the choice of words such as "too repulsive to mention" that there is a clear hierarchy of acts and of those who perform them. Even though he attempts to present a detached "scientific" account of sexual dreams, and although in most cases even appalling dreams of incest have interpretations in the "normal" range, the author and his translator clearly struggle with their revulsion when they have to discuss certain practices. It is as if oral sex at the time was equivalent to notions of deviation connected to pederasty in our times. We do not know to what degree this spectrum of good and bad sexuality that originated in Greek morality also represents an early Islamic discourse. It was probably translated at first with no special attention paid to discrepancies between the text and sexual imagination of the time among Arabs or other groups under Islamic rule. We must also assume some proximity between these ideas of late Hellenic antiquity and those of the interpreter, Ḥunayn Ibn Isḥāq, a Christian of the early Abbasid era. In any case, it is a starting point from which we can trace developments in the Ottoman period.

Other early sources of dream interpretation come from an Arab lineage. One of the earliest is Ibn Sīrīn, some of whose interpretations were mentioned earlier. A member of the successor group to the Companions of the Prophet, born in the first Islamic generation (34h/654), he was known primarily as a trustworthy transmitter of the Prophet's sayings and deeds. After a while he became known for his accounts of dreams and was hailed as a paragon of interpretation wisdom. In the first centuries of Islam, many works were written bearing his name, and today it is difficult, perhaps impossible, to disentangle all the apocryphal Ibn Sīrīns from the historical one. For our purposes, however, it is not necessary to make these absolute distinctions. What matters is that nobody at that early stage cared to make distinctions between his writings and those of his emulators. They all came to be treated as a single corpus of texts. In fact, we may take what is known as the work of Ibn Sīrīn to be a collective product of several people in the first three centuries, and therefore more representative of a formative discourse.

The various Ibn Sīrīns devote less space than Artemidorus to dreams about intercourse. Unlike Artemidorus, they usually discuss all kinds of intercourse under one heading, usually with titles such as: "About Marriage/Intercourse *[nikāḥ]* and what it concerns, including sexual intercourse *[mubāshara]*, divorce, jealousy, corpulence, purchase of slave-women, fornication *[zinā']* and male-to-male sex *[liwāṭ]*, the immoral junction of people *[al-jamʿ bayn al-nās bi'l-fasād]*, the imitation of men by women *[tashabbuh al-mar'a bi'l-rijāl]*, effeminacy *[takhnīth]*, and the sight of the female vulva *[naẓar al-farj]*." It is difficult to discern any order in the discussion, and themes are repeated in different places in the text.[63]

The contents are not much different from those in Artemidorus. Intercourse is seen as an exchange, a contest, or a war, in which the adult penetrating male should, all other things being equal, have the upper hand. In most cases, male dreams of penetrating other partners, male or female, are good omens. Still, some changes can be perceived. More attention is given to women and to their dreams, although usually within the same framework. Dreams of marriage to a man, even if the female dreamer is married, are a good omen for her. Marriage to a dead man is a bad omen, for her property will be lost. For a man, though, dreams of marriage to a dead woman are a good sign, for he will inherit money. Homoerotic sex may be beneficent for the penetrated in certain cases. For instance, a jailed man who dreams he is the penetrated party in male intercourse will be freed.

In the following centuries, after the translation of Artemidorus and the writings of the Ibn Sīrīns, interpretations were slowly adapted to the mores and nuanced discourse of Abbasid, Fatimid, Mamluk, and Ottoman societies. Interpreters kept the tradition of discussing all kinds of intercourse, and of openly contemplating even remote and unacceptable practices, but the semantic meanings of categories and concepts shifted, as did the interpretations offered for some of these dreams.

In al-Nābulusi's work, several centuries later, the first thing that is apparent is a different arrangement of material. Alphabetical arrangement of symbols replaced the division into chapters prevalent in Artemidorus, Ibn Sīrīn, and in other books attributed to early interpreters.[64] This appears to be merely a different classification method, but it may also reflect a deeper motivation. Some of the categorizations offered by Greek/Byzantine and early Islamic authors may have lost their intrinsic logic. They may have even become unintelligible, to the extent that al-Nābulusi saw no point in adhering to them. In the field of sexual imagery, as in other facets of human existence, Greek categories of licit/illicit and natural/unnatural no longer reflected the then current Islamic discourse of sexuality. This is not to say that sexuality in the Ottoman period had no prohibitions or taboos. These taboos were simply cast in a different mold and did not correspond to the older classification. Many of the things considered unnatural or repulsive by Artemidorus assumed a more neutral flavor, or were not an issue of contention any more, only to be replaced by others that were. Legal practices became illegal; unconventional ones were now performed without hindrance. Rather than go on changing headings and rearranging material that became obsolete, al-Nābulusi chose to dispense with the old classification altogether, and to replace it with a lexicon format. In this new packaging, the structured discourse presented by Artemidorus was broken down into numerous smaller entries. Partly for this reason, al-Nābulusi's attitude toward sexual practices is much more elusive, and has to be sought between the lines or in "hyper-connections" between terms, things, and actions. In the absence of explicit headings and discussions, only the subtle use of language and the kinds of term used to describe certain actions may indicate the value that the interpreter attaches to them.

We may begin by noting that most discussions of intercourse in this later Ottoman compilation appear under five headings: *zinā', liwāṭ, mujāmaʿa, nikāḥ,* and *zawāj*.[65] This arrangement reflects the well-known division of human actions in *sharīʿa* law into five categories: obligatory *(wājib, farḍ);* recommended *(sunna, mandūb, mustaḥabb);* indifferent *(mubāḥ);* reprehensible, disapproved *(makrūh);* and forbidden *(ḥarām)*.[66] While some actions are specifically ordained or strictly forbidden by God, and need therefore be performed or, on the contrary, abstained from, others are more loosely defined as positive, negative, or neutral, without incurring any prescribed punishment or reward. The five headings chosen by al-Nābulusi and his contemporaries represent the rungs in this ladder. *Zinā'*, fornication or adultery, is, of course, strictly forbidden. *Liwāṭ,* sodomy or homoerotic sex, though reviled, does not necessarily incur the ultimate *ḥadd* penalty reserved for crimes against God. *Mujāmaʿa,* simply intercourse, is neutral. *Nikāḥ,* which means both legal intercourse and marriage, is clearly tilted to the positive side. *Zawāj* is marriage with almost no sexual subtext, and is considered close to divine commandment, if not strictly so. In a further indication of his own awareness of the meaning of his choice, al-Nābulusi urges the dream interpreter to be attuned to the words used by the dreamer: "Sometimes the dreamer will say *'tazawwajtu'* (I got married) and sometimes *'nakaḥtu'* (I took in marriage/had intercourse with). Their interpretation may be different.

That is why we mentioned *'zawāj'* under 'Z,' and *'nikāḥ'* under 'N.' This is also true for similar issues."[67]

In the tradition of his predecessors, al-Nābulusi seldom suggests a sexual interpretation for a sexual dream. Dreams of *zinā'* are usually interpreted to be negative symbols, pertaining to treason or theft, but they may also be positive indications. For example, a sultan dreaming of illicit intercourse of the *zinā'* type and of receiving punishment for it should expect to strengthen his rule—an interesting comment on morality and government. If a person who waits for high office *(āhil li'l-wilāya)* has such a dream, office will be bestowed upon him, but he will rule unjustly.[68] It is interesting to note that the only instance where a dream of *zinā'* has an actual sexual connotation is when the dreamer, male or female, dreams not of the act itself, but of the koranic verse condemning adulterers.[69]

*Liwāṭ,* though reserved for male love, is also ambiguous in its contents.[70] An adult male who sees himself penetrating a boy will become a laborer or will lose his property to an enemy, although some say that he will eventually overcome his enemy. If a person sees himself having intercourse with a small child, he will receive money that is due him or do something that is improper for him. If he sees himself penetrated by an unknown man, an enemy will overcome him, or, if he has no enemies, his honor or property will be damaged. If, on the other hand, the man in the dream is known to him, they will join forces in order to do something hateful. If a man dreams of having sexual relations with the sultan as the penetrating party, he will gain much money and property, but if he is the penetrating party all his property will be lost.[71]

*Nikāḥ,* legal sexual intercourse, carries an auspicious interpretation in the realms of politics and society. Such dreams are often indications of victory over rivals, of release from worry or trouble, of carrying out justice and of receiving religious wisdom. It seems that for al-Nābulusi the choice of the word by the dreamer—*nikāḥ, mujāmaʿa,* or *zinā'*—is more important than assessing the moral value of the act itself. Under the heading of *nikāḥ* he includes dreams of prohibited intercourse with one's mother or with other forbidden women *(muḥarramāt)* and dreams about non-Muslim men having intercourse with Muslim women. The third category, *mujāmaʿa,* is perhaps most interesting. Here al-Nābulusi discusses hetero- and homoerotic dreams together, as well as dreams of sex with oneself, with other males, and with children of both sexes. In most cases these are indications of enmity and rivalry, but, again, the outcome is usually not directly related to the position of the dreamer.

While al-Nābulusi uses the religious classification into degrees of recommended and disapproved, he consciously refrains from automatically attaching religious values to sexual acts. It seems that for him the crucial value of these categories lies in the fact that they form part of a cultural lexicon capable of conveying the dreamer's own attitude toward the dream. When a dreamer admits to having dreamt about *nikāḥ*, it is immaterial to al-Nabulusi whether the act is strictly in accordance with religious definitions. If one dreams of having homoerotic intercourse and yet calls it *mujāmaʿa*, this should indicate that the dreamer himself does not attach negative significance to the dream, and therefore interpretation should note and make use of this fact. Al-Nābulusi says as much himself. For the believer, he says, a dream of honey may mean the sweetness of the Koran, while for the profligate *(fāsiq)* it is a symbol for this world of sin and its pleasures.[72] He accepts this as a part of life, and rather than trying to rebuke the sinner for impure thoughts, he seems to acknowledge them on a par with those of the righteous believer.

On yet another plane, this may indicate that it was quite normal for al-Nābulusi's contemporaries not to see certain acts as intrinsically immoral, even when they were prohibited by the *sharīʿa*. Just as it was evident for Artemidorus (and Ḥunayn bin Isḥāq) that oral-genital contact is taboo, it appears that in the minds of Ottoman dream interpreters, sexual attraction, heteroerotic or homoerotic, with women in dominant positions or with men on top, was never unnatural or reprehensible in and of itself. Law sometimes forbade sexual acts, but they were still within the bounds of nature and normalcy. Sex in the Ottoman period became a multifaceted affair, sometimes forbidden, to be sure, but seldom fettered by psychological inhibitions.

## DREAMS IN THE OTTOMAN ERA'S UNCONSCIOUS

It is clear, if we compare al-Nābulusi to Artemidorus, that by the seventeenth century serious changes had occurred in the evaluation of sexual dreams, and thus also in sexual discourse. Using Artemidorus's categories of nature, custom, and law as our starting point, we may say that the category of "nature" as understood by antiquity lost almost all its meaning for early modern Middle Easterners. Al-Nābulusi and his audience do not seem to be aware of any natural order of things sexual in the universe. Right and wrong in sexual intercourse do not constitute part of any binding cosmology, and modes of intercourse are not seen as intrinsically imprinted with social value. Al-Nābulusi makes no mention of the term and never uses it to refer to sexual relations.

If we take Artemidorus's second category, "custom," to mean a set of unwritten norms prevalent in society, here too the differences are meaningful. The moral tone embodied in "custom" is attenuated. Al-Nābulusi's interpretation does not maintain Artemidorus's careful balance between gender, age, and social status, on the one hand, and position in intercourse, on the other. He does defer to people of higher economic and social status, signified by titles such as *ʿālim,* sultan or governor. But while intercourse is still primarily interpreted as an exchange of political or economic power, connections between these and the social hierarchy are not always simple and self-explanatory.

It is the third category offered by Artemidorus, that of law, that seems to supersede all others in the dream interpretation script of the early modern Middle East. We noted earlier that in order to explain the basics of interpretation, al-Nābulusi and his contemporaries had recourse to the science of *ḥadīth* and to the principles of *sharīʿa* jurisprudence. The same principles guided scholars in their attempts to interpret the language of the libidinal unconscious. They conceive of the disposition of the dreamer as emerging from an almost intuitive grasp of the range of prohibitions available to the Muslim, believed to be somehow inculcated in the souls of dreamers. Dreams are seldom judged good or bad purely on the basis of visual content, but the quasi-legal evaluations that the dreamer applies to his images—forbidden, reprehensible, neutral, recommended, obligatory—are intrinsic to the evaluation. This awareness of law goes beyond the issue of language. Legality seems to be the principal determinant of right and wrong, good and bad. As a sexual script, while dream interpretation obfuscates the relationship between position in intercourse and social status, it reinforces another—that between sex and law.

Yet the same sources suggest that people in Ottoman cultures, at least in the major Islamic centers, viewed sex and sexuality in a way that is unfamiliar to us. Images interpreted by most modern psychologists as latent symbols of sex were, almost as a rule, interpreted to mean other things, and often symbolized social and political relations. One explanation for the total absence of sexual interpretations for "Freudian" symbols may be that although images were believed to originate from within, from the person's store of images and connotations, they were not believed to represent an inner self, and therefore there was no connection between the image and the dreamer's psyche. But as we have seen, this was not the case. Dream interpreters assumed a relationship between the dreamer's world and the dream. A better explanation would be that nonsexual alternatives for sexual desires were not needed. Overt sexual imagery was natural, and even illegitimate acts did not carry the stigma of guilt and deviation or mental disorder attached to them in modern societies. Sexual elements in dreams were not disguised at the latent level, because there was no need to distort or censor them at the manifest level.

An absence of "Freudian" symbolic meanings attached to images reminiscent of the penis and the vulva does not mean that nonsexual objects were never assumed to have sexual value. Images of enclosed spaces, and especially containers of all kinds, from bottles and glasses to wells and cisterns, very often represented women, with a clear allusion to their sexual organs and their wombs. Enclosed spaces like the *ḥammām*, although never used by both sexes at the same time, also carried connotations of women and sex. Memories of male childhood in the ladies' bath may have influenced the unconscious in dreams, but the connection of women to receptacles for fluid and connotations of purity and impurity may also have been part of the sexual lexicon of the unconscious. One can surmise that inhibitions in this society were not attached to the sexual act, but to the desecration of the person of woman, and to a breach of the very strict boundaries separating the sexes.

Precisely because they carried no intrinsic burden of guilt or deviation, at the latent level dreams of copulation were rarely sexual. Unless they bore unequivocal proof of sexual desire, particularly when the male dreamer experienced nocturnal emission, they were never interpreted as such at the manifest level. This is why a leading interpreter such as al-Nābulusi needed to devise a scale of right and wrong based not on the nature of the act itself, but rather on the dreamer's choice of words in referring to it. If the dreamer defined the act as illegal sex, then it probably meant that at the latent level, the act of copulation referred to an illicit dealing (which does not necessarily mean that the interpretation is negative). If he or she described it as a licit or even as an approbated act, the interpreter would take it to mean that the dreamer had been thinking of better things.

## DELETING DANGEROUS DREAMS

In the later nineteenth and twentieth centuries, things changed again. Intellectually, the whole genre seems to have withered away. New books contained very little innovation. They are mostly copied versions of the older ones, sometimes rendered in simpler language. One reason for this may be that the classic science of dream interpretation lost its prestige with the advent of modernity. A respectable area of study enjoying a privileged place among the Ottoman intellectual elite gradually became part of yesterday's world, associated with backwardness and tradition. Dreams lost their power of divination, and their charm as keys to the mysteries of the world faded with the emergence of a new "scientific" outlook. Later, new discourses, among them the emerging field of psychology, created different scripts, and these in turn shaped new discursive and social power relations. Intellectuals devoted themselves to other fields of inquiry, and little effort was invested in updating dream language and in bringing it into line with modern assumptions about sex. As a result, modern compilations of dream interpretations mostly ignored the sexual changes that took place in the Middle Eastern and Ottoman world with the advent of modernity.

On the other hand, the heteronormalization of love, as well as other influences, began to impinge on representations of the Middle Eastern unconscious, just as it did on other scripts. Several sexual choices, especially same-sex intercourse and pederasty, came to be seen as a deviation from a norm, and later as unnatural or abnormal behavior. In nineteenth- and early-twentieth-century dream interpretation manuals, and in texts abridged and adapted from older books, changes may be found mainly in the careful pruning of discussions relating to homoerotic practices and of some of the more candid discussions of incest.[73] Compilers of dream interpretation manuals woke up to another reality where such imaginings were forbidden even in dreams.

CHAPTER 5

# Boys in the Hood

## *Shadow Theater as a Sexual Counter-Script*

Previous chapters discussed a number of sexual scripts that, while very different from one another, had one thing in common: legal discussions, dream interpretation manuals, and medical treatises all represented a formal kind of knowledge and, in a sense, high culture. Though not always officially sanctioned, and sometimes even at odds with one another, they embodied authority in its myriad forms: state power, religious influence, hegemonic scientific knowledge, and high social status. The script to which we now turn, that of the Ottoman shadow theater, offers another dimension, a rare excursion into a very different cultural narrative, one that may be described as a counter-script. Unlike the textual traditions we have examined in previous chapters, this group of texts bears the imprint of the view from below or, to be more accurate, from the sidelines.

In the theater, society presented itself to itself. It was here that it created its world of laughter, made its critique of state and religion known to the authorities, and presented an alternative. Just as in the medieval carnival, shadow theater was an activity in which high and low took part on an equal basis. *Ulema* and peasants, *efendi*s and Gypsies watched it together. Some plays originated in the palace and found their way to the street. Others, conceived in local coffeehouses, were performed in the sultan's harem, transmitting the norms and wishes of the populace and poking fun at the state and its servants. Thrice removed from reality, once through the stage, then through the puppets, and finally through their projection on a flat screen, it was a safety valve for venting popular dissatisfaction, but a lot more, too. Ephemeral and elusive though they were, the shadows poked fun at morality and voiced a truth about society that hides within fiction.

In his research on Rabelais and the culture of the Middle Ages and the Renaissance, Bakhtin offers a different vantage point concerning the relationship between high and low culture. Comic and carnivalesque spectacles in the premodern world, he says, stood in marked opposition to the rites of the church and the state, and deliberately represented a world opposed to the one suggested by these authorities. They seem to have constructed, alongside the official world, another kind of life to which all people belonged at certain periods of the year. Understanding this duality is essential to understanding the medieval world and the world of the Renaissance.[1] "This temporary suspension, both ideal and real, of hierarchical rank created during carnival time a special type of communication impossible in everyday life. This led to the creation of special forms of marketplace speech and gesture, frank and free, permitting no distance between those who came in contact with each other and liberating from norms of etiquette and decency imposed at other times. A special carnivalesque, marketplace style of expression was formed which we find abundantly represented in Rabelais's novels."[2] In other words, this carnival culture created an alternative world, just as real, side by side with the one created by church and state, and this alternative world was crucial for medieval civilization as a whole. But Bakhtin adds another dimension to his portrayal. This is not merely a popular culture set against a high one, he says. All men (perhaps we should take the liberty here of adding "and many of the women") were part of this culture. Carnivals were a parody of religious rites and beliefs, a critique of the state and its servants, but at the same time they were part of an integrated culture. White-collar clerics and state functionaries participated alongside the bourgeois and peasants. During festivals, "c'est la vie même qui joue et, pendant un certain temps, le jeu se transforme en vie même" (life itself is at play, and, for a while, the game transforms itself into actual life). This is a "parallel life" for the people, a liberating experience, set apart from current affairs and hierarchies, privileges, taboos, and laws, yet uniting high and low. Carnival laughter is not an isolated individual reaction. It is a sense of the ensemble of people. It is universal, encompassing all who participate and watch. It is also ambivalent: joyous and sarcastic, negating and affirming at the same time.[3]

Bakhtin has been criticized for some of his assumptions, for his tendency to idealize the carnival, for ignoring tensions and inequalities in early modern spectacles, and for his disregard for the many different varieties of carnival. Later critics emphasized the fact that he ignored the sometimes cynical use of carnival by the state to vent protest and minimize resistance.[4] Yet at least in relation to the shadow theater tradition in the Ottoman Middle East, his work manages to convey a sense of social leveling and a shared culture that finds its expression in the staged event.

In our quest for the sexual scripts of the period, Karagöz cannot be overrated. We should bear in mind that most of the population of the Middle East until the late nineteenth century could not read and that even if they had been taught to do so, the majority had little access to books. Thus, almost the only authoritative text-bound scripts available to the public, apart from sermons at the mosques, were shadow theater plays. Whether accepted at face value as guides to sexual debauchery or understood for what they purportedly were—a satire of morality and social injustice—it was Karagöz and Hacivat who talked to the people about their sexuality and its limits. Before we analyze this profane sexual script, however, let us begin with a description of shadow theater and its place in the public arena.

## SHADOW THEATER IN THE OTTOMAN EMPIRE

Projected onto a flat screen, the shadow theater, most commonly known as Karagöz, as Hayal Oyunu, or as *hayal-ı zill* (*ḥayāl al-ẓill* in Arabic), is a precursor of cinema and television. Usually a large curtain of dark material is set up. In the middle of the dark curtain, a smaller rectangular aperture is covered with white cotton cloth and lit from behind, in the past usually by candles or lanterns "that smoke abominably."[5] A flickering light shines on the puppets, which are made of thin, translucent, smoothly dressed, and richly painted camel leather. The leather is then perforated, so that the picture projected on the screen is not a uniform black shadow, but rather a cartoonlike image in full color. The puppeteer manipulates the puppets by means of long sticks, which he hides by placing them at a direct angle to the source of light. He also plays all the roles in the play, frequently as many as twenty, and usually sings songs as well.

Historians still debate the origins of the Ottoman shadow play. Many probable sources were suggested, from an ancient Turkic tradition, perhaps borrowed from China, India, or the Mongols, to the influence of Greek and Byzantine theater. Some highlight the contributions of Italian commedia dell'arte, the heritage of Iberian Jews, and that of Gypsies around the empire.[6] Yet it appears that the most probable source for the specific form finally developed by the Ottomans originated in the Mamluk sultanate. Before the Ottoman conquest of the Arab lands, a local type of shadow theater, sexually promiscuous in nature, thrived in Mamluk Egypt and Syria. The puppets and the techniques were similar to those evolved by the Ottomans and, as we shall see, some of the contents of older plays were still used by the Karagöz-Hacivat duo in their adventures. In an oft-quoted passage, the Mamluk historian Ibn Iyās recounts how Sultan Selim "the Grim," the Ottoman conqueror of Egypt, attended one such performance in Cairo, in which the tragic end of Tuman Bay, the last Mamluk sultan, was reenacted. He enjoyed it so thoroughly that he decided to pack up both theater and performer and bring them back to Istanbul with him.[7]

Two other Ottoman theatrical traditions already extant in the empire enriched the imported Mamluk version. *Meddah*s, storytellers, were an old and revered form of popular entertainment that provided a developed mode of narration and vocal expertise, on which the shadow theater could rely and build. The second tradition, Orta Oyunu, was a popular street theater in which the crowd is seated around a circular stage on which the play is performed. The contents of the plays are similar to those of the Karagöz. Through the years Orta Oyunu probably contributed a great deal to the development of contents and positioning in the shadow play, and its own plots and characters must in turn have been enriched as a result of its contact with shadow theater.

By the seventeenth century, Karagöz theater was already a well-established and immensely popular art form, though contested inside the Ottoman world. Many European travelers from the sixteenth century onward witnessed it, and most of them seem to have been shaken by the lewd plays and by what Dr. John Covell, who visited the empire in the 1670s, describes as "the beastly brutish language."[8] It appears that Europeans of the time had already lost their sense of carnivalesque language and the lewd laughter of days past, immortalized by Rabelais. Pocqueville, a century later, does not hide his disgust at the vulgarity of the play:

> It cannot be said that they have any shews or dramatic spectacles: for we ought not to give that name to the indecent scenes of the puppet-shew kind, which those men, so jealous of their wives, cause to be represented in their families. "The hero of the piece" said M. Sevin, whose words I quote, "is an infamous wretch whom they call Caragueuse, and who appears on the stage with all the attributes of the famous god of Lampsacus.[9] In the first act he gets married, and consummates the ceremony in the presence of the

> honest assembly: in the second act his wife lies in, and the child immediately begins a very filthy dialogue with its father."[10]

For the local elite, the plays obviously had a deeper significance. Evliya Çelebi devotes several pages of his travel book *Seyāhatnāme* to the shadow theater. In his exposé he finds it necessary to begin by discussing the birth of comedy in the world, from the stories of Cain and Abel to this day. Coming to the Ottoman era, he tells a fantastic story of a court jester, a certain Kor Hasan, who was a favorite of Sultan Yıldırım Bayezid ("the Thunderbolt") in the late fourteenth century. One day, he says, the sultan was furious with the *ulema* for their corruption and abuses. He arrested several hundred of the highest-ranking clerics and was determined to burn them all at the stake. Many of his closest advisers pleaded with him to spare their lives, but to no avail. Then Kor Hasan decided to try his hand. He put on the costume of a Greek Orthodox patriarch and entered the sultan's chambers. Seeing him, the sultan laughed "until he was powerless." "What is this dress?" he asked. "My Sultan! I have to go to the land of the infidels, and it seems to me this dress would help me in my mission," replied Kor Hasan. "Where is it that you are going?" asked the sultan. "I will go to the Christian king of Istanbul, my sultan."[11] "What will you do there, a curse be upon you?" "I have heard," replied Kor Hasan, "that some eight hundred authors, compilers, heads of the schools of law, the kadi of Bursa, the chief mufti, the able jurists, are all to be burned at the stake. I told myself that when no competent *ulema* are left, we might as well take the priests of the Christian nation. You will most certainly send your slave to bring over forty or fifty such priests. Send this poor soul wearing this dress to the Christian king. Our city Bursa will once again be alive with priests, and they will return to their old places on Keșiș Dağı [Priest Mountain, the local name for Uludağ, a famous mountain near Bursa]."

With his stand-up act, Kor Hasan managed to convince Yıldırım, who had been unwavering until that day. "Ya Hasan!" cried the sultan, "for the sake of my forefathers, since these people were unjust and oppressive, I decided to burn them all. But for those nice words of yours I will forgive them." Kor Hasan lifted his hand and swore an oath of loyalty to the sultan. "If they do no more evil, they will be freed, but if they stick to their injustice, the sentence will be carried out." He took a written order proclaiming the sultan's pardon and hurried to the prison. Opening the gates of the prison wide, he cried, "Hey, *ulema!* The sultan has given you his pardon at the request of a poor undeserving and ridiculed *mukallid* [mimic] like me." As they heard the news, the *ulema* began to thank him profusely. "Oh, our friend Hasan, may the almighty show you happiness! May you never know a day of sadness. May the lord keep the chain of your offspring until the end of time." Thus, concludes Evliya, Kor Hasan, the fountainhead of all mimics, was accepted and revered by all *ulema*.[12]

True or false, Evliya does not recount this story merely for our reading pleasure. In his time, and throughout the period from the sixteenth to the nineteenth centuries, a heated debate raged around the shadow theater. Many, especially in the circles of the orthodox *ulema,* viewed its vulgarity and open sexuality with disdain and apprehension. They demanded that the plays be censored or prohibited, and some insisted that men of faith should not attend these lewd performances. Once again it was Ebüssuud Efendi, Sultan Süleyman's mentor and the brilliant şeyhülislam of the sixteenth century, who made a first attempt, in the following *fetva* he issued, to reconcile such an earthly and profane form of art with the gravitas required of *ulema:*

> Question: One night a shadow play was brought to a gathering, and Zeyd, who is *imam* and *hatib,* stayed in that gathering. Would it be in accordance with *[sharīʿa]* law, if he saw the play until the end, to dismiss him from his position as *imam* and *hatib?*
>
> Answer: If he watched the play in order to learn its moral lesson *[ibret],* and thought about it with a tame mind *[ehli hal fikri ile tefekkür etti]* it is forbidden [to dismiss him].[13]

As Evliya's lengthy and carefully constructed preamble demonstrates, the debate around the legitimacy of Karagöz plays flared up again in the late seventeenth century. Later sources describe a similar attitude of suspicion. Indeed, during the nineteenth century, in the Tanzimat period, almost all plays were censored, and direct references, mainly visual, to overt sexuality were omitted. The versions we possess for most of the plays, from the nineteenth and the early twentieth centuries, have gone through a process of cleansing, which we will discuss later.[14]

This ongoing centuries-long debate shaped some of the discourse in the plays themselves and had an influence on their content. But in true Ottoman fashion, even as the debate continued, a vague live-and-let-live compromise was reached and adhered to until the explosion of the nineteenth century. The ideas expressed in Ebüssuud's *fetva* became the standard justification for the plays' free-spirited attitude. To mollify the moral majority, shadow theater had become a metaphor for the world. Our lives, sinful, petty, or virtuous as they may be, are a mere passing shadow on a screen, whereas the Creator, like the puppeteer, stays behind when our light is gone. One of the earliest *gazel*s, poems recited in the plays, brings these ideas to the forefront:

> Look, oh Wise One, with your ever truth seeking eyes, and behold the skies where the pavilion of the shadow-theater has already been pitched
> Gaze upon the spectacle, which the Master-Showman of the Universe has displayed to your view
> From behind His screen, through the men and women He has created
> It is He who, casting all the figures in their proper roles,
> Causes each to speak in the words and manner appropriate thereto.
> See—all those figures are but passing shadows
> And it is God's wrath or beauty, which manifests itself through them
> Gaze upon this spectral screen and fail not to remember
> That He who created it can likewise destroy it.
> And what remains is forever Himself alone.
> By his very nature the initiate to pantheism must grasp these concepts
> And those who cannot detach themselves from the plurality
> Will never appreciate the meaning of my words.
> Şeyh Kuşteri has shown us the meaning of unity and of plurality.
> Oh Birri, gaze in your wisdom on the shadow theater, and benefit thereby![15]

These verses demonstrate the way in which shadow theater was appropriated, mainly by Sufis at the time, as a metaphor or even an embodiment of their ideas about the relationship between our world of the senses and the imaginal/imaginary one suggested by Ibn al-ʿArabi. ʿAbd al-Ghanī al-Nābulusi, our protagonist from chapter 4, may have played a role here, too.[16] Some of the puppeteers themselves were known Sufis, and we have records of several authors and operators (*hayalcı*s) who belonged to the powerful Nakşibendi order.[17] In a sense, questions of morality concerning shadow theater, just like similar issues pertaining to legal matters, dream interpretations, and poetry, have become an arena in the struggle for the interface of religion and sexuality in Ottoman society.

Be that as it may, in the eighteenth and nineteenth centuries the shadow theater was probably the most popular public entertainment in Istanbul and in the other Turkish-speaking Ottoman cities. Its fame spread far and wide and reached Greece, Syria, and North Africa, where local versions were created. In Egypt it appears that Karagöz did not fare so well. Having exported the shadow theater in the sixteenth century to Istanbul, a couple of centuries later the Egyptians received back a Turkish-language version that was popular only among the Turkish-speaking elite.

In his *Manners and Customs of the Modern Egyptians,* E. Lane writes: "The puppet show of 'Kara Guooz' has been introduced into Egypt by Turks, in whose language the puppets are made to speak. Their performances, which are, in general, extremely indecent, occasionally amuse the Turks residing in Cairo, but, of course, are not very attractive to those who do not understand the Turkish language. They are conducted in the manner of the 'Chinese shadows'; and therefore only exhibited at night."[18]

## THE PLAYS

As far as we know, all Karagöz plays until the twentieth century have a similar basic structure. As the lamp is lit, the screen is adorned with a colorful translucent showpiece *(göstermelik):* a ship, a neighborhood, or a caravan walking through the desert. Music starts playing, and tension builds through the rows of spectators. At this point the showpiece is removed, the music is hushed, and Hacivat (originally Haci Ayvad), oozing righteousness, appears on the screen with a short introductory part called the *giriş* (introduction, entrance). This is the first of four modular parts, which may be removed and interchanged according to circumstances. Hacivat usually declaims a poem of virtue and faith (known as *perde gazeli,* the screen poem), sometimes pledging allegiance to the sultan, and, in the spirit of compromise with the *ulema,* he summons the audience to witness a play of moral virtue.

At that point the voice of Karagöz, at first just a set of incomprehensible murmurs from backstage, gets louder until he appears on the screen, with mocking remarks about Hacivat and his piety, making fun of its haughty moral tone. Thus begins the second part, the *muhavere* (dialogue), which consists of rapid exchanges of witticisms and mutual mockery "emphasizing the tension between the superficial formal knowledge of Hacivat, and the commonsense and incomprehension of Karagöz."[19] This part, often the most radical and anarchic, pokes fun at authority and convention in all its guises. Coming right after Hacivat's pious *perde gazeli,* the rapid dialogue of the *muhavere* sets the tone for the play itself.

Sometimes the *muhavere* prefigures some of the contents of the play, but most often the main story is detached from the previous two parts. It is in this third part, the *fasıl* (episode), that the story line emerges. Other characters appear on the screen, and the plot slowly thickens toward its denouement. Our discussions will revolve mainly around these stories, although other parts of the play, mainly the *muhavere,* may be just as bawdy, or even more so. Plays usually end with another autonomous part, called *bitiş* (ending). This once again is a dialogue between the two protagonists, albeit more violent than the *muhavere*. They swap puns and jibes, accompanied, often, by one-sided kicks and slaps, as the betrayed, humiliated Karagöz once again shows his displeasure with his conniving friend who got him into trouble.

Although Evliya Çelebi describes the contents of one or two plays and there are short descriptions in travel literature, the first serious excerpts we possess are from the nineteenth century.[20] Traditionally, shadow theater plays were passed from master to disciple in oral form, and were written down only in the last decades of the Ottoman Empire. The source for most of the important plays is the meticulous work of the German scholar Hellmut Ritter. Ritter recorded the plays with the last court puppeteer, Nazif Bey, in his multivolume work *Karagös, Türkische Schattenspiele,* produced during and after the First World War.[21] This was preceded by the work of the Hungarian scholar Ignacz Kunos, who studied several plays in the late nineteenth century.[22] Similar anthologies, though much less inclusive, were written and published anonymously in the empire at the beginning of the twentieth century,[23] and by Hayalī Memduh and Hayalī Küçük Ali, two of the last famous puppeteers, in the wake of the establishment of the Turkish Republic in the early 1920s.[24] Finally, the Turkish scholar Cevdet Kudret collected thirty-seven shadow theater plays and many excerpts in the richest anthology, titled simply *Karagöz,* which today serves as the standard source for these plays. While some are complete, up to forty or fifty pages long, others are very short pieces, and can best be described as sketches of longer plays or as the debris of older ones.[25]

Thus, even plays considered part of the ancient repertoire *(kar-ı kadim),* which we find mentioned in pre-nineteenth-century texts, appear as detailed theatrical productions only toward the end of the Ottoman era. While older layers are still evident in both linguistic usage and temporal landmarks, the plays were clearly changed. "Modern" Turkish and French terminology; references to technological innovations such as the steam engine, the cinema, and the train; and references to new structures such as the Galata Bridge all attest to these changes. Nineteenth-century censorship also took its toll, cleansing the plays of what, at the time, were considered vulgar or improper references to sexuality and to "uncivilized" behavior.

At some basic level we can still delineate differences between older plays and modern ones, sometimes influenced by European theater.[26] *Ab-*

*dal Bekçi,* an "old" play, can thus be contrasted with *Bahçe* (Garden), a play written probably at the end of the nineteenth century or even at the beginning of the twentieth.[27] Based, as most plays are, in the local quarter *(mahalle), Abdal Bekçi* describes a life of debauchery and moral laxity in an old neighborhood with its classic figures—the "woman" *(zenne)* and her black maid, the night watchman, the drunkard *(sarhoş),* the ever-present dandy (Çelebi), and the semimythical elf characters *(beberuhi'ler).* Court positions, guild names, titles, and honorifics are old style. Anachronisms notwithstanding, the language of *Abdal Bekçi* is mainly old Ottoman laced with Persian and Arabic, the poems retain older styles and rhymes, and, as we shall see, vulgar speech, laced with sexual innuendos, is relatively unfettered.

In the new *Bahçe* play, the story is taken out of the local quarter, the language is modernized, new titles and honorifics are used, and in the *muhavere* new institutions, unknown previously, make an appearance. Karagöz tells Hacivat of his half-dreamt experience, with a clear jab at the cinema hall: "When I tell you this, you will go mad," he says. "In this building I arrived at, I began to walk, swaying to and fro. No matter how far I went, the same things happened. Someone called out: 'Hey, bearded guy, come here.' I looked around. All around me there were these red and blue, showily dressed *'matmezeller'* (mademoiselles), eighty or ninety years old, tugging and trying to seduce me." Lost in the giant whorehouse, he hears them shouting, "Where's your dick? Show us your stork!" Finally he finds his way out and immediately stumbles on an almost identical institution: "Suddenly, I'll be damned, all these *madamlar, müsyüler, matmazeller, efendiler, beyler, ağalar,* dandies, bums, and hooligans. The whole nation is there . . . all buying tickets. I am not sure, is it called a *'sinematograf'* or a *'minagotoraf'*?"[28]

A brave new world of sexuality and erotica beckons, elegantly incorporated into the dying art of the shadow theater. Yet even this modern play maintains the same basic plan of four autonomous parts, and the poems, sometimes sung by newly introduced dancing girls, now called *dansöz* (from French *danseuses*), retain the form of old-style *gazel*s and *şarki* poems. The new and the old are thus inextricably mixed even in the new plays, making our task more difficult. We have to assume, therefore, that the plays are multilayered archeological sites in which the older strata were corrupted, and that even plays positively identified as old reflect at base nineteenth-century cultural values, modes of thought, and, of course, sexual discourse. Their value for earlier times is at best a conjectural assumption.

## THE CAST

Most of the characters on screen were well known to the audience. Each had his or her own characteristics; each had his or her predilections, typical behavior, social norms, and vernacular speech. Understanding sex in shadow theater begins with acquaintance with the cast.

The two main protagonists are Karagöz and Hacivat. Karagöz, who gave his name to the entire institution, is known to be a resident of Istanbul. He is part of the lower classes and has no connection to state authority, apart from short stints as watchman or neighborhood strongman, which always end in tragedy. It is said that he is a Gypsy by origin, and that his father was a blacksmith or tong maker, who left him nothing but a broken furnace.[29] His language is simple. He feigns ignorance of educated speech and often mocks his friend's use of high language by finding rhyming vulgar equivalents. This mockery leads to defiance of all kinds of authority. Nerval, a nineteenth-century French writer and traveler who visited Istanbul, recounts the story of a play he witnessed, which sums up this aspect of Karagöz's character:

> In the period when police regulations instructed for the first time that one could not stay outside without a lantern after dark, Karagöz appeared with just a bare hanging lantern, boldly taunting the powers that be, because the regulation did not specify that the lantern should hold a candle. He was arrested by the guards and released when his claim was found to be legally sound, and we see him appearing once again, with a lantern holding a candle that he didn't bother to light. Karagöz appropriates freedom of speech and always defies injustice, the sword, and the whip.[30]

Of all the puppets, Karagöz is the one endowed with most capacity for movement. Additional holes in the marionette allow the puppeteer to move his hands, and sometimes other parts of his body, notably his penis. Sexually, Karagöz is a shameless omnivore. At one point, when Hacivat interrogates him about a woman he was chasing and asks: "Was she pretty?" Karagöz answers, "To be honest, I haven't really seen her. But what does it matter? She's a woman."[31] Although most often found chasing women of all sorts (and usually failing miserably), he is definitely not a homophobe. He does not recoil from casual homoerotic encounters of both an "active" and a "passive" nature. In many of the plays we find Karagöz cross-dressing, and disguising himself as a woman in order to carry out one of the impossible schemes he and Hacivat hatch.

Hacivat is the eternal sidekick. He is the elusive mastermind behind the schemes that always get the pair into trouble. Unlike Karagöz, Hacivat seems to be modestly wealthy and relatively educated and acculturated, although it is clear in some plays that his education and cultural patina are superficial. In that sense, as in many others, Hacivat is a fake, whose mask, once removed, satirizes an entire social stratum of the bourgeoisie. Behind the highbrow talk and the use of sophisticated words hides a simple crook, sometimes a pimp procuring whores, sometimes a dealer in real estate trying to deceive his customers into buying worthless property. It appears that unlike his longtime accomplice, Hacivat is sexually restrained. Yet he seems knowledgeable enough in matters of debauchery and fornication, and he does not shrink from the occasional sexual encounter or short affair. He is the sounding board for Karagöz's exploits, and although he does not always participate, he rarely criticizes.

Both Hacivat and Karagöz are married, and both have children. Their wives do not appear on screen very often, but their voices (mainly that of Karagöz's wife) are heard from backstage. The relationship between the husbands and wives is not a simple one, and definitely not one that bears any resemblance to the stereotypical depiction of women in Islamic societies. The women talk back, scold their husbands harshly for their behavior, sometimes throw them out of the house, and once in a while threaten to leave. In one or two cases, there are threats or hints that they may have lapsed into prostitution. Husbands are not totally devoid of authority, but this is a negotiated precarious power, contested on a regular basis and occasionally overturned.[32]

Female independence, authority, and freedom find their ultimate expression in the main female character in the play, Zenne. *Zenne,* a general term denoting woman in Persian and Ottoman, contains an inherent contradiction. It creates a female character that is anonymous and yet all-encompassing. Sometimes *zenne*s have names, but they are still referred to in the script as "the woman." In the traditional literature on shadow plays, these women are often described as prostitutes, women of loose morals. As Tietze writes, "Her profession, the oldest, assures her of an unchallenged position in society." The *zenne* in all her guises may be any woman, but she is also a female mirror image of the men on stage. If the women are prostitutes, so are the men. Since there are rarely virtuous men or chaste women on stage, including the wives of the main protagonists, this seems to be a description of all humankind.[33] Yet it is also true that *zenne*s, unlike the wives, are respected, independent, opinionated, and sometimes wealthy. This depiction of women, as I will show later, is one point where this subdiscourse differs from all others.

Another popular character is Çelebi, a rich, opulently dressed dandy who appears in many plays and is always in search of women and sex. Çelebi, sometimes known as Miras Yedi (Eater of His Inheritance),[34] is the representative of the aristocracy. He is well mannered and usually soft-spoken, courteous, and educated (certainly more substantially than Hacivat). Seemingly a cut above our two heroes, he is no less scheming and devious, and his moral attitude leaves much to be desired. In modern plays he is often the symbol of super-westernization and is ridiculed for his affectation of French and Greek words and dress codes.

There are a host of other characters in the play: ethnic types such as the Albanian (Arnavut), the Turk (Türk), the Persian (Acem), the Arab (Arap), and the Jew (Yahudi). Neighborhood types include the addict (Tiryaki), the drunkard (Sarhoş), the watchman-bully (Tuzsuz Deli Bekir), who is the voice of authority, and a host of mythical creatures—jinns (Cin) and elves (Beberuhi). Sometimes carrying private names, they are nevertheless representatives of a group, and their typical jargon, speech impediments, and ludicrous accents are mocked throughout the play.[35] All are male and all want the same things—lots of sex and money. None among them displays more virtue than the rest.

All these characters have apparently been on the Karagöz stage since the very outset. In Evliya's description the same characters appear. Yet their style and attributes evolved somewhat during the eighteenth and nineteenth centuries. This evolution is evident first of all in their dress. In a well-researched section of his book, Siyavuşgil follows changes in the puppets' attire. This is most noticeable in the character of Çelebi, whose ancient puppets wear a turban and an old-style fur-lined coat. We see him changing into the westernized *alafranga* costume favored by Sultan Mahmud II, and then sporting an elegant fez and a Sherlock Holmes–style checkered coat in the early twentieth century.[36] Çelebi's image changes in other ways as well. In the later nineteenth century, he appears more often as the Levantine, "*mösyö*" something or other, a mixture of Istanbul urban toreador and Greek merchant, speaking turkefied French and Greek *(vre, bonsuvar, küzinyer, kalo kalo)*. Although he follows political and social trends in Ottoman society, Çelebi does not change fundamentally. He is still a recognized member of the elite, still well educated (even Hacivat begins to include French words in his speech), and still an ardent womanizer. The same is true for Zenne's dresses, which follow changing fashions and become more daring, exposing some of her cleavage in French style. Zenne is usually unveiled (probably since we meet her at home or in the immediate neighborhood) and when she does wear a veil, it is made of flimsy transparent tissue.

## THE STAGE, THE AUDIENCE, AND THE OTTOMAN PUBLIC SPHERE

The screen of the shadow theater is, in fact, a window on the old urban neighborhood. "This screen, with its manifold characters, its atmosphere, its events and its intrigues, is nothing other than one of the old neighborhoods (*mahalle*s) of Istanbul in days gone by."[37] In many ways the quarter or neighborhood was self-contained. It had its own mosque, shops, and inns, a coffeehouse, sometimes a school or a toddlers' *kuttab*, perhaps a convent or a synagogue. Ottoman law regarded the *mahalle* as a legal entity in certain matters, such as reporting crimes and observing morality, and, later, in the nineteenth century, as responsible for reporting vagabonds, vagrants, and new arrivals.[38]

It is here that most of the action takes place and the story unfolds. The houses of Karagöz and Hacivat are adjacent, their upper windows overlooking the neighborhood square. The drunkard and the addict, the night watchman and the Albanian tough guy, the Jewish merchant and the Armenian money-lender are part of the scene. If they do not reside there, they frequent the neighborhood for their work. Others are newcomers who upset the balance of the place and bring excitement and anxiety. Such is Zenne, who is in most cases an outsider, coming to rent an apartment in the neighborhood for some reason, or simply newly established there. Çelebi, the gallant admirer, is also an outsider, usually unknown to the boys, although they are all familiar with his type. The *mahalle* functions as a living tissue, engulfing the newcomers and changing as a result.

This seems to be a major Ottoman-era innovation in the shadow theater. Earlier versions, such as the Mamluk one (notably in the plays of Ibn Dāniyāl), offer a different kind of setting for the play. It is either more private, such as the interior of an unidentified house, or more public—a nonexistent public arena such as a city square. The atmosphere in most of these earlier plays is dreamlike, removed from daily reality. Spectators must have found it hard to identify the setting and thus to identify with the story.[39] The Ottoman version as it evolved in the seventeenth and eighteenth centuries brought the play down to earth, closer to the majority of the spectators.

This evolution would probably not have been possible had it not been for the evolution of the coffeehouse. It is there, in the newly established coffeehouses of the post-suleymanic era, that the plays assumed a new role. Being shaped by the new enthusiastic audiences, shadow theater plays contributed their share to the emergence of a new public sphere. Karagöz plays became society's way of expressing itself, of presenting itself to itself, and of creating that alternative world of the carnival. Just as the emergence of the public sphere in eighteenth-century England was "rooted in new kinds of social space and institution—the coffee-house, the clubroom, 'Grub Street,' the assembly rooms of the spas and resorts, the salon, the pleasure gardens of Vauxhall and Ranelagh and the tea-gardens such as those popular resorts of Chelsea,"[40] the Ottoman equivalent was rooted in the neighborhood cafés and tea houses. In an Islamic society, where alcohol consumption was limited and sometimes frowned on, the coffeehouse, which was also a venue for smoking and table games, was the ideal venue, at least for the male public. I believe it is this fusion—of an art form that requires precisely that kind of space and an institution that addresses the needs of a growing bourgeois class and serves as a meeting place for city folk—that amplified the impact of Karagöz as a cultural product and as a discourse.[41]

Little by little, with no manifest intention on the part of playwrights and puppeteers, the plays acquired a different nature. Episodes connected by loose threads became more cohesive, and the middle part, the "episode" *(fasıl),* emerged as a play in its own right. The familiar sight of the *mahalle* substituted for the surreal atmosphere of the Mamluk play. Everyday people—Karagözes and Hacivats—replaced metaphorical characters and abstract symbols of social values. In the austere reality of the Ottoman Empire, with its emphasis on law and order, its frequent official processions of royalty and guilds, and its clear hierarchical social divisions, shadow theater emerged as a new form of social critique. As Europe left its medieval carnival heritage behind, the Ottoman world reintroduced Bakhtin's alternative "world of laughter" through Karagöz, a world mocking the rites of church and state, yet open and inclusive enough to admit them. It was the ultimate alternative to state intervention, to the *ulema*'s control of public life and morality. It was an alternative world of promiscuity, lawlessness, and freedom.[42]

## SEXUALITY IN THE HOOD

What, then, did Ottoman urban society choose to present to itself (or to represent itself as) regarding its conceptions of gender and sexuality? In what way did the script of Karagöz plays resonate with that of other subdiscourses? How was it different?

In answering these questions, we should remind ourselves once again that in the plays examined, the temporal boundaries are vague at best, and we cannot be sure about the dynamics of the script. That is to say, we cannot pin down exactly when these concepts were formed or became current and what changes occurred in them through the years. We will have to extrapolate from insufficient data and to assume that as they found their way to the twentieth century, some of the plays represent an older layer, notably that of the mid-nineteenth century, and many contain heavy residue from even earlier periods. Another caveat we must mention at this point is that analysis of the Karagöz would be relevant primarily to the main urban centers in the Turkish-speaking provinces of the empire, with a clear emphasis on Istanbul itself, where most of the plays were written and where most take place. Application of this moral subdiscourse to other parts of the Ottoman state, including Arab urban centers, is tenuous at best.

While other scripts, even heterodox Sufi ones, are clearly critical of promiscuous sexual behavior, whichever way they define it, shadow theater pays only minimal lip service to extraneous morality, mainly in the form of the *perde gazeli,* the screen poem. Describing the ephemeral nature of the play, the *gazel* evokes the fragile nature of human life itself, in contrast to the everlasting God, and therefore the need for humility, moral virtue, and religious devotion. But it is clear to the reader and the spectator from the beginning that this is an expected intervention, a fig leaf that fails to hide a libertarian text. Emplotted as a comedy rather than an epic or a tragedy, the Karagöz story ends on an upward note and the sinning heroes never really fall. Spectators know that Karagöz and Hacivat will live to ride another day, and the overall tone is therefore not one of castigation but of casual jest, of well-disposed storytelling. Although the devious scheme is sure to fail and gunpowder may blow up in their faces, our cartoonlike characters will come out unscathed. The crowd identifies completely with Karagöz when he dresses as a woman to enter the *hamam* on ladies' day, when he tries to climb a wall to peek through a window, and when he is entertained by the beautiful Zenne.

The first thing to notice in the Karagöz sexual script, the point of departure for the whole subdiscourse, is the different portrayal of women and men as gendered categories. While some scripts, such as law and medicine, do not preoccupy themselves with the moral portrayal of men and women, and others, notably medieval literature, draw a clear gender boundary between virtuous men and voracious women, the shadow theater describes both genders as sexually libidinous and promiscuous, always on the lookout for sex and pleasure. Most known medieval literary models construct a dangerous woman, the embodiment of *fitna,* a constant danger to the morality of men and even to the moral order of the world.[43] Many of the male protagonists in this literature, on the other hand, are described as virtuous and sexually contained. Although weaker ones sometimes succumb to the wiles of women, others, the true heroes, often succeed in remaining pure, retaining their virtue, *muruwwa,* which also translates as "manliness" in the classic sense of the word. The world becomes a constant battleground between woman, an earthly, corporeal, satanic creature, and man, a spiritual being adorned with the faculties of reason and devotion. As shown earlier, this has become one of the main themes of Sufi erotic literature, promoting a spirit of homosociality and even homoeroticism in Sufi poetry. The medical script, while suggesting a one-sex continuum for men and women, also contributes to this view by portraying women as failed versions of men.[44]

The shadow theater strikes a very different balance between men and women. It retains the earthy portrayal of women, and Zenne, the essence of woman, is always an unabashed flirt, on the lookout for lovers and sex, turning tricks and setting snares for men. All male characters in the play, however, are just as promiscuous, and make no attempt to retain their virtue, save their souls, or evade Zenne's traps. Quite the opposite: they willingly walk in, and insist on staying even when Zenne tires of their company. Karagöz himself, with whom the audience identifies most of all, is totally devoid of inhibitions in this respect. In *Abdal Bekçi,* to take but one example from an older layer of plays, the scheming Zenne gives a password to her lover, Çelebi, to call out to her when he is at the door so she can let him in. Karagöz, who hears only the first part of the password, spends hours under the window trying to figure out the rest and get admittance to the lady's chambers.[45] Hacivat, the seemingly educated and outwardly moral protagonist, is no less a rascal when it comes to hatching schemes and getting to see naked ladies in the public bath, or to procuring women for desperate *çelebi*s who wander into the neighborhood.[46] Other men follow suit, and those who are not interested in sex have other vices, notably greed, presented in the play as worse than the crime of lust.

Another characteristic of these plays is the marginalization of homoerotic sex. Homoeroticism does not vanish completely, but it holds only a minor place in the sexual practices of our heroes. Karagöz never misses a chance to exchange pederastic puns, to offer himself jokingly as a sexual partner to Hacivat or to other men, or to invert the meaning of ordinary words such as *to ride* or *to give* and uncover their sexual connotations. Even when his son utters an awkward phrase, Karagöz interprets it as having sexual innuendoes. He often calls his friend "*oğlan pezevenği*" (boy pimp, bugger). Homoerotic tendencies are not shameful or forbidden. They are taken in stride and regarded as part of "normal" sexuality. Yet very seldom do we find reference to actual homoerotic affairs between men that go beyond simple jokes or dirty language. The only insinuations of actual sexual attraction (apart from a kiss that Karagöz receives from Deli, the madman, who ends up biting his tongue) refer to meetings with dancers, *köçek*s, who are usually men dressed up as women, famous for their beauty and feminine behavior. Karagöz sometimes mistakes them for women (as in the plays *Bahçe* and *Meyhane*) and tries to seduce them. In one such play *(Sahte Esirci)*, Karagöz falls for a black slave girl, Sünbül, who turns out to be a man in disguise trying to lead a band of thieves into his house.[47]

Female homoeroticism is also referred to once in a while. In the play *Hamam,* there is a lesbian couple that falls out and then makes up with a lot of mutual excitement.[48] In a hilarious part of *Buyük Evlenme* (The Great Wedding), Karagöz, whose elaborate ploys have gone awry as usual, meets a group of women who are on their way to arrange a wedding in which he is to be the bridegroom. Not recognizing their interlocutor, the women ask him for details about Karagöz. "He's a thief and a scoundrel," says Karagöz, trying to dissuade them from participating in the wedding he was lured into. "Well, so are we," they reply. "He roams the area of Beyoğlu every night in search of action," he says. "Wonderful, so do we," they reply. "He hardly leaves the *hamam.*" "—Oh, so he must be very clean." "All right," says the exasperated Karagöz finally. "He's a pederast *[mahbub dost]!*" "Well, we are women lovers also *[zen dost]*," they answer, leaving him gaping and speechless.[49]

When compared with other scripts, the limited space allocated to homoerotic practices in the Karagöz is puzzling. In other discourses we have examined, there is either very little differentiation between homoerotic and heteroerotic practices or a marked preference for homoeroticism. This attenuation of same-sex relationships also stands out against the background of Mamluk plays, which are almost entirely homoerotic and rarely mention heteroerotic relations. Moreover, the most famous plays, written by Ibn Daniyāl and al-Safadi in the fourteenth century, make homoerotic relations their main focus, to the exclusion of all others.[50]

One reason for the change may be that these plays were censored in the nineteenth century by the government or by the authors (or, most probably, by both). As a result of a change in sexual discourse, direct allusions to same-sex exploits were expurgated. This is borne out by the fact that in other Ottoman scripts the same phenomenon occurs around the same time. We see dream interpretation books censored in the same way, with embarrassing evidence of homoerotic dream symbols and their interpretation cleansed wherever possible. Another clue we may have to a richer past is the many casual references to homoerotic practices. Every major play contains at least one jesting reference to pederasty or homosexuality. These references may be the residue of an earlier layer containing much more explicit reference to such practices.

Yet another explanation, which does not entirely rule out the former, could be that our instinctive modernist assumptions are misleading. We tend to assume that homoerotic practices are at some level construed as shameful even by premodern societies, and whenever they rise to the textual surface it is a sure sign of a homoerotic cultural tendency so powerful that it eclipses the more "acceptable" heteroerotic one. In premodern Middle Eastern society, as in many others, however, homoerotic practices were not stigmatized as something that should be suppressed, not even unconsciously. High-culture texts such as Sufi poetry, classic literature, and theological discussions sometimes *preferred* male homoerotic metaphors to heteroerotic ones, because the introduction of women, in and of itself, was far more sensitive. The more acceptable script would therefore be homoerotic, even when referring to both sexes. Ottoman shadow theater, being an insolent counter-script, a mirror of the wild world of promiscuity, would thus display sexual tendencies with less inhibition than other scripts. If this hypothesis is true, then shadow theater's tendency toward heteroeroticism is a more uninhibited display of sociocultural tendencies than certain other scripts may be. Its inherent heterosexuality is not an inhibition, but rather a sign of audacity.

This leaves us with the comparison between Mamluk and Ottoman shadow theater. If it is the case that an overt heteroerotic stance is a less restricted version of sexuality, and if the theater is the natural venue for it, why do Mamluk plays dwell so much on homoeroticism? Perhaps the answer lies in the changing nature of the theater and the audience. It is difficult to know what the Mamluk setting was for performance of the plays. We do know, however, that fourteenth- and fifteenth-century Egypt did not have coffee-drinking and pipe-smoking institutions such as those we find in later centuries. If we add to this the high language in which these Mamluk plays were written (usually classical Arabic, sometimes in the highly poetic *qasīda* and *zajal* form, with some vernacular mixed in),[51] we may arrive at the tentative conclusion that Mamluk spectators were mainly high-class patrons and their entourage in sumptuous mansions, and that the plays were written with them in mind. It was improper, in such company, to present the carnival in all its coarse heteroerotic glory. Male-female sex and love were therefore secondary to homoerotic and, of course, homosocial values. If we are to take at face value the stories of Evliya and others about the patronage of sultans and grandees in the sixteenth and seventeenth centuries, we may even draw a course of development here. Imported from the Mamluk court in Egypt, Karagöz theater started out as a high-class venture, and initially evolved within the palace walls. But soon it found its way out and established itself as a popular art form. With the change wrought in the public sphere as it emerged in the coffeehouse and the *mahalle*, the audience changed, the language became more vernacular, and manners were not strictly observed. Male-female love and sex could finally, audaciously, be presented on stage.

Another rich vein in Karagöz literature is that of crossing gender boundaries.[52] This is especially interesting in light of similar tendencies in seventeenth- and eighteenth-century English theater. In England, Dror Wahrman notices a shift in conceptions of gender in the late eighteenth century. With a growing conviction that gender roles (and perhaps sex itself) are assumed rather than innate, early-eighteenth-century plays take their spectators on forays across gender lines. Such forays became more daring from play to play until the 1770s. The female knight became a popular stage character, as did the woman disguised as a man, and, on the other side, the homebound male. Later in the century a shift occurred in English theater. Cross-gendered behavior went out of fashion, ushering in a consolidation of gender definitions. This, Wahrman assumes, probably had to do with the rise in England of a scientific outlook that assumed a biologically preordained sexuality.[53]

In Karagöz plays gender crossing is a more of a male domain. While stories of amazons and women warriors were popular in Arabic and Turkish literature, they were not as popular in the comic theater. Here women do not usually disguise themselves as men or take on male occupations. There may be several reasons for this. First, Ottoman society was accustomed to men dressed as women. *Köçek* dancers were very popular at weddings and ceremonies and the idea of a man dressed as a woman and imitating her gait and gesture was not altogether bizarre or unsightly. Another thing we should take into account is the comic effect. Women in Ottoman society were expected to wear veils in public. This was not always adhered to, but it was quite common. The comic possibilities inherent in the situation—a man moving around unnoticed, the moustache peeking from under the veil, the shame of discovery, the improbable inversion of gender hierarchies—are endless.

Apart from the special case of the *köçeks,* contained and located in the genderial twilight zone to the extent that they may be seen as transsexuals, cross-dressing in the plays did not imply a change of gender or a different sexuality. On the contrary, it was meant to show, once again, the absurdity of crossing gender lines and the necessity of adhering to the basic sexual definitions. Whereas in early-eighteenth-century England "gender identity was represented as hinging at least in part on external markers—clothes—that could be easily donned,"[54] Karagöz plays emphasized the opposite: gender identity does not change easily, even if one dresses up and tries to imitate the other sex. Mobility on the gender spectrum was not impossible, but was difficult to handle.

This quasi-permeability of gender boundaries does not seem to have changed through the centuries. A cross-dressed Karagöz appears in the oldest plays we have on record, and since in some cases the whole story hinges on the comic opportunities inherent in the change of costume, we may assume that this was part of the script even in older versions that we do not possess. The same ploy is used in new plays. Thus, in the modern play *Aşçılık* (Cooking), the lady, here called *Hanım* rather than the archaic *Zenne,* convinces Karagöz to wear a woman's dress and a scarf in order to enter her house unnoticed. Realizing the danger, Karagöz does so with trepidation, only to be exposed and ridiculed by the ruffian Bekri Mustafa.[55]

One noticeable shift from earlier centuries to the later nineteenth century concerns the graphic presentation of sexual organs on the screen. Partial records of early plays attest to the use of straightforward sexual presentation. This is also borne out by preserved seventeenth- and eighteenth-century Karagöz puppets with enormous movable phalluses. In scraps of certain old plays, such as *Kanlı Nigar* (previously known by the name *Civan Nigar*), Karagöz has an erection that is noticeable on screen. In an early version of *Sünnet* (Circumcision), Karagöz is circumcised and again flaunts his penis in full view.[56] In one scene of a play described by Gerard de Nerval during his visit to Istanbul in 1843, "d'une excentricité qu'il serait difficile de faire supporter chez nous" (of an eccentric nature that would be difficult to support in our part of the world), Karagöz, asked to watch over the wife of an acquaintance, decides to disguise himself as an itinerant holy man, and lies on his back on the pavement. Suddenly his enormous penis rises in the air and stands like a pole. Indeed, passersby mistake it for a pillar. Women on their way back from washing tie a clothesline to it to dry their laundry. Horse riders tie their horses to it, and so on.[57]

Apparently these graphic descriptions and some of the coarser language were eradicated by the censorship of the Tanzimat very soon after Nerval's visit. Another French visitor witnessed the period of change. This was Théofile Gautier, who attended what he describes as an uncensored and very rude play in 1854, and expresses shock at the promiscuity performed in front of young children:

> The garden was full of people when we arrived. Children and little girls were there in particular abundance; and their appreciation and enjoyment of a performance much too gross for description was by no means the least singular part of the exhibition.
>
> Karagheuz is often sent for to perform in the harems; the females witnessing the exhibition from curtained and latticed "boxes" or enclosures; which is singularly at variance with the severity of restriction imposed upon the females throughout the Orient, and would seem to indicate, as has been so often alleged—that in their degradation of her to a position purely animal, the Turks care to secure only the persons of their females, and pay no regard whatever to the cultivation or degradation of their moral faculties.[58]

It is fortunate, he says, that these plays have lately come under some sort of censorship that forces the performers to curb their primitive urges:

> It ought, however, to be mentioned, that, among other consequences of the reform, the performances of Karagheuz have been submitted to "the censorship"; and that much which was rather extreme in action has been reduced to words, and the words themselves very freely excised; for, in truth, in its original form, the representation could hardly have been described to European readers; although, as performed before an audience consisting entirely of men, and those men Turks, it used to be considered quite proper, and in no way censurable.

It appears, if we are to believe Gautier, that the main reason for censorship was the opening of the public arena to children and women. This may well have been the case, as this move coincided with the emergence of the idea of the family and with the growing visibility of children. As fathers began to take their children out on holidays, to bring them along to their coffeehouses and regular haunts, something had to be done about the unadulterated sexual approach of the theater. Coupled with the sense of shame that Ottomans in general felt about their sexual mores at the time, censorship was probably applied by the performers and authors themselves, even before the state intervened.

## A NEW SEXUAL GEOGRAPHY

While reform-minded Ottomans effectively toned down the overt sexual range of their script and visual display in the mid-nineteenth century, later Karagöz plays demonstrate that the quest for sexual gratification continued unabated in the city. Earlier plays locate male-female encounters in such traditional places as the *hamam,* the ferryboat, the stagecoach, and picnic grounds on the outskirts of the city, but late-nineteenth-century shadow plays introduce a new and unfamiliar landscape. The theater presents a new sexual map wherein the new European-style quarters of the bourgeoisie and the rapidly developing suburban neighborhoods function as venues for a new type of sexual activity that ranges from prostitution to sites where men and women could meet.

Prostitution had been known in the Ottoman empire since its early days, and edicts and *fetva*s were published frequently to try to contain what authorities viewed as a problem for moral order and public health. Several times during the sixteenth century prostitutes were expelled from Istanbul, Damascus, and other cities, and in a famous edict they were forbidden to follow the army as it marched to and from the front. In sixteenth-century regulations, procurers are warned against the use of slave girls as prostitutes in hostels around the empire. One common practice to circumvent laws against prostitution was to sell a slave girl to a customer, and then buy her back the next morning. From the point of view of the *Sharīʿa,* this type of transaction, though reprehensible, was not illegal, and the authorities were forced to promulgate special *kanun* regulations prohibiting such practices. But common though it may have been, prostitution was not usually practiced in formal establishments intended for that purpose. In many plays, the lone damsel, Zenne, living in a rented house in the neighborhood and socializing with men, embodies the older variety of prostitution, with blurred boundaries between companionship and sexual favors. The later nineteenth century introduced the brothel as a commercial enterprise, which authorities seemingly ignored but perhaps even encouraged as a form of state control. The theater was quick to grasp the comic possibilities and to mock the brothel as a new locus of sexual debauchery, sending Karagöz and Hacivat there instead of to their old haunts.

Side by side with the brothel, Karagöz introduces us to other coordinates in the new underground sexual layout of the city. Traditionally, Islamicate societies had their own outlets for extramarital sex, at least for males. Men could marry several women; richer men could own slaves and exploit them sexually; many public baths also functioned as meeting places for same-sex encounters. But as slavery declined in the nineteenth century and polygamy was frowned on in certain urban circles, a new institution appeared. The mistress, the kept woman, along with the *garçonierre,* a clandestine apartment for amorous activities, made their entrance. In the new plays written in the late nineteenth and early twentieth centuries, mistresses, often called *metres* (from French, *maîtresse*), a word unknown in the earlier lexicon, appear frequently, taking over from the *zenne.*[59] At the same time, the male *çelebi* makes his new debut as a gigolo in the service of rich women.

Already dotted with whorehouses and sprinkled with love-nests, the new fashionable streets of Pera, Istanbul's urban center, were now in need of new venues for extramarital and premarital encounters of the modern kind. A favorite location, in the middle of the old city, was Kalpakçılar Sokağı (Street of the Fur Hat Vendors) in the Covered Bazaar, to which young men and women went to catch a glimpse of their loved ones. Soon such hangouts were cropping up mainly in the European-style northern neighborhoods and on the Asian side of the city. Built in the mid-nineteenth century, the Galata Bridge over the Golden Horn allowed more freedom of movement between the old city and the suburbs, and became a catalyst for some of these developments. The bridge itself is the site of several amorous meetings on the shadow screen.[60] Beyoğlu, a quarter of the new European city, was also notorious for its sexual attractions and free spirit. Another such area was Fenerbahçe on the Asian side. At the time it was famous for its public garden where men and women went to seek sexual partners.

But has shadow theater really changed? In a hilarious scene of *The Great Wedding,* Karagöz, who goes to Fenerbahçe precisely for this purpose, exchanges complex signals with a veiled woman he meets there, and finally convinces her to come home with him, only to discover to his dismay and astonishment that the woman he went to such lengths to seduce was none other than his wife.[61]

CHAPTER 6

# The View from Without

## *Sexuality in Travel Accounts*

Books and manuscripts written by travelers from Europe to the Ottoman Middle East provide us with yet another perspective on sexuality. Compared to the intimate internal scripts examined so far, the travelogue, an external vantage point often replete with bias and ignorance, has significant drawbacks. Yet for all their shortcomings, travel accounts can add a further dimension to our understanding of the sexual world. Things that are transparent to locals, or not deemed worthy of mention, may be new and exciting—or anathema—to strangers. Outsiders would therefore notice phenomena that insiders neglect or gloss over. Bringing their own biases and concepts along on the journey, travelers also bring into focus the differences between their culture and the one observed, allowing us to follow the parallel development of discourses in European and Ottoman culture.

In the framework of this study, however, travel literature is even more crucial. As I will contend in this chapter, travelogues, both those written by Europeans visiting the Ottoman world and those written by Middle Easterners traveling to Europe, had a profound impact on conceptions of sexuality and gender in the region during the latter part of the nineteenth century, an impact that had far-reaching implications and that reverberates in Middle Eastern society to this day.

### EARLY FORAYS AND HAZY CONSTRUCTIONS

Accounts of travel to the Orient have been transformed by academic authors in the last two decades into the epitome of Western encroachment on the Islamic East. The travelogue, it is claimed, became the first and foremost means of otherization, creating European self-images in contrast to those of an invented or deliberately distorted image of the East. A pervasive subtext, and often the text itself, used sexuality as a leitmotif, metaphor, or synecdoche for the East. Perverted morality stood for the Orient's passivity, laziness, cowardice, and submission.[1] Feminizing it, showing its depraved and abnormal sexuality, made it easier for European discourse to justify colonizing the Islamic world and to rationalize its subjugation, as well as to define the sexual "other" within society.[2]

Yet as Irvin Schick pointed out, ridiculing the other's sexual morality was not necessarily a Western invention, and did not emerge only as a result of the Imperialist mindset. A type of literature that classifies others sexually with negative attributes has been part of the literature of cosmology and wonder, Eastern and Western alike, for many centuries. Characterizations of other races and ethnic groups in terms of their wisdom, courage, loyalty, and the like were basic staples in premodern descriptions of the world. In most cases this "xenological discourse" had very little to do with actual travel, and was simply a means of constructing social space. In Schick's words, "The abstracting, archetype-making impulse present in much erotic writing is singularly well suited to construct spatial differentiation." The colonial project was added later, building its premises and linking itself to the xenological discourse.[3]

Yet travel literature concerning the Ottoman Middle East in the sixteenth and seventeenth centuries, though an offspring of these medieval xenological typologies, should not be seen as part of a yet-to-come colonization project. Early travelers seem to have been motivated by a curiosity about the other, which somehow managed, for a while, to tone down the stereotypes so prevalent in the xenological genre. Their depiction of Middle Eastern morality, though grudging, was not always predisposed to condemn. The reason may have been a sense of familiarity. Rather than be appalled by an alien sexuality, visitors perceived this Islamicate outlook as not very different from their own. Where differences were obvious, such as in the way women dressed in public or in concepts of social segregation, Western European travelers did not necessarily see such customs as deficient and sometimes commended Muslims for their piety and ethics.

Ogier Ghiselin de Busbeq, the Habsburg ambassador to the Porte from 1554 to 1562, who left one of the most penetrating descriptions of the Ottoman Empire in the sixteenth century, has little to say about the sexual mores of the "Turks." What he does say, however, suggests respect for their piety, if not admiration:

> I will now pass to another topic and tell you about the high standard of morality which obtains among the Turkish women. The Turks set greater store than any other nation on the chastity of their wives. Hence they keep them shut up at home, and so hide them that they hardly see the light of day. If they are obliged to go out, they send them forth so covered and wrapped up that they seem to passers-by to be mere ghosts and specters. They themselves can look upon mankind through their linen or silken veils, but no part of their persons is exposed to man's gaze. The Turks are convinced that no woman who possesses the slightest attractions of beauty or youth can be seen by a man without exciting his desires and consequently being contaminated by his thoughts. Hence all women are kept in seclusion.[4]

Beyond the occasional reference to Turks, Arabs, and other "Moors" as heretics and infidels, travelers seem to have been genuinely intrigued by the behavior of local men and women. Thus, George Sandys, a seasoned traveler writing in 1610, discusses Turkish harems with hardly any reference to sexual promiscuity or debauchery. His only snide remark suggesting a problem of morality refers to the sultan executing ten of his pages for this "ordinary crime [of sodomy], if esteemed a crime . . . in that nation."[5] Thomas Dallam, the master organ maker sent from England to set up an organ in the royal court at the turn of the sixteenth century, is even more circumspect and reveals astonishment only at the way women dress in the streets: "The Turkishe and Morishe weomen do goo all wayes in the streetes with there facis covered, and the common reporte Goethe thare that they beleve, or thinke that the weomen have no souls. And I do thinke it weare well for them if they had none, for they never goo to churche or other prayers, as the men dothe."[6]

Later, at the end of the seventeenth century, an adventurous traveler from France recounts that, dressed as a Turk, he overheard some of his compatriots speak indecently about Turkish women. Their attitude was so outrageous and wrong that despite being a European alien he felt he had to react. Still posing as a local, he addressed them: "Know gentlemen . . . that by both reason and custom [our women] are much more reserv'd than yours. And though there may be some who perhaps may think bad enough, yet there is such good order taken throughout this empire, that they are deprived thereby of opportunity to act."[7]

Here we can perhaps glimpse the turning point. While Grelot the adventurer, well acquainted with Ottoman Anatolia, gallantly defends the good reputation of Ottoman women and morality, his interlocutors make fun of them, revealing an emerging discourse that would become more pronounced in later years. In the course of the following decades, these two approaches—one more favorable and open to local discourse, the other hostile and unflattering—would develop into two distinct discursive threads in contest with each other for the truth about the Ottoman soul.

In Europe things began to change in the course of the seventeenth century. A new heteronormal morality was beginning to form in people's minds. Sexual acts and proclivities were divided into natural and unnatural, normal and abnormal, Christian and heathen.[8] This was coupled with and affected by a new political attitude toward the Ottoman Middle East. Whereas late-sixteenth-century travelers to Istanbul still hoped to discover the reasons for their societies' weakness and for the Ottomans' strength, a century later Europeans celebrated their rising power vis-à-vis their rivals. Now, discussing Ottoman culture and politics, their emissaries became bold and even disdainful. The sense of awe and fear that pervaded Europe in the sixteenth century gave way to a critical approach, exposing weaknesses and corruption.

Paul Rycaut, several times ambassador to the Sublime Porte, is perhaps one starting point for this emerging critical discourse. His book, a meticulous and often favorable account of the Ottoman state and its governing elites, written in the 1660s, is manifestly outspoken when it comes to sexual mores. Describing the pages in the imperial palace in a moralizing and sarcastic tone, Rycaut ridicules their "platonick" love for one another:

> Since in the fore-going chapter we have made mention of the amorous disposition that is to be found among these youths each to other, it will not be from our purpose to acquaint the reader, that the doctrine of Platonick love hath found Disciples in the Schools of the Turks, that they call it a passion very laudable and virtuous, and a step to that perfect love of God, whereof mankind is only capable, proceeding by way of love and admiration of his image and beauty enstamped on the creature. This is the coulour of virtue, they paint over the deformity of their depraved inclinations; but in reality this love of theirs, is nothing but libidinous flames each to other, with which they burn so violently, that banishment and death have not been examples sufficient to deter them from making demonstrations for such like addresses; so that in their Chambers, though watched by their eunuchs, they learn a certain language with the motion of their eyes, their gestures and their fingers, to express their amours; and this passion hath boiled sometimes to that heat, that jealousies and rivalries have broken forth in their Chambers, without respect to the severity of their guardians, and good orders have been brought into confusion, and have not been again redressed, until some of them have been expelled from the seraglio with the Tippets of their vests cut off, banished into the Islands, and beaten almost to death.[9]

The overtones of the local Sufi-orthodox dispute can clearly be heard in Rycaut's discussion of homoerotic practices among the pages of the palace, but even more evident is the sarcastic and deprecating tone with which he approaches the subject.[10] In this description the Topkapı palace becomes a den of sexual intrigue and repressed urges, where sultans and viziers spend their time ogling young pages with unveiled passion and scheming to seduce them. The pages, in turn, work their charms to ensnare rich old patrons, enjoying their presents, patronage, and, eventually, a share of their fortune and power. This "sickness," though common everywhere, writes Rycaut, is all but pervasive among the Janissaries and the Bektashi Sufi order of which they are part.[11]

In his long and vitriolic description, sexual depravity is by no means restricted to men alone. Although men are allowed to marry several women and have sex with as many concubines as they wish, their wives are "accounted the most lascivious and immodest of all women, and engage in the most refined and ingenious subtleties to steal their pleasures." Debauchery, then, is rampant according to Rycaut. By all accounts, men's almost unlimited access to women and women's lustful ways, so ordained by the Prophet to increase the number of people in Islam's domain, should have increased the number of Muslim believers manifold. Yet demographic growth has been lagging, and the lands of the Ottomans are not densely populated. The reason for this glaring discrepancy, writes Rycaut, must be their "accursed vice of sodomy."[12]

Though he recounts them with passion, it is never clear what the source of Rycaut's stories is or how well documented they are, if at all. Venturing a guess based on foreign travelers' almost total exclusion from local private lives, we could say that they are hearsay and unfounded rumors more than anything else.[13] But that is beside the point. What matters more is the sheer volume and tone of this description. The choice of words—*depraved, deformity, libidinous flames, licentious, gangrene*—leaves no room for ambiguity and clearly moves us away from the former deferential discourse into the realm of another, far more judgmental mode of writing.

## FROM DEPRAVED MORALITY TO DEPRAVED GOVERNMENT

In the following years this condemnatory mode remained unchanged in its premises. Yet as a new moral code emerged in Western literature, based on subtle hints understood by writers and their readership, travelers began to use oblique, cynical allusions to sexual mores instead of blatant critique. They often resorted to the use of barely concealed euphemisms.

This new tone of benevolent disdain is clearly present in Baron de Tott's memoirs. A Frenchman of Hungarian origin, de Tott spent almost two decades in the empire, where he assisted in the building of fortifications, set up a mathematics school for the Ottoman navy, and built the new rapid-fire artillery force in the 1760s and 1770s. Well acquainted with the different military corps, he tells the story of a squabble between two units, the Janissaries and the navy: "The Janissaries of the company of the Lasses had for some time before been at variance with the troops employed on board the fleet. The quarrel began in one of the taverns of Galata, where a boy, of about thirteen or fourteen, used to dance to bring custom to the house. As he equally pleased both parties, the dispute concerning him rose to a great height, and, the one successively taking him from the other, they at length publicly declared war, of which Galata became the seat."[14] This faintly mocking, tongue-in-cheek description of ubiquitous military homosexuality is representative of this new vein in travel literature. We all know what these Turks (or Muslims or Arabs) are like, de Tott seems to be implying. There is no point in pushing home the argument, so let us revel in the hilarious sight of two army units waging war for the love of a boy.

In the same period another theme was added to the discourse. The condition of women, their isolation and seclusion, which early travelers considered one of the more positive attributes of the Ottoman Middle East, came to be seen as a sign of cruelty. Desperate to evade their lot, women were prone to run away, forfeiting their property and risking death. In his memoirs, de Tott discusses the lamentable fate of prostitutes in the empire, and his discussion turns to the fate of other women:

> But I speak of those women of a more exalted rank, whom an irresistible furey overpowwers, and who escape secretly from their prisons. These unfortunate creatures always carry off with them their jewels, and think nothing too good for their lover. Blinded by their unhappy passion, they do not perceive that this very wealth becomes the cause of their destruction. The villains to whom they fly, never fail, at the end of a few days, to punish their temerity, and insure the possession of their effects by a crime, which, however monstruous, the government is least in haste to punish. The bodies of these miserable women, stript and mangled, are frequently seen floating in the port, under the very windows of their murderers; and these dreadful examples, so likely to intimidate the rest, and prevent such madness, neither terrify nor amend.[15]

In his *Geography of Perversion*, Rudy Bleys claims that there was no basic change in Western attitudes toward Islamic sexuality from the eighteenth to the nineteenth centuries. But a close reading of travelogues reveals that in the middle decades of the nineteenth century, especially in the course of the Tanzimat period, when change was rapid and pervasive, nuances of attitude among travelers branched out into two distinctive subdiscourses, and the debate between them was conscious and determined. While some chose to depict local sexuality as an instance of a different but no less moral outlook, in other accounts sexual behavior in the Ottoman world assumed an all-embracing character as an endemic vice that represents not only a morally depraved society but also morally corrupt politics.

Before we go on to describe the consolidation of the condemnatory discursive thread, it is important to review the development of the other one, which has remained largely unnoticed or perhaps has been silenced over the years. Sympathetic to Ottoman sexual morality and well aware of distorted depictions in other travel accounts, some travelers advocated a different view of local morality. They rejected accusations of depraved sexuality and steered clear of unfounded accusations. This is meaningful in two ways. First, it reminds us that, like most other discourses on sex, travel literature was never completely unified. Second, the existence of these different strands indicates that the condemnatory mode was not only widespread but also deliberate.

Lady Mary Wortley Montagu's views on the relative independence of Ottoman women are well known, as is her aim of contrasting this independence with the condition of women in her own society.[16] Such liberal views, however, were not restricted to women. They can be found among travelers from all Western countries in the late eighteenth century and throughout the nineteenth century.[17] Charles White, writing in the 1840s, is perhaps the best example. Rather than make a point of women's relative independence in the Ottoman state, White, upholding the social and sexual values of his class and gender, emphasizes their propriety and sense of decency. In his very detailed description of social and commercial life in the empire, spanning three volumes, he seldom alludes to any divergent customs or deviant sexuality of the Ottomans. In fact, when discussing Ottoman sexual mores, he compares them favorably to those of the English, stressing respectability and devotion:

> In short, with the exception of novel-reading, lovemaking, love-letter writing, and receiving the visits of the male sex, ladies of rank at Constantinople pass their time much as the ladies of other great capitals, with this difference, also, that they are more united in their families, more respectful to their parents, more obedient to their husbands, and infinitely less per-

verted in mind and principle than that which is considered the fashionable portion of the female population of Paris, London, or Vienna. It may also be observed that, among the unfortunate inmates of the female lunatic asylums, few instances occur of the malady being traced to the passions.[18]

White, however, represents a minority of travelers. Others stand in stark opposition to his compassionate discourse, and they undoubtedly outnumber the other group. One of the most observant travelers in the first half of the nineteenth century was Adolphus Slade, a navy officer who spent relatively long periods of time in the Middle East, spoke some Turkish, and was a frequent guest of the local gentry.[19] On the whole his account seems well informed, balanced, and often empathetic. His judgment on Ottoman sexual behavior, however, is severe and unrelenting to the point of overshadowing his other views.

In his travelogue, as in those of many other visitors to the Ottoman world, the derisive tone and unconcealed condemnation are in sharp focus, and taken a step further than in earlier travel accounts. This is no longer an ethnographic account of strange customs among the heathen, but rather a closely knit discussion that makes a clear connection between sexual habits and the failure of government. Slade makes his point in numerous ways: "sodomy" is not only widespread, it is also the underpinning of political culture. The evidence is to be found even in the slave market: "Boys fetch a much higher price than girls for evident reasons: in the East, unhappily, they are also subservient to pleasure, and when grown up are farther useful in many ways; if clever, may arrive at high employments; whereas woman is only a toy with Orientals, and, like a toy, when discarded, useless."[20] The flip side of "sodomy" is the sexual abuse of women, to which Slade alludes with a dramatic sleight of hand: "At evening [the 'Osmanley'] may honour the ladies with his presence. We will not draw the harem curtains; a description of the bizarre and multiplied sensualities behind it, would rather offend than amuse."[21]

The outlines of a two-pronged attack, on woman's sexual enslavement and on the political consequences of rampant sodomy, are thus firmly set in place. Unwavering, Slade now focuses on Sultan Mahmud II himself, and on his "depraved" practices, to which he alludes sometimes obliquely: "He is greatly influenced by the favourites of the day, who enjoy his intimacy in a degree unwitnessed in western courts since the reign of Henry III of France."[22] In other places the accusations are barely disguised rhetorical questions: "Or, if there be a man in the empire—a modern Koprugli[23]—qualified to undertake the task [of reforming the empire], is it likely that he will be found among the ministers of Mahmoud II, who are, four fifths of them, bought slaves from Circassia, or from Georgia—whose recommendation was a pretty face—whose chief merit, a prostitution of the worst of vices, whose schedule of services, successful agency in forwarding their master's treacherous schemes against his subjects?"[24]

Could these be simply the perversions of Mahmud II? Is he to blame for this state of affairs? Slade makes certain to tell us that this is the rule among the Ottoman elite, not an exceptional tendency of the monarch. Here he is at his cynical best, describing a party he was invited to by senior officials. As the music, the wine, and the dancing boys warmed up the atmosphere,

> some of the guests tore off their upper garments—fire in their eyes, froth on their beards—joined the dancers, their turbans half unrolled flying out as they reeled round the apartment, and but for the presence of the bey scandalous displays would have ensued. One grey-beard actually seized a handsome lad belonging to the cadi with felonious intent. The struggle was sharp between them, and the company stifled with laughter at beholding the grimaces of the drunken old satyr. The lad's eye at length caught mine—blushing till his very ears tingled, he broke away, letting the other fall on his face.[25]

But conscious of his society's sexual mores, or perhaps of the way they may be viewed by the European guest, the bey in charge prudently tells Slade afterward that this behavior takes place "only once in a way" and pleads with him not to remark on it. Slade, ironically, promises to do as bidden and then proceeds to describe the scene to us in minute detail.

Male-to-male sex is thus rampant. No longer a personal predilection of individuals, in Western travel literature it has become much more—a disease of the state, a corrupt form of government. Four-fifths of the state's government ministers are slaves bought for the pleasure of the sultan, with no qualifications for government except their good looks. But sodomy is only one manifestation of the depravation that has lodged itself in the Ottoman soul. Drowning in their perverted desire, local state officials can only watch and gape at the marvel of European mixed dancing: "The Osmanleys left their sofas and their pipes to gloat their eyes on the mazes of the waltzers, and, but for their pelisses, might have joined them. The old capidgi bashi[26] was in a state of ravishment, which the sameness of his harem had failed to produce. 'Wonderful!' he emphatically exclaimed, 'I have lived fifty seven years and seen nothing like this; now that I have seen a *ballo* I will die content.'"[27]

As it emerges from Slade's descriptions, echoed by so many other travelers, the political system prevalent in the empire is neither absolutist monarchy nor Oriental despotism. It is sodomy. And in the same vein, the key to the entire social structure is the bizarre sexuality of the harem. Slade's contemporary, Walter Colton, a U.S. naval officer, seeks a quasi-psychological explanation for these "travesties." In his view, they all emerge from a lack of innate morality. While simple folk are expected to respect all laws and never stray from the straight path, the leadership is forgiven all travesties: "[The Turk's] morality flows from a different source; he is governed by motives which fluctuate with his condition, and seem to lose their force as he ascends in the scale of despotical power. He will practice, as a general, what he condemns in the humble subordinate; and applaud the Sultan for an act which, if committed by a private citizen, would curdle his blood with horror."[28]

Lacking a moral compass, living in blissful ignorance of right and wrong, Turks, Arabs, and Orientals are presented as beyond the boundaries of "moral" civilization. Governed by sodomy and debauchery, their only law is social and political domination. In the absence of an innate moral code, social etiquette and the behavior of people depend on their positions in the social order. The powerful and the mighty are allowed everything; the poor and the meek, nothing.

Distorted descriptions of this kind, reiterated relentlessly by English, French, American, and German travelers, could not have failed to leave their mark on their object.[29] While dwelling so much on ideas of "alterity" and the discursive construction of the Orient as a distorted mirror image of the West, we may fail to notice that the influence of such travelogues on Middle Eastern culture was even more critical. But before we go on to describe the impact of these tropes, we should examine another set of travelers, those going from East to West, from the Middle East to Europe, and their constructions of the different moral codes.

## OTTOMAN MORALITY AND EUROPEAN MATERIALITY

While European visitors to the Middle East were busy casting Ottomans and Arabs in the role of the sexually depraved, early travelogues written by Middle Eastern Muslims visiting Europe also brought forth themes pertaining to the status of women and, more comprehensively, to sex and gender. A similar curiosity, tinged with religious rancor but with no accompanying sense of inferiority, disdain, or envy, is present in the reports of Ottomans sent to Europe from the seventeenth to the beginning of the nineteenth century.

In Iran and the Persianate world, a special type of discourse emerged, which Tavakoli-Targhi labels "Euro-erotic" or "eurotic." Many nineteenth-century travelers viewed Europeans as nymphomaniacs and effeminates, and Europe as a "heaven on earth" where all sexual wishes may be gratified. This discourse made it possible for Persians to put their own sexuality in perspective, to reify their culture, and later to condemn Europeans for their depraved morality.[30] One result of this ability to contemplate their own culture reflexively was the resignification of dress and space, including the emergence of the veil as a symbol of repression and seclusion, on the one hand, and of steadfast allegiance to Islamic values in the face of the Western onslaught, on the other hand.

Early travel accounts from the Ottoman world to Europe did not register the kind of reaction evident in such Persianate accounts. In this sense the Ottoman encounter with the European world diverges from the Safavid and Qajar experiences.[31] Travelers to Europe from the Ottoman world who wrote travelogues (until the nineteenth century practically all of them were Turkish speakers from the Ottoman center) never fail to notice the sexual, social, and gender differences, and seem to be intrigued by them, but no sense of surprise is evident, and no "heaven on earth" fantasies are evoked by such sights. If such a reaction were registered, on a lower emotional scale, it was only in the very early voyages, such as those of Yirmisekiz Çelebi Mehmet Efendi in the first decades of the eighteenth century.[32]

This somewhat less fervent appraisal of Europe by Ottoman travelers may have had to do with the fact that inhabitants of most Ottoman urban centers were closer to Europe and had centuries-long commercial and cultural ties with the West. Though more cautious about public displays of unveiled women and mixed company than their mother communities in Western Europe, inhabitants of the European quarters of Galata and Pera north of Istanbul, and similar areas in other commercial cities such as Izmir, Aleppo, Thessalonica, and later Alexandria, Tunis, and Beirut, did not always conform to Ottoman Islamic social codes. For the Ottomans the European West was alien, yet far more familiar and ubiquitous than for the Persianate world.[33] Yet this familiarity notwithstanding, the emergence of the travelogue as a new literary genre in the Ottoman world ended up producing an effect that was very similar to the one described by Tavakoli-Targhi and Najmabadi for Iran and the Persianate world.

In the account of his early-seventeenth-century trip to France, Yirmisekiz Çelebi Mehmet Efendi recorded positive observations in his short ambassadorship. He was certainly aware of cultural differences, and he refers to strange eating habits and to the frequent presence of women in the public sphere, yet he remarks on them with a certain humor and detachment, devoid of any allusions to sexual promiscuity or paradisiacal gratification. Although some of the customs he encountered were anathema to an Ottoman member of the elite, he adapted himself to them with relative ease and carried himself as a gallant French gentleman. His reaction to women's presence in the public sphere was one of mixed appreciation and apprehension: "In these lands, women's commands are enforced. So much so that France is the paradise of women. They have no hardships or troubles at all—it is said that they obtain their wishes and desires without any resistance whatsoever."[34]

Yet it was not until such journeys into Europe had reached some critical mass, and travelogues had been written and published, that Ottoman Middle Eastern society started reflecting on these issues in terms of sexuality and modernity. In this case there is no doubt that the introduction of the printing press in the nineteenth century and the printing of travel literature were crucial factors. No longer a faraway, exotic place in the western marches, Europe was now viewed as a locus of dynamic change and as a powerful rival. What went on in there had immediate consequences for the inhabitants of the Middle East, and Europeans' approach to sexuality became an issue of concern. Little by little an "Occidentalist" counter-discourse evolved, which attempted to unravel the experience of travelers and to demonstrate Europe's dark side as well as its possible contribution to Ottoman culture.[35]

Juxtaposed with this emerging discourse, the encounter with European travelogues mainly through translations from European languages to Turkish, and eventually Arabic, created a powerful dialectic.[36] A number of travelogues were indeed translated, and even if in many cases the sexual aspects were toned down or censored, enough was left to convey European condescension toward local sexual practices. Ottoman readers were aghast when looking in the mirror set up for them by this genre. In many of their own travelogues the need to counter this European discourse and to present an equally valid Ottoman one are evident. One outcome was the appearance of Ottoman travelogues on the empire's own "Oriental" backyard, the Caucasus and in Central Asia, reproducing the themes of European voyagers, presenting to themselves the strange otherness, the quaint sexual morality, and the backwardness of their own East. Another was a kind of reprisal action—Turkish and Arab visitors to Western Europe painstakingly sought to demonstrate the moral decrepitude of European culture in contrast to their own high moral standards.[37]

This is evident in the travelogues of many Turkish- and Arabic-speaking travelers in the later nineteenth century. Ahmed Midhat, a famous author, playwright, and traveler, visited Western Europe in 1889, the year of the great World Exposition in Paris. In his book *Avrupa'da bir Cevelan,* Midhat persistently presents the gap between European superiority in science, technology, and material achievement, and its moral inferiority.[38] Although his descriptions of European social and sexual morality are often self-contradictory, he focuses on the corruptibility of Western women as ultimate proof of Ottoman Muslim preeminence. In Vienna one night he listens to a coffee-shop owner describe the plight of the numerous young "fallen women." Some of them, says the *Kahveci,* come from respectable families. Their fathers and brothers may have gone broke or lost their money in card games. These girls, educated and well mannered, leave their houses devoid of any means of existence. They become musicians and singers and even play in theaters and casinos for a while, only to finally "fall to the street" *(sokağa düşmek),* where their only option is prostitution. "Now I understand," says Midhat, in a tone that does not fall short of Slade's cynicism, "why all these female singers and musicians end up in Istanbul in their multitudes and then move on to Izmir, Thessalonica, and even to Syria."[39] His views about the pitfalls of Westernization, the evils of Europe, and the supremacy of Ottoman morals are thus vindicated.

Simultaneously with their condemnation of European morality, Midhat and other travelers defended Islam and Ottoman culture against what they saw as a distorted representation of Islamic morality. A scantily dressed dancer appearing as a Muslim Arab at the Paris exhibition infuriates him. Commenting on a paper presented at an academic conference in Stockholm, he criticizes the images of voluptuous harem odalisques, and attributes them to poetic imagination rather than to serious academic research. In his depiction, the Ottoman and Arab world became a refuge of morality and social welfare.

A similar description of European decadence and rampant prostitution appears in many other travelogues written by Arabs and Turks. Even the Lebanese modernist Jurji Zaydān, traveling from Cairo at the beginning of the twentieth century, was so affected by the sight of pervasive prostitution that, in his words, "our good opinions about European women were reversed, and we wanted to return to our *ḥijāb* and [women's] ignorance *(juhl)*."[40] Another malady he mentions is that of foundlings, babies discarded by their mothers. There are eighteen thousand such foundlings in Paris alone each year, he says, and it is all the result of an excess of liberty and a disdain for religion *(min natāj al-ifrāṭ fi'l-ḥurriyya wa'l-fuṭūr fi'l-dīn)*. If this is the outcome of European modernity and liberalism, says Zaydān, we should beware of it and keep to our own morally superior values. Women were made to take care of home and children, he concludes. They need to be educated to fulfill that role, but having a woman work in manly occupations takes her away from what she was made for *(khārij ʿamma khulikat lahu)* and leads to nothing but trouble.[41]

Mehmed Enisi, an Ottoman officer on a military expedition to Europe at about the same time, describes a discussion he had with a French officer aboard a ship they were both traveling on. Strolling on deck, the two soldiers argue about the status of women in their societies. The Frenchman accuses Muslims of imprisoning their women. "Aren't they bored behind those bars all day long?" he asks. "We call it concealment *[tesettür]*, not prison," responds Enisi, and goes to great lengths to explain how important women's role is in the Islamic household, and how much they contribute to educating the children and looking after the house.[42] Having convinced the French officer, he now goes on the attack. "Our women," he says, "are protected from misfortunes that French and other women of the 'free' world are exposed to." He talks of French women leaving their houses and running away with strangers, and about prostitution and fallen women. He also brings up the same problem of foundlings that Midhat and Zaydān mention. "Let's leave your customs to you and ours to ourselves," he concludes. "Our women find nothing useful in your customs."[43]

The end result of this counterattack, however, was a pendulum movement striking back at the Ottoman world, and shutting down entire sexual discursive fields. On the one hand, the Occidentalist reaction drove home the claim about the superiority of local morality. Readers of Turkish and Arab travelogues were convinced that their sexual and moral conduct was something to be proud of. On the other hand, molding morality to fit the new standard presented as superior, necessitated far-reaching changes in attitudes toward sex and sexuality. In other words, while reassuring themselves that their culture was still superior to that of Europe, the travelers, as well as the entire book-reading population, needed not only to find fault with Europe but also to redefine their own morality to fit these new standards, or to create an ethics of sex that heretofore was absent from discourse.

## THE TREE OF KNOWLEDGE

Over the years, from the seventeenth to the nineteenth centuries, the discourse presented in travel literature gained a good deal of power in Western elite circles. It was perhaps the greatest single discursive influence shaping European ideas about sexuality in general and about morality in the Ottoman Middle East as a crucial part of this construction. This powerful discourse found its way back to strike at the inhabitants of the Middle East in myriad ways.[44]

In *Colonialism and Its Forms of Knowledge,* Bernard Cohn suggests that through "investigative modalities" typical of Western culture—defining a body of information, ordering and classifying it, and then publishing it in reports, statistics, histories, and so on—an interaction was initiated that ended up causing an immense shift in the epistemological underpinnings of this region. Investigative modalities of this kind "unknowingly and unwittingly invaded and conquered not only a territory but an epistemological space as well." The study of linguistics, for instance, led to a new comprehension of language and its relationship to forms of identity that in time permeated the region. Classification of languages into Indo-European and Semitic families reshaped definitions of self and other. Attempts at understanding and ordering of local legal systems such as the *sharīʿa* created rigid new concepts of legality where law previously had been soft and malleable. Objects imbued with deep cultural content were reified as antiquities or art, and complex codes of behavior "were reduced to a few metonyms."[45] Nothing that was developed independently and unwittingly in the colonized world prior to that fatal period remained intact.

For sexuality and sexual discourse in the Ottoman world, the main investigative modality until the mid-twentieth century was travel literature. Unlike other fields, where such investigations began only with some form of colonization, in this case the probing began long before any massive European presence was felt. It was an investigative mode that never remained aloof from or impartial toward its subject. But just as gathering information about roots, verbs, and nouns changed perceptions of language, travelers' descriptions of sex and morality imprinted the local significance of right and wrong in sexual comportment.

A new European sexual morality came into being in the seventeenth and eighteenth centuries, and we may assume that early travelers' tales of "Oriental" sexuality, accurate or not, played a part in this transformation. As we have observed, the emerging European sexual outlook brought about a change in the tone of travelogues and changed the basic assumptions of the Orientalist discourse. It suggested new classifications into normal and deviant, natural and unnatural, moral and immoral, which were alien to the Ottoman Middle East. Decades of traveler investigations cast in this new terminology in all European languages and translated into Turkish and Arabic,[46] left an indelible mark on European images of Ottoman sexuality and their effect on local sexual discourse was devastating.

European travelers to the Middle East, fed on such a cultural diet, arrived with preconceived notions and mindsets. Their writings made Ottoman sexuality into a palpable "thing" for the inhabitants of the Middle East. Moreover, these sexual practices, tendencies, and preferences, formerly unquestioned and part of the fabric of culture, were made tangible through reflection in a funhouse mirror. Turks and Arabs were engulfed in a sense of shame and foreboding.

In a revealing paragraph in his autobiographical contemplations, Cevdet Paşa, the great scholar, legal expert, and leader of reform, describes the turning point. In the late 1850s, he writes, in the wake of the Crimean War, a change could be perceived in people's moral conduct. It was no longer fashionable, for example, for men to conduct amorous affairs with boys or other men:

> With the increase of women lovers the number of boy-beloveds decreased and the sodomites *[qavm-i lūṭ]* seem to have disappeared off the face of the earth *[sanki yere batdı]*. Ever since then the well-known love for and relationships with the young men of Istanbul was transferred to young women as the natural order of things *[Istanbul'da öteden berü delikanlılar içün ma'rūf mu'tād olan aşk u alāka, hāl-ı tabi'isi üszre kızlara müntakil oldu]*. . . . None remained of the group among the upper classes *[kübera]* known for their love of boys, such as Kāmil and Āli Paşa and their entourages. Faced with the disapproval of foreigners, even Āli Paşa made a reluctant attempt to hide his pederasty *[kübera içinde gulampārelikle meşhur Kamil ve Āli Paşalar ile anlara mensūb olanlar kalmadı. Halbuki Āli Paşa da ecānibin i'tirāzātından ihtirāz ile gulāmpareliğini ihfāya çalışordu]*.[47]

This tendency to disavow former sexual inclinations and supersede them with others swept the entire elite. Even the sultan himself was not immune. Cevdet can barely hide his sarcasm when describing Sultan Abdülhamid II's change of heart:

> And the great Sultan Abdülmecid *Han,* although truly born as a *padishah* with sublime royal traits, is he not part of humanity? This wind has also bent him *[Bu ruzgār anı da çarptı].* In this spirit of revolution in the world, he decreed that some women are to be loved and desired *[Alemin bu inkilābātı arasında, o dahi kadınlardan baʿzılarına mahabbet ü rağbet buyurdu].* He also commanded people to regard as permissible *[halāl]* activities that were formerly forbidden *[harām].* No one objected to this, but His royal health caused growing concern from day to day with the abundance of friendships with women *[Fakat nisvān ile kesret-i musāhabetinden nāşı vücud-ı hümāyūnlarına günden günne zaʿf gelmesi bādī-i endişe idi].*[48]

Thus began the journey to suppress established sexual discourses, silence them, and replace them with others. None of the discursive scripts presented in previous chapters—medicine, law, Sufi literature, dream interpretation, shadow theater—were spared. As we have seen, they all either disappeared in the late nineteenth century or were transformed into almost sterile genres in which sex and sexuality are seldom discussed, and even then always obliquely.

But as with several other facets of modernity, the attempt to change, silence, dissimulate, or censor did not emerge from deep conviction. The old sexual discourses (to the extent that they previously were, in some deep sense, unified) were now dismembered, but a new meta-discourse did not emerge in their stead. As Laqueur and Foucault rightly point out, old modes of discussing sexuality disappeared during the nineteenth century but were soon replaced by new ones. These changes in sexual discourse, however, came about in Europe only as a result of sweeping social and political changes, including a new role for women in the public sphere; the need to increase control over the population; new definitions of masculinity, femininity, sex, and gender; and new conceptions of private space. In the Ottoman world, the process was reversed. Changes in sexual discourse preceded changes in society and politics. The sense of embarrassment felt toward the old sexual discourse could not, in and of itself, produce a new one. As familiar sexual scripts collapsed under the onslaught of the travelogue, no new ones came to take their place. The Ottoman and Arab lands experienced unprecedented transformation: sexual discourse moved out of the textual sphere and into the arena of male and female intimate circles, while a curtain of silence descended on the sexual stage.

# Conclusion

## *Modernity and Sexual Discourse*

Looked at from our perspective, premodern Middle Eastern sexual discourse was surprisingly frank and outspoken. To us it may be more akin to latter-day television series such as *Sex and the City* or *Will and Grace* than to most nineteenth- and twentieth-century sexual discourse, with one major difference. Although some of this discourse was attuned to the needs and sexual preferences of women, it was a singularly male voice.

The set of discourses or "scripts" examined here was congruent with the great variety of male and female sexual preferences. The spectrum was restricted by religion and social regulation, to be sure, but very few of its varieties were seen as inherently flawed. Arising from a one-sex biological paradigm in which women were believed to be imperfect men, ideas of sexuality in the period reveal none of our fixed, rigid boundaries distinguishing heterosexuals from homosexuals, and almost no sense of deviation from a compelling norm. As early shadow theater manifests, there was no sense of shame attached to sex. The penis was an actor on stage, and coarse Rabelaisian language was ubiquitous. It was very different from the prevalent, almost sanctimonious, public sexual discourse in most of the Islamicate world in the last decades.

So much so, in fact, that at one point in the seventeenth century it seemed as though the religious establishment itself might succumb to popular homoerotic practices and that some influential sects might succeed in making such practices part and parcel of mainstream religion. Reading seventeenth-century debates about gazing at the beauty of young men may be misleading. From our heteronormalized viewpoint, we tend to construe these as debates about right and wrong in everyday sexual conduct. But the violent struggle that ensued in the great urban centers of the Ottoman Empire in the seventeenth century between Sufis and orthodox *ulema* was not about the permissibility of same-sex relations. Though legally frowned on, these were taken to be part of life and usually ignored. The debate was about the place accorded to such relationships in the religious scheme.

In the event the more radical Sufi views were eschewed, and the strict orthodox dogma, which saw such practices as theologically abominable, triumphed. Afraid of a resurgence of Sufi devotional erotica, *ulema* treated all matters relating to sexuality coming from Sufi circles as suspect. Although the orthodox establishment fought to defend the ramparts of Islamic theology and its own privileged status, and not to challenge social patterns of behavior as such, its victory may have signaled the beginning of a process that in the late nineteenth century accelerated the disintegration of premodern sexual discourse.

From the mid-eighteenth to the mid-nineteenth centuries, this process coincided with what later became the main instigator of discursive change: the two-pronged criticism of sexual morality by European travelers to the Middle East and by Middle Eastern travelers to the West. Sexual mores in Western Europe had changed in previous centuries. In medicine and popular belief, the one-sex paradigm had been replaced by a clearer two-sex one, the hazy boundaries between heterosexual and homosexual had solidified, new conceptions of sex and power had replaced older notions, and a set of new scripts had emerged to control deviant sexual behavior. These changes were related in various ways to political and social changes and to new conceptions of gender relations. They were soon integrated and fashioned into a subtle meta-discourse that created a clear, new, and comprehensive sense of bounded sexuality with a heteronormal center and "deviant" margins.

Guided by this new clarity and its inherent sense of righteousness, travelers to the Ottoman Middle East were appalled when they witnessed firsthand what they perceived as uninhibited sexual discourse in a society they pictured as conservative. In addition to the greatly exaggerated stories about debauched harem practices, and to rumors about widespread female adultery punished by jealous husbands, travelers found the unabashed homoerotic culture of coffeehouses and public baths, as well as the bawdiness of Karagöz and his friends, too lurid for their tastes. In travelogues, often translated into Turkish and Arabic, this sense of repugnance laced with mockery at heathen manners was made evident. In a world under Western European influence, such disdainful descriptions hit hard. Moreover, as in many other cases of colonialist investigative modalities, the main effect of travel literature was reification of culture in general and of sexual discourse in particular. A previously invisible part of life suddenly became an object for observation and comparison with other cultural norms.

By and by, a local counter-narrative emerged. Middle Eastern travelers to Western Europe found European morality just as wanting. Critiques of Western promiscuity had appeared before, at the time of the Crusades and during Napoleon's invasion of Egypt, for example, but now they were revisited with new vigor. Young prostitutes roaming city streets and the huge numbers of deserted babies and foundlings in Vienna and Paris were described as major failures of European culture. But along with the comforting belief that Europe was not all it was cracked up to be and that the Islamic world and the Ottoman state had a clear moral advantage, this Occidentalist counter-narrative forced a move away from the old sexual discourse at home. In countering the European argument, Ottoman writers presented their own society's morality as based on rigidly defined social spaces, on the seclusion of women to save them from the fate of their European counterparts, on a heterosexual ethic, and on conservative values.

Life, at least on the discursive plain, now had to conform to a literary ideal of superior morality. It needed to be distanced from the sexual scripts embraced by previous generations. Homoerotic discourse, formerly part of the cultural center, was marginalized. Even heterosexual discourse assumed a much more subdued role in society. Authors of Karagöz plays first removed the physical evidence: puppets no longer appeared on stage with exposed penises, and overt scenes of copulation were replaced by descriptions and insinuations. In a second phase, the words themselves were censored by authors and authorities.

Similar developments occurred in other discursive fields. Dream interpretation manuals, which until the nineteenth century had referred to dreams of homosexual, extramarital, or incestuous relations as a normal part of people's unconscious, were now reprinted in abridged or purged editions. The entire category of same-sex relations was diluted and sometimes removed altogether. The very widespread religious literature on homoerotic practices, both treatises vilifying love for beardless youths and those condoning the practice as a spiritual experience, encountered a similar fate. In literature, while the *Thousand and One*

*Nights, The Perfumed Garden,* and *The Delight of Hearts* became popular in the West, they all but disappeared from Middle Eastern libraries. The bodily mechanics of intercourse and the attributes of the sexual body, once analyzed in detail in treatises of anatomy and physiognomy, were banished from medical discourse. State laws and regulations, which formerly discussed sexual offenses in explicit language, now chose circumspect terms with which to refer to the same crimes. The only discursive field where discussions of sexuality remained more or less constant was orthodox jurisprudence. Yet even these discussions, centered as they were on the legal aspects of sexual transgression, seem to have lost their sparkle. Rather than debating and reformulating the law as they had done for centuries, jurists were content to reproduce previous discussions verbatim.

The introduction of the printing press in the Arab- and Turkish-speaking worlds at the beginning of the nineteenth century added impetus to the process by changing attitudes toward the written text. Formerly books were written, compiled, and copied by hand, with no regard to copyright or contents. Prices were high, circulation in most cases was relatively insignificant, and by default the only people with free access to books were members of the religious and governing elites. As elsewhere in the world, printing made books cheaper and more accessible to the masses, and thus enhanced literacy. Texts that in the past were read by a chosen few, beyond the reach of the unprivileged, now found themselves in the public arena. The spread of printing was accompanied by the rapid decline of guilds of copiers and calligraphers. Gradually manuscripts disappeared from the markets. Their prices shot up, and they were much in demand by collectors and libraries at home and abroad. The array of erotic literature necessarily diminished. Only books deemed fit to be read by the masses were now printed; other books, including erotica and discourses on sex, were relegated to archival ivory towers.

During a relatively short span of time an entire cultural silencing mechanism was galvanized to cleanse the discourse of anything deemed sexually improper. The effort was not merely top-down. Although the state did indeed do its share of silencing, this was not simply a state project. Small power streams of self-censorship by publishers, authors, buyers, puppeteers, and *ulema* joined together to hush up sexual discourse to the point where it became almost extinct. By the beginning of the twentieth century the transformation was complete. A veil of silence had descended on sex in Middle Eastern culture.

Michel Foucault begins his *History of Sexuality* with a critique of our misconceptions of the Victorian era. We tend to think that the entire period from the beginning of the nineteenth to the mid-twentieth centuries was a time of sexual repression. As the story goes, a previously free-spirited attitude toward sex was suddenly shackled and sexual practices repressed. Ever since, the story continues, authors and thinkers have been trying to rid society of its shackles. In fact, claims Foucault, the situation is the reverse. Sex was not silenced in the Victorian era. It exploded in myriad discourses—in psychology, in medical discourse, in education manuals, and in the idea of the panopticon—all of which were means to create new ways of discussing sex under the guise of keeping it under wraps. Secrecy was part of the discourse itself.

But in the late Ottoman Middle Eastern world, and at least until the emergence of a new nation-state culture in the 1940s, no such new set of discourses replaced the vanishing ones. Even state institutions in charge of censorship, it seems, did not produce a discourse delineating what was permissible and what was not. Other localized oral sexual scripts evolved—neighborhood networks and coffeehouse cultures—but they did not assume another, textual form. A possible reason for this silence is that the old scripts did not disappear because they were inadequate. They may have been silenced, but not necessarily because people saw sexuality in different terms now. For quite a number of years following the dissolution of Ottoman-era sexual scripts, the heteronormalized view of sexuality remained on the margins of culture, and a certain tension was apparent between the now discarded scripts, still accepted by large segments of society, and new imported ideas, which may have been considered more proper but were nevertheless alien.

This book ends with the demise of the Ottoman Empire and the disappearance of its world of ideas. It would take another book to document the transformation of sexual discourse in the Middle East during the twentieth century and the emergence of a heteronormalized culture. It may be an irony of history that just as Middle Eastern Islamicate cultures have come to terms with heteronormalized sexual discourse, Western cultures are once again distancing themselves to develop a sexual culture reminiscent of that practiced by the Ottomans several centuries ago.

# Notes

INTRODUCTION. SEX AS SCRIPT

1. Abu al-Fatḥ al-Dajjāni, *Al-ʿiqd al-mufrad fi maḥabbat al-amrad* (Princeton University, Firestone Library, Cat. no. 1952); W. Caskel, "ʿAbd al-Ḳays," in *Encyclopedia of Islam,* 2nd edition (Leiden: Brill, 1960–2002), vol. 9, pp. 72–74.

2. G. H. A. Juynboll, "Al-Shaʿbi," in *Encyclopedia of Islam,* vol. 9, pp. 162–63.

3. I use Hodgson's term *Islamicate* instead of *Islamic* (Marshall G. S. Hodgson, *The Venture of Islam: Conscience and History in a World Civilization* [Chicago: University of Chicago Press, 1976]). By using this term, Hodgson tried to differentiate between phenomena that stem from the religion of Islam *(Islamic)* and those that arose in predominantly Islamic lands but are not a direct consequence of religion *(Islamicate).* Unfortunately, use of the latter term has not spread beyond the narrow circle of social historians of Islamic societies.

4. Ṣalāḥ al-Dīn Al-Munajjid, *Al-ḥayāt al-jinsiyya ʿind al-ʿArab* (Beirut: Dār al-kitāb al-jadīd, 1975 [1958]); Y. Al-Masri, *Le drame sexuel de la femme dans l'Orient Arabe* (Paris: Lafont, 1962); Fatima Mernissi, *Al-sulūk al-jinsi fi mujtamaʿ Islāmi ra'smāli* (Beirut: Dār al-Ḥadātha, 1982); Charles Pellat, "Djins," in *Encyclopedia of Islam,* vol. 2, pp. 550–52.

5. Abdelwahab Bouhdiba, *Sexuality in Islam* (London: Routledge and Kegan Paul, 1985), p. 232.

6. Ibid., p. 30.

7. Ibid., p. 115.

8. Fedwa Malti-Douglas, *Woman's Body, Woman's Word: Gender and Discourse in Arabo-Islamic Writing* (Princeton, NJ: Princeton University Press, 1991), p. 91.

9. See Stephen O. Murray and Will Roscoe, *Islamic Homosexualities: Culture,*

*History, and Literature* (New York: New York University Press, 1997). For a discussion of *hetero-normal* and similar terminology, see Afsaneh Najmabadi, *Women with Mustaches and Men without Beards: Gender and Sexual Anxieties of Iranian Modernity* (Berkeley and Los Angeles: University of California Press, 2005).

10. J.W. Wright and Everett K. Rowson, eds., *Homoeroticism in Classical Arabic Literature* (New York: Columbia University Press, 1997).

11. Everett K. Rowson, "Two Homoerotic Narratives from Mamlūk Literature: al-Ṣafadi's Lawʿat al-shākī and Ibn Dāniyāl's al-Mutayyam," in *Homoeroticism in Classical Arabic Literature,* ed. Wright and Rowson, pp. 158–91.

12. Ibid., p. 184.

13. One rare instance where court cases proved to be an important source of insight into sexuality is Leslie P. Peirce's *Morality Tales: Law and Gender in the Ottoman Court of Aintab* (Berkeley and Los Angeles: University of California Press, 2003). Through meticulous work in the court archives of ʿAyntāb (Antep), Peirce provides us with a detailed description of sexual discourse in an Ottoman village society. Unfortunately, as my own research in the court archives of Jerusalem and Nablus has taught me, these are rare cases indeed, and most court protocols (*sijill*s) are almost bereft of discussions referring to sexuality and sexual crimes.

14. J. W. Wright Jr., "Masculine Allusion and the Structure of Satire in Early ʿAbbāsid Poetry," in *Homoeroticism in Classical Arabic Literature,* ed. Wright and Rowson, pp. 1–23.

15. Ibid., p. 16.

16. Steven M. Oberhelman, "Hierarchies of Gender, Ideology, and Power in Ancient and Medieval Greek and Arabic Dream Literature," in *Homoeroticism in Classical Arabic Literature,* ed. Wright and Rowson, pp. 55–93.

17. Basim Musallam, *Sex and Society in Islam: Birth Control before the Nineteenth Century* (Cambridge: Cambridge University Press, 1983).

18. Paula Sanders, "Gendering the Ungendered Body: Hermaphrodites in Medieval Islamic Law," in *Women in Middle Eastern History: Shifting Boundaries in Sex and Gender,* ed. Nikki R. Keddie and Beth Baron (New Haven, CT: Yale University Press, 1992), pp. 74–95.

19. John Gagnon, *Human Sexualities* (Glenview, IL: Scott, Foresman, 1977), p. 6; Jeffrey Weeks, *Sexuality* (New York: Tavistock Publications and Ellis Horwood, 1986), pp. 57–58.

20. Weeks, *Sexuality,* p. 58.

21. Foucault, *The History of Sexuality* (New York: Pantheon Books, 1978), vol. 1, pp. 83–84: "The pure form of power resides in the function of the legislator; and its mode of action with regard to sex is of a juridico-discursive character." For Foucault's definition of power in this context, see ibid., pp. 92–96.

## CHAPTER 1. THE BODY SEXUAL

1. It should be noted, in this respect, that most physicians and medical theoreticians in the Ottoman period were also *ulema,* or at least well versed in legal and theological matters, as well as other scientific disciplines. See Adnan Adıvar, *La science chez les turcs ottomans* (Paris: Maisonneuve, 1939), pp. 37–39.

2. In many classifications of the sciences by *ulema,* medicine figures as one of the second rank of sciences. See Hajji Khalifa, *Kashf al-ẓunūn,* Lexicon bibliographicum et encyclopaedicum, Arabic text with Latin translation by G. Flügle, 7 vols. (Leipzig: R. Bentley, 1835–58), vol. 2, p. 125; and Youssef Mourad, *La physiognomonie arabe et le kitāb al-firāsa de Fakhr al-Dīn al-Rāzi* (Paris: Librairie Orientaliste Paul Geuthner, 1939), pp. 23–26. Through the ages, however, medicine acquired a status of independence that made it autonomous of religious truth to some extent.

3. Basim Musallam, *Sex and Society in Islam: Birth Control before the Nineteenth Century* (Cambridge: Cambridge University Press, 1983), pp. 54–55.

4. H. Laoust, "Ibn Kayyim al-Djzawziyya" in *Encyclopedia of Islam,* 2nd edition (Leiden: Brill, 1962–2002), vol. 3, p. 821b; E. Geoffroy, "Al-Suyūtī," in *Encyclopedia of Islam,* pp. 913–19.

5. Emilie Savage-Smith, F. Klein-Franke, and Ming Zhu, "Ṭibb," in *Encyclopedia of Islam,* vol. 10, p. 451b. See also Emilie Savage-Smith, "Medicine," in *Encyclopedia of the History of Arabic Science,* ed. Roshdi Rashed and Regis Morelon (London: Routledge, 1996), vol. 3, pp. 903–62.

6. Adıvar, *La science,* pp. 15–16; J. Walsh, "Hadjdji Pasha," in *Encyclopedia of Islam,* vol. 3, p. 45a; Osman Şevki Uludağ, *Beşbuçuk asırlık Türk tababeti tarihi* (Ankara: Kültür Bakanlığı Yayınları, 1991 [1925]), pp. 179–81.

7. Adıvar, *La science,* p. 17; Uludağ, *Beşbuçuk asırlık,* p. 179.

8. Şerefeddin Sabuncuoğlu, *Cerrāhiyyetü'l-haniyye,* ed. Ilter Uzel (Ankara: Dil ve Tarih Yüksek Kurumu, 1992), pp. 271, 300.

9. Muḥammad Amin bin Faḍlallah al-Muḥibbi, *Tarikh Khulāsat al-āthār fi a'yān al-Mi'a al-ḥādiya 'ashara* (Egypt: 1284H), vol. 2, pp. 240–42; Raşit Efendi (Muhammad bin Mustafa Rashed), *Tarih-i Raşıt* (Istanbul: Matbaa-yı Amire, 1282H), vol. 1, p. 96; Adıvar, *Osmanlı Türklerinde İlim* (Ankara: Remzi Kitabevi, 1982), pp. 122–23, 131–32; E. Kahya and A. D. Erdemir, *Bilimin Işığında Osmanlıdan Cumhuriyete Tip ve Sağlık Kurumları* (Ankara: Türkiye Dıyanet Vakfı Yayınları, 2000), pp. 179–84; Uludağ, *Beşbuçuk asırlık,* pp. 195–96.

10. Adıvar, *La science,* p. 127; Uludağ, *Beşbuçuk asırlık,* pp. 196–97.

11. Adıvar, *La science,* p. 146; Uludağ, *Beşbuçuk asırlık,* pp. 206–7.

12. Shams al-Dīn al-'Itāqi, *The Treatise on Anatomy of Human Body and Interpretation of Philosophers (Tashrīḥ al-abdān),* trans. Esin Kahya (Islamabad: National Hijra Council, 1990), pp. 9–12.

13. Ṣāliḥ Ibn Naṣrallah Ibn Sallūm (d. 1670), *Ghāyat al-Itqān fi Tadbīr Badan al-Insān (The Greatest Thoroughness in Treatment of the Human Body),* Reşid Efendi 698 and Şehid Ali Paşa 2062 in the Süleymaniye Library and Add. 3532 in the Cambridge University Library. For the Turkish translation, see mss. Browne Or. Ms. P. 27 in the Cambridge University Library and Garret 1181H and New Series 998 in the Princeton University Library. See also Manfred Ullman, *Islamic Medicine* (Edinburgh: Edinburgh University Press, 1978), pp. 50–52; and Savage-Smith, Klein-Franke, and Zhu, "Ṭibb," p. 457b. Thanks are due to Miri Shefer, who pointed out these manuscripts in her lecture "The Ottomanisation of Arab-Muslim Medicine in the Sixteenth and Seventeenth Centuries" (Gabriel Baer forum, Tel-Aviv University, December 2002). For Galenic principles in the Ottoman Empire, see also Daniel Panzac, *La Peste dans l'empire*

*ottoman, 1700–1850* (Louvain: Peeters Editions, 1992), pp. 286–90; and Adıvar, *La science,* p. 129.

14. Uludağ, *Beşbuçuk asırlık,* pp. 191–92.

15. Mehmet Ataullah Şanizade, *Hamse-i şanizade* (Istanbul: Darüt-Tibaatü'l-Amire 1235 [1820]). I used the copy at the Süleymaniye Library (Pertev Paşa 516). Part 4, on surgery procedures, was also published in Arabic at Bulāq in 1828 by direct order of Mehmet Ali.

16. Charles White, *Three Years in Constantinople* (London: Henry Colburn, 1846), vol. 1, pp. 126–37. For a description of the state of affairs several years earlier, see Adolphus Slade, *Records of Travels in Turkey, Greece, etc., and of a Cruise in the Black Sea with the Capitan Pasha, in the Years 1829, 1830 and 1831,* 2 vols. (London: Saunders and Otley, 1832), pp. 173–74.

17. Yıldırım, *Türkçe Basılı ilk Kıtaplani,* pp. 448–49; Adıvar, *La science,* p. 159.

18. This "longing" or "desiring soul" is one of three that animate the body in classical Islamic-Greek medicine. See Ullman, *Islamic Medicine,* pp. 56–64. For the Ottoman period, see, for example, Eşref bin Muḥammed, *Hazā'inü's-saʿādāt* (Ankara: Türk Tarih Kurumu, 1960), folio 44a.

19. Thomas Laqueur, *Making Sex: Body and Gender from the Greeks to Freud* (Cambridge, MA: Harvard University Press, 1990). For a critique of Laqueur's theory in the European context, see Joan Cadden, *Meanings of Sex Difference in the Middle Ages: Medicine, Science and Culture* (New York: Cambridge University Press, 1993), p. 3.

20. Laqueur, *Making Sex,* pp. 122–28. See also Sabuncuoğlu, *Cerrāhiyyetü'l-haniyye;* and Paula Sanders, "Gendering the Ungendered Body: Hermaphrodites in Medieval Islamic Law," in *Women in Middle Eastern History: Shifting Boundaries in Sex and Gender,* ed. Nikki R. Keddie and Beth Baron (New Haven, CT: Yale University Press, 1992), pp. 74–95.

21. Ibn al-Nafīs did more than sum up Ibn Sina. His works contain several new concepts, including the first known description of the lesser circulation of the blood (between the lungs and the heart). These and other discoveries exposed the first cracks in the Galenic paradigm and presented a challenge to its teachings, but the challenge was not carried to its conclusion. It seems that many Ottoman authors of medical tracts felt that humoral medicine failed to supply answers to such new challenges, and their explanations sometimes seem half-hearted, but no alternative presented itself until the nineteenth century. See *The Islamic Sciences,* pp. 163, 180; Ullman, *Islamic Medicine,* p. 68; and Adıvar, *La science,* p. 52.

22. Savage-Smith, Klein-Franke and Zhu, "Ṭibb."

23. See also Ullman, *Islamic Medicine,* pp. 55–60.

24. Ibid., p. 57.

25. For several Ottoman examples of humoral differences, see Seyyid Süleyman el-Hüseynī (Cami ve müellifi), *Kenzü'l-Havass* (Istanbul: Demir Kitabevi, n.d.), vol. 3; Mustafa Iloğlu (derleyen), *Gizli Ilimler Hazinesi* (Istanbul: Aktaş Matbaası, 1968); Keykavus (Ahmet Ilyasoğlu Mercimek), *Kābusname,* ed. Atilla Özkırımlı (Istanbul: Milli Eğitim Basimevi, 1974), pp. 223–24; and al-ʿItāqi, *Treatise on Anatomy,* pp. 25–35.

26. Ullman, *Islamic Medicine,* pp. 55–60.

27. Mourad, *La physiognomonie arabe,* p. 89. See also Nil Sarı, "Osmanlı sağlık hayatında kadının yerine kısa bir bakış," in *Sağlık alanında Türk Kadını,* ed. Nuran Yıldırım (Istanbul: Novartis, 1998), pp. 451–65.

28. Ibid., p. 26.

29. *Ehlak-ı zahirden ehval-ı batiniye istidlal etmek ibarettir. Kiyafet Name,* manuscript, Süleymaniye Library, B. Vehbi 918, folio 2a. This compilation, based on earlier texts in Persian and Arabic, exists in many copies and versions in the Süleymaniye, some attributed to Ak Şamsuddinzade Hamdallah Ahmed Çelebi (or variations of that name); see Esad Efendi 3797/9, Esad Efendi 3814/5, Esad Efendi 3613/12, Haci Mahmud Efendi 2043, Haci Mahmud Efendi 3902/3, Mihrişah S. 185/8, Şehid Ali Paşa 1840/3, Murad Buhari 330/4, and many others.

30. Fakhr al-Dīn al-Rāzi, *Kitāb al-firāsa,* quoted in Mourad, *La physiognomonie arabe,* p. 90. See also Moris Gorlin, ed., *Maimonides "On Sexual Discourse"* (New York: Rambash Publishing, 1961), p. 68.

31. Murat Bardakçı, *Osmanlıda Seks: Sarayda Gece Dersleri* (Istanbul: Gür Yayınları, 1992), pp. 77–79 (from Nasreddin-i Tūsī, *Bahname-i Tūsī,* Istanbul üniversitesi Kütüphanesi, t.y. 2706).

32. Keykavus, *Kābusname.* See also *Kiyafet Name,* folio 28b.

33. See Musallam, *Sex and Society,* pp. 40–52.

34. Eşref bin Muḥammed, *Hazā'in,* folio 44a. See also Ibn Kamāl Pasha (Kemal Paşa Zade), *Rujūʿ al-shaykh ila sibāh fi al-quwwa ʿala al-bāh* (Cairo: Bulāq, 1309H), pp. 4–9; and V. L. Menage, "Kemal Pasha Zade," in *Encyclopedia of Islam,* vol. 4, p. 879b. See also Gorlin, *Maimonides "On Sexual Discourse,"* pp. 69–70.

35. Kadizade Islamboli Ahmed bin Muhammed Emin Efendi, *Cevhere-i Behiyye-i Ahmediyye fi şerhi vasiyet al Muhammediyye* (Üsküdar: n.p., 1218), p. 209.

36. Eşref bin Muḥammed, *Hazā'in,* folio 44b.

37. Al-ʿItāqi, *Tashrīḥ al-abdān,* p. 116.

38. Eşref bin Muḥammed, *Hazā'in,* folio 44b.

39. Al-ʿItāqi, *Tashrīḥ al-abdān,* p. 118.

40. Eşref bin Muḥammed, *Hazā'in,* p. 53. On the same subject, see another early-sixteenth-century scholar: Selim S. Kuru, "A Sixteenth Century Scholar, Deli Birader, and His Dāfi'ü'l gumūm ve rafi'ü'l humūm" (Ph.D. dissertation, Harvard University, May 2000), p. 162.

41. The earliest treatise on syphilis in the Islamic world was written in Persian by ʿImad al-Din al-Shirāzi in 1569. Savage-Smith, Klein-Franke, and Zhu, "Ṭibb," p. 457a.

42. Eşref bin Muḥammed, *Hazā'in,* folio 45b. On masturbation, see also Kuru, "A Sixteenth Century Scholar," pp. 247–50.

43. Peter Brown, *The Body and Society: Men, Women, and Sexual Renunciation in Early Christianity* (New York: Columbia University Press, 1988), p. 19.

44. Ibid.

45. Ibid., pp. 432–34.

46. Eşref bin Muḥammed, *Hazā'in,* folio 44a, and see a more detailed ex-

planation on folio 65a. The theory of semen as an essence collected from all organs originates in Hippocrates' writings. Aristotle elaborated this idea and describes semen as an essence of blood. For an earlier Islamic example (Al-Kindi), see Giuseppe Celentano, *Due Scritti Medici di Al-Kindi* (Naples: Instituto Orientale di Napoli, 1979), p. 21. See also Ibn Kamāl Pasha (Kemal Paşa Zade), *Rujūʿ al-shaykh,* pp. 2–8. Kemal Paşa Zade complicates the picture even more when he speaks of two different "semens." One is the same as that described in the quotation from Eşref bin Muḥammed, and the other is a lubricant needed to prevent irritation in the penis. One consequence of excessive intercourse, he says, is a burning itch caused by the depletion of the lubricating semen. See also Gerrit Bos, *Ibn al-Jazzār on Sexual Diseases and Their Treatment: A Critical Edition of Zad al-musafir wa-qut al-hadir* (Provisions for the Traveler and Nourishment for the Sedentary) (London: Kegan Paul International, 1997), pp. 240–42; and Gorlin, *Maimonides "On Sexual Discourse,"* p. 67.

47. Ibn Kamāl Pasha (Kemal Paşa Zade), *Rujūʿ al-shaykh,* p. 4. On *pneuma,* see also Bos, *Ibn al-Jazzār on Sexual Diseases*, p. 240. On erection and the connection between the heart, brain, liver, and testicles, see Bos, *Ibn al-Jazzār on Sexual Diseases*, p. 241. Early humoral medicine assumed that *pneuma* flows in the veins. It seems that later medical tracts, including those written in the Ottoman Empire, no longer believed this to be the case. As a result, *pneuma* has become a vague term that is used sparingly and uncomfortably, and endowed with little functionality. See also Al-ʿItāqi, *Tashrīḥ al-abdān,* pp. 114–15.

48. Koran, Surat al-ʿAlaq (XCVI).

49. Al-ʿItāqi, *Tashrīḥ al-abdān,* p. 118. This claim is repeated also on p. 119 (p. 236 in facsimile).

50. Eşref bin Muḥammed, *Hazā'in*; Al-ʿItaqi, *Tashrīḥ al-abdān,* pp. 121–22.

51. Al-ʿItāqi, *Tashrīḥ al-abdān,* p. 115.

52. In Franz Rosenthal, "Ar-Rāzī on the Hidden Illness," in *Science and Medicine in Islam: A Collection of Essays* (Aldershot: Variorum Reprints, 1990), pp. 52–53. Al-Rāzi takes his evidence from the world of mules, conceived through intercourse between asses and horses. Horses' semen is obviously more powerful than asses', he says. Now, if the male parent is an ass, the female mule (formed by the more powerful female semen) is better than the male, but if the male parent is a horse, then the male mule would be much superior to the female.

53. Ibid., pp. 54–55. This is echoed by many physiognomy books of the Ottoman period, as we will see.

54. Ibid.

55. Ibid., p. 50.

56. For one partially successful attempt to explain this, see Stephen O. Murray, "The Will Not to Know: Islamic Accommodations of Homosexuality," in *Islamic Homosexualities: Cultures, History and Literature,* ed. Stephen O. Murray and Will Roscoe (New York: New York University Press, 1997), pp. 14–54.

57. Al-ʿItāqi, *Tashrīḥ al-abdān,* p. 116 (p. 229 in facsimile).

58. See Sanders, "Gendering the Ungendered Body."

59. Sabuncuoğlu, *Cerrāhiyyetü'l-haniyye,* pp. 271, 300.

60. Named after Gabriel Fallopius, who described them in the sixteenth century. See Laqueur, *Making Sex,* p. 97.

61. *Keylos* (from Greek, *chyle*) is medieval medicine's term for the essence of food "cooked" in the body to become semen.

62. Şanizade, *Hamse-i şanizade*, vol. 1, pp. 90–91.

63. Felix von Niemeyer, *Ilm-i emraz dahiliye* (Istanbul: Mekteb-i tibbiye-i askeriye matbaasi, 1300 [1882]); Osman Saib Efendi, *Ahkamül-emraz* (Istanbul: Matbaa-i amire, 1252 [1836]).

64. Antun Klūt Bayk, *Kunūz al-Siḥḥa wa-yawāqīt al-minḥa* (Beirut: Dar Lubnan li'l-ṭibā'a wa'l-nashr, 2004); Antūn Bartīlīmī Klūt, *Durar al-Ghawal fi amrād al-aṭfāl* (Cairo: Bulāq, 1260 [1844]).

65. Michel Foucault, *The Birth of the Clinic* (London: Tavistock, 1973), pp. 162–66.

## CHAPTER 2. REGULATING DESIRE

1. Michel Foucault, *The History of Sexuality* (New York: Pantheon Books, 1978), p. 84.

2. See N. Calder, "Uṣūl al-Fiḳh," in *Encyclopedia of Islam*, 2nd edition (Leiden: Brill, 1960–2002), vol. 10, p. 931b.

3. Some of these systems were known as the *maẓālim* court, the *iḥtisāb*, and the *jināyāt* court.

4. Wael Hallaq, "The Qadi's Diwan (Sijill) before the Ottomans," *Bulletin of the School of Oriental and African Studies* 61, no. 3 (1998): 416–36.

5. Uriel Heyd, *Studies in Old Ottoman Criminal Law*, ed. V. L. Menage (Oxford: Clarendon Press, 1973), pp. 1–3; Uriel Heyd, "Kanun and Sharī'a in Old Ottoman Criminal Justice," *Proceedings of the Israel Academy of Sciences and Humanities* 3, no. 1 (1967): 1–8; Halil Inalcik, "Kanūn," in *Encyclopedia of Islam*, vol. 4, pp. 556–59. The word *kanun* had several meanings in the Ottoman Empire. Among them were provincial codes and simple orders of the sultan. In this chapter, unless otherwise stated, the term will refer to collected volumes of prescriptions and law edited in the imperial palace.

6. See Richard C. Repp, *The Müfti of Istanbul: A Study in the Development of the Ottoman Learned Hierarchy* (London: Ithaca Press, 1986).

7. Inalcik, "Kanūn," p. 560; Heyd, *Studies in Old Ottoman Criminal Law*, pp. 2–3, 192; Katib Çelebi, *The Balance of Truth (Mizanül hakk)*, trans. G. L. Lewis (London: George Allen and Unwin, 1957), pp. 128–29.

8. Frank Vogel, "Siyāsa shar'īyya," in *Encyclopedia of Islam*, vol. 9, pp. 694–96; Heyd, *Studies in Old Ottoman Criminal Law*, pp. 198–99. Among the most prominent *fuqāhā* who developed the doctrine were Ibn Taymiyya, his student Ibn Qayyim al-Jawziyya (d. 1350), and the Ottoman scholar Dede Efendi (d. 1565), whose work influenced Ottoman lawmakers in the sixteenth century.

9. The *nişancı* (seal bearer) was one of the viziers in the imperial divan. Among his duties was the verification that all state documents were written in accordance with law and protocol.

10. *Şeyhülislam* was the title of the chief mufti of the Ottoman Empire, who was also a senior member of the imperial divan.

11. Katib Çelebi, *The Balance of Truth*, p. 128.

12. Repp, *The Müfti of Istanbul*, p. 61; Katib Çelebi, *The Balance of Truth*,

pp. 128–29; Heyd, "Kanun and Sharī'a," pp. 3–4; Heyd, *Studies in Old Ottoman Criminal Law,* pp. 25–27.

13. *Kanunnāmes* were collections of *kanun* regulations that often had a preamble delineating proper application in court.

14. Heyd, *Studies in Old Ottoman Criminal Law,* pp. 151, 181–82; Inalcik, "Kanūn," p. 560. Some court cases from sixteenth- and seventeenth-century Anatolia demonstrate that it was, indeed, *kanun* law that was applied by the kadis. See *Şer'iye Sicilleri* (Istanbul: Türk Dünyası Araştırmaları Vakfı, 1989), pp. 104–7. In one case of adultery, the husband wishes to divorce his adulterous wife; in another, the husband of an adulterous wife demands compensation from her lover. In none of the cases is there any demand for *şeriat* punishment. See also Leslie P. Peirce, *Morality Tales: Law and Gender in the Ottoman Court of Aintab* (Berkeley and Los Angeles: University of California Press, 2003).

15. Fleischer, *Bureaucrat and Intellectual,* p. 291.

16. The discussion that follows is informed by Colin Imber, "Zina in Ottoman Law," in *Studies in Ottoman History and Law* (Istanbul: Isis Press, 1996), pp. 175–206, which looks at the same questions from a different vantage point.

17. Daniel Boyarin, *Carnal Israel: Reading Sex in Talmudic Culture* (Berkeley and Los Angeles: University of California Press, 1995), p. 28.

18. For my description of the *şeriat*'s treatment of sexual transgression and family law, I relied on the following texts: Muḥyi al-Dīn Abu Zakariyya al-Nawawi, *Kitāb al-majmū': Sharḥ al-muhadhdhab li'l-Shirāzi* (Beirut: Dār al-Turāth al-'Arabi, 1995), vol. 22; Aḥmad al-Wansharīsi, *Al-Mi'yār al-mu'rib wa'l-jāmi' al-mughrib fi fatāwa 'ulamā' Ifrīqya wa'l-Andalus wa'l-Maghrib* (Rabāt, Morocco: Dār al-Gharb al-Islāmi, 1981); Abi al-Ḥasan al-Baṣri, *Al-ḥāwi al-kabīr fi fiqh madhhab al imām al-Shāfi'i* (Beirut: Dār al-Kutub al-'Ilmiyya, 1994); *Mu'jam al-fiqh al-ḥanbali: Mu'jam al-mughni fi al-fiqh al-ḥanbali, mustakhlas min kitāb al-mughni li'ibn Qudāma* (Beirut: Dār al-Kutub al-'Ilmiyya, 1973); Taqi al-Dīn Aḥmad 'Abd al-Ḥalīm Ibn Taymiyya, *Majmu' fatāwa shaykh al-islām Aḥmad ibn Taymiyya,* ed. 'Abd al-Raḥmān Muḥammad Ibn Qāsim (Saudi Arabia: n.p, n.d.); and Ibrāhim al-Ḥalabi, *Multaqa al-abḥur* (Beirut: Mu'assassat al-Risāla, 1989). The latter appears to have been the favorite of Ottoman kadis until the nineteenth century. Views presented by these sources are by and large corroborated by a different set of sources quoted by Colin Imber in "Zina in Ottoman Law."

19. There were, of course, many other sources in use, and it is difficult to say with certainty which were the most important authorities at each point in time.

20. The principle of *kafā'a* (marriage to one's equal, socially or economically) is, admittedly, an obvious exception, but this too is a recommendation, and no punishment is prescribed for those who marry above or below their social or economic bracket. See, for example, al-Ḥalabi, *Multaqa al-abḥur,* vol. 1, p. 246.

21. The Romans saw sexual positions in which women were on top as serious moral transgressions. See Peter Brown, *The Body and Society: Men, Women, and Sexual Renunciation in Early Christianity* (New York: Columbia University Press, 1988), pp. 5–11. In Renaissance Venice, to take another example, anal intercourse was seen as a very serious offense. See Guido Ruggiero, *The Boundaries of Eros: Sex Crime and Sexuality in Renaissance Venice* (New York: Oxford University Press, 1985), pp. 109–13. See also chapter 4.

22. Abdelwahab Bouhdiba, *Sexuality in Islam* (London: Routledge and Kegan Paul, 1985), pp. 30–31.

23. Imber, "Zina in Ottoman Law," p. 176.

24. Ibid., pp. 176–77.

25. Koran, 27:55.

26. Al-Basri, *Al-ḥāwi al-kabīr,* pp. 222–26.

27. Ibn Taymiyya, *Majmuʿ fatāwa shaykh al-islām Aḥmad ibn Taymiyya,* pp. 179–80; Imber, "Zina in Ottoman Law," p. 179.

28. Al-Nawawi, *Kitāb al-majmūʿ*, vol. 22, p. 58; Ibn Taymiyya, *Majmuʿ fatāwa shaykh al-islām Aḥmad ibn Taymiyya,* p. 181–82; *Muʿjam al-fiqh al-ḥanbali,* pt. 2; al-Basri, *Al-ḥāwi al-kabīr,* pp. 222–23; al-Wansharīsi, *Al-Miʿyār,* vol. 2, pp. 208–10; al-Ḥalabi, *Multaqa al-abḥur,* vol. 1, p. 334.

29. Al-Nawawi, *Kitāb al-majmūʿ*, pp. 63, 48; al-Baṣri, *Al-ḥāwi al-kabīr,* p. 224.

30. *Muʿjam al-fiqh al-ḥanbali.*

31. Ibn Taymiyya, *Majmuʿ fatāwa shaykh al-islām Aḥmad ibn Taymiyya,* pp. 181–82; *Muʿjam al-fiqh al-ḥanbali;* al-Nawawi, *Kitāb al-majmūʿ*, pp. 58, 26, 27.

32. Al-Nawawi, *Kitāb al-majmūʿ*, p. 27; al-Ḥalabi, *Multaqa al-abḥur,* vol. 1, pp. 334–35.

33. Heyd, *Studies in Old Ottoman Criminal Law,* pp. 167–69; Inalcik, "Kanūn," pp. 556–59. See also Colin Imber, *Ebu's-Su'ud: The Islamic Legal Tradition* (Stanford, CA: Stanford University Press, 1997), p. 44. Imber argues correctly that the source for many of the *kanun*s is legal custom *(örf).* Ömer Lutfi Barkan mentions several previous *kanunnāme*s that the Ottomans knew and probably learned from, such as the law codes of Uzun Hasan, the Pādişah of the Ak-Koyunlu, the laws of Kayitbāy, the Mamluk sultan of Egypt, and those of Dulgadir. See Barkan, "Kanun-Name," in *Islam Ansiklopedisi* (Istanbul: Maarif Basimevi, 1955), vol. 6, pp. 193–94. The point I would like to stress here, however, is that those other legal systems were already influenced by the *şeriat,* and even custom is not an immutable ancient code. In many parts of the Ottoman Empire, after hundreds of years of Islamic rule, custom appears to have absorbed some of its basic principles from the *şeriat.* To a certain extent it was restructured to fit some of the basic concepts of the *şeriat,* or at least what most common people assumed would be consistent with Islamic law.

34. Heyd, *Studies in Old Ottoman Criminal Law,* pp. 44–53. See also Ahmed Akgündüz, *Osmanlı Kanunnameler ve Hukuki Tahlileri* (Istanbul: Hilal Matbaası, 1992), vol. 4, pp. 293–96.

35. Akgündüz, *Osmanlı Kanunnameler,* vol. 4, p. 361. According to Akgündüz, about 90 percent of general *kanunnāme*s in Turkish libraries are copies of this one.

36. Ibid., vol. 4, p. 366.

37. Ibid., vol. 4, pp. 366–67; Heyd, *Studies in Old Ottoman Criminal Law,* pp. 109–30.

38. Information in these tables is based on Heyd, *Studies in Old Ottoman Criminal Law,* and on Akgündüz, *Osmanlı Kanunnameler,* vol. 4.

39. In this respect, see also Imber, *Ebu's-Su'ud,* p. 50; and Akgündüz, vol. 4, pp. 296, 366.

40. Heyd, *Studies in Old Ottoman Criminal Law,* pp. 55–93, 95–131. See also Leslie P. Peirce, "Seniority, Sexuality and Social Order: The Vocabulary of Gender in Early Modern Ottoman Society," in *Women in the Ottoman Empire: Middle Eastern Women in the Early Modern Era,* ed. Madeline Zilfi (Leiden: Brill, 1997), pp. 170–71.

41. Heyd, *Studies in Old Ottoman Criminal Law,* p. 97.

42. Imber, "Zina in Ottoman Law," p. 192.

43. See al-Ḥalabi, *Multaqa al-abḥur,* vol. 1, pp. 336–41; Ortayli, "The Family in Ottoman Society," in *Analecta Isisiana X: Studies on Ottoman Transformation* (Istanbul: Isis Press, 1994), p. 130. Ortayli claims that "throughout Ottoman history there was only one instance where *recm* [stoning] was decided upon and carried out."

44. Dror Ze'evi, *An Ottoman Century: The District of Jerusalem in the 1600s* (Albany: State University of New York Press, 1996), pp. 177–78. Cases that the court dealt with had to do with suspicions of prostitution, rape, or sexual liaisons that were too obvious to disregard. See also Imber, "Zina in Ottoman Law," pp. 190–92, for Ebüssuud's *fatāwa* concerning intent to commit fornication.

45. See also Peirce, "Seniority, Sexuality and Social Order," p. 187. Peirce, seeing this as a question of male honor, rightly remarks that the same *kanun* imposes a cuckold tax *(köftehorluk)* on a married man whose wife was involved in an adulterous affair, and that the father of a boy yielding to a pederast is to be punished.

46. Dror Ze'evi, "*Kul* and Getting Cooler: The Dissolution of an Elite Collective Identity in the Ottoman Empire," *Mediterranean Historical Review* 11, no. 2 (December 1996): 177–99.

47. Ortayli, "The Family in Ottoman Society," pp. 129–30; Leslie Peirce, "Fatma's Dilemma: Sexual Crime and Legal Culture in an Early Modern Ottoman Court," *Annales—Histoire, Sciences Sociales* 53, no. 2 (1998): 291–346.

48. Halil Inalcik offers yet another explanation. In his view, since so many laws had to do with the agrarian system and the *timar,* and these systems went through serious changes, there was no point in adhering to the *kanun,* and its importance declined. Inalcik, "Kanūn," p. 561.

49. *Ceza Kanunname-i Hümayun* (Arabic version), Süleymaniye Library, Hüsrev Paşa no. 826.

50. *Kanunname-i Ceza,* Süleymaniye Library, Hidiv Ismail Paşa no. 35, no. 157, and no. 121. The last copy is an Arabic translation.

51. *Kanunname-i Ceza,* p. 45, reg. 197.

52. Ibid., p. 45, reg. 199. *Kürek* (paddle) used to mean work on the galleys as punishment, but at this period it probably meant any kind of imprisonment with hard labor.

53. Ibid., p. 45, reg. 200.

54. Ibid., p. 46, reg. 202. For other examples, see reg. 188, 205–6.

55. Ehud Toledano, *The Ottoman Slave Trade and Its Suppression* (Princeton, NJ: Princeton University Press, 1980).

56. Ze'evi, "*Kul* and Getting Cooler."

57. Haim Gerber, *State, Society and Law in Islam: Ottoman Law in Comparative Perspective* (Upper Saddle River, NJ: Pearson Addison Wesley, 2000);

Ibn ʿĀbidīn, *Radd al-muḥtār ʿala al-darr al-mukhtār* (Beirut: Dār Iḥyāʾ al-Turāth al-ʿArabi, n.d.).

## CHAPTER 3. MORALITY WARS

1. One such study, albeit problematic, is G. H. Bosquet, *L'Ethique sexuelle de l'Islam* (Paris: G. P. Maisonneuve et Larousse, 1966); Bouhdiba also devotes the first chapters of his *Sexuality in Islam* (London: Routledge and Kegan Paul, 1985) to classical Islamic sexual doctrine. See also Basim Musallam, *Sex and Society in Islam: Birth Control before the Nineteenth Century* (Cambridge: Cambridge University Press, 1983).

2. Joseph Norment Bell, *Love Theory in Later Hanbalite Islam* (Albany: State University of New York Press, 1979), pp. 88, 144, 200–201.

3. J. Spencer Trimingham, *The Sufi Orders in Islam* (London: Oxford University Press, 1973), pp. 14, 103. One indication for the late appearance of *ṭarīqas* would be to check the formal establishment dates of the ones that were most popular in the Ottoman period: Qādiriyya (1166), Rifāʿiyya (1182), Shādhiliyya (1258), Badawiyya (1276), Mawlawiyya (1276), Naqshbandiyya (1389), and Bektashiyya (1337). These dates are often based on the death of the eponymous founder, and in most cases a true order only developed several decades after his death.

4. Alexander Knysh, *Islamic Mysticism: A Short History* (Leiden: Brill, 2000), pp. 265–80.

5. Trimingham, *Sufi Orders,* p. 104. See also Madeline C. Zilfi, *The Politics of Piety: The Ottoman Ulema in the Postclassical Age (1600–1800)* (Minneapolis: Bibliotheca Islamica, 1988), pp. 165–66.

6. Zilfi, *Politics of Piety,* pp. 274, 278–80. See also Ahmet Yaşar Ocak, "Oppositions au soufisme dans l'empire ottoman aux quinzième et seizième siècles," in *Islamic Mysticism Contested: Thirteen Centuries of Controversies and Polemics,* ed. F. de Jong and B. Radtke (Leiden: Brill, 1999), p. 610; and Trimingham, *Sufi Orders*, p. 69. On the early history of the Malāmatiyya, see Sara Sviri, "Hakīm Tirmidhī and the Malāmatī Movement in Early Sufism," in *The Heritage of Sufism,* ed. L. Lewisohn (Oxford: One World Publications, 1999), vol. 1, pp. 583–613.

7. See J. Schacht, "Abu'l Suʿūd," in *Encyclopedia of Islam,* 2nd edition (Leiden: Brill, 1960–2002), vol. 1, p. 152a; Ocak, "Oppositions au soufisme," pp. 610–12; and John Kingsley Birge, *The Bektashi Order of Dervishes* (London: Luzac, 1937).

8. Dror Ze'evi, *An Ottoman Century: The District of Jerusalem in the 1600s* (Albany: State University of New York Press, 1986), pp. 69–70; Muḥammad Amīn Ibn Faḍlallah Al-Muḥibbi, *Tārīkh Khulāṣat al-āthār fi Aʿyān al-qarn al-ḥādi ʿashar* (Cairo: Bulāq, 1284H).

9. Bell, *Love Theory,* pp. 44, 98, 125, and many other places; A. Ateş, "Ibn al-ʿArabī," in *Encyclopedia of Islam,* vol. 3, p. 707b; Ocak, "Oppositions au soufisme," p. 611; Zilfi, *Politics of Piety,* pp. 37–38. In fact, Ibn al-ʿArabi did not use the term *waḥdat al-wujūd;* it was invented by his followers to explain his ideas.

10. William C. Chittick, *The Self-Disclosure of God: Principles of Ibn al-ʿArabi's Cosmology* (Albany: State University of New York Press, 1998), pp. 12–16; Knysh, *Islamic Mysticism*, pp. 168, 268.

11. Annemarie Schimmel, *Mystical Dimensions of Islam* (Chapel Hill: University of North Carolina Press, 1975), p. 291.

12. M. Milson, *A Sufi Rule for Novices: Kitāb ādāb al-murīdīn of Abu al-Najīb al-Suhrawardi* (Cambridge, MA: Harvard University Press, 1975), pp. 33, 47, 75–76; J. During, "Samāʿ," in *Encyclopedia of Islam*, vol. 8, p. 1018a; Knysh, *Islamic Mysticism*, pp. 322–24.

13. Milson, *Sufi Rule*, pp. 47, 75–76.

14. Ocak, "Oppositions au soufisme," p. 611 (from Düzdağ, *Seyhülislām Ebussuud Efendi Fetvāları*, p. 86).

15. Khayr al-Dīn al-Ramli, *Al-fatāwa al-Khayriyya li-nafʿ al-bariyya* (Cairo: Bulāq, 1300H), vol. 2, pp. 179–80. Compare with Shams al-Dīn Muhammad Ibn ʿUmar Al-Ghamri al-Wāsiṭi, *Al-ḥukm al-maẓbūṭ fi taḥrīm fiʾl qawm Lūṭ* (Cairo: Dar al-Saḥāba li'l-Turath, 1988), p. 108. For *ḥadīths* about singing and music playing and the debate about the Prophet's attitude to them, see ʿAbd al-Raḥmān Ibn ʿAli Ibn al-Jawzi, *Al-Nafīs fi takhrīj aḥādīth Talbīs iblīs*, ed. Yahya bin Khalid bin Tawfīq (Cairo: Maktabat al-tarbiya al-Islāmīya, 1994), pp. 162–65.

16. Al-Ramli, *Al-fatāwa*, vol. 2, pp. 179–81.

17. Abdellah Hammoudi, *Master and Disciple: The Cultural Foundations of Moroccan Authoritarianism* (Chicago: University of Chicago Press, 1997). For a much earlier but related description of relationships between masters and disciples, see Milson, *Sufi Rule*, p. 56.

18. Hammoudi, *Master and Disciple*, pp. 91–97, 138–41.

19. Ibid., pp. 138–39.

20. Even Evliya Çelebi, the famous Ottoman traveler, recounts how, when he was born, a Sufi master of the Mevleviye visited his house, took some bread out of his own mouth, and fed it to the baby (Evliya) as a blessing. See Evliya Efendi, *Narrative of Travels in Europe, Asia and Africa in the Seventeenth Century*, trans. Joseph von Hammer (London: Parbury, Allen, 1834), part 2, pp. 15–16.

21. Cornell Fleischer, *Bureaucrat and Intellectual in the Ottoman Empire: The Historian Mustafa Ali (1541–1600)* (Princeton, NJ: Princeton University Press, 1986). For an interesting description of contemporary Sufi *dhikr* ceremonies, see Michael Gilsenan, *Saint and Sufi in Modern Egypt: An Essay in the Sociology of Religion* (Oxford: Clarendon Press, 1973), pp. 156–87.

22. Hamid Algar, "Reflections of Ibn ʿArabī in Early Nakshbandī Tradition," *Islami Araştırmalar* 5, no. 1 (January 1991): 1–20; R.S. Humphreys et al., "Ṭarīḳa," in *Encyclopedia of Islam*, vol. 10, p. 243b; F. De Jong, "Khalwatiyya," in *Encyclopedia of Islam*, vol. 4, p. 991a; G.L. Lewis, "Bayramiyya," in *Encyclopedia of Islam*, vol. 1, p. 1137a; Abdulbaki Gölpinarlı, *Melamilik ve Melamiler* (Istanbul: Devlet Matbaası, 1931).

23. See Zilfi, *Politics of Piety*, p. 168: "It was not simply deviance but the *popularity* of deviance that first alerted the Kadizadelis" (my emphasis).

24. About al-Amāsi, see Hajji Khalifa, *Kashf al-ẓunūn* (Leipzig: R. Bentley

for the Oriental Translation Fund of Great Britain and Ireland, 1835–58), vol. 1, p. 191.

25. Sinān al-Dīn Yūsuf al-Amāsi (al-Wāʿiz), *Tabyīn al-maḥārim,* manuscript, Princeton University, Firestone Library, Hitti Cat. no. 927, folios 135a, 142b. See also Abu al-Fatḥ al-Dajjāni, *Al-ʿiqd al-mufrad fi maḥabbat al-amrad,* manuscript, Princeton University, Firestone Cat. no. 1952, folio 7b.

26. See Bell, *Love Theory,* pp. 19–21, 26, 30–31, 44, 88, 125–27, 139–44. Aḥmad bin Muḥammad, *Rushd al-labīb fi muʿāsharat al-ḥabīb,* manuscript, Bibliothèque Nationale, Mss. Arabes 3051. See Hajji Khalifa, *Kashf al-ẓunūn,* vol. 1, p. 237.

27. Apart from the treatise described at length here, see Al-Amāsi (al-Wāʿiz), *Tabyīn al-maḥārim;* al-Wāsiṭi, *Al-ḥukm al-maẓbūṭ;* and Taqi al-Dīn Aḥmad ʿAbd al-Ḥalīm Ibn Taymiyya, *Ḥijāb al-mar'a wa-libāsuha fi'l-Islām* (Cairo: n.p., [1974]). There are many others that are also well known, including books by Ibn Qayyim al-Jawzīya and Al-Suyūṭi. For Turkish treatises, see Kadizade Islamboli Ahmed bin Muhammed Emin Efendi, *Cevhere-i Behiyye-i Ahmediyye fi şerhi vasiyet al Muhammediyye* (Üsküdar: n.p., 1218); A. Faruk Meyan, ed., *Birgivi Vasiyetnamesi (Kadizade Şerhi)* (Istanbul: Bedir Publishing, 1977); and Ergün Hiçyılmaz, *Eski Istanbulda "Muhabbet"* (Istanbul: Cep Kitapları, 1991).

28. Al-Dajjāni, *Al-ʿiqd al-mufrad fi maḥabbat al-amrad.* There is another copy at the Hebrew University, no. APAR 338. About the author, see Moshe Perlman, "A Seventeenth Century Exhortation Concerning Al-Aqsā," *Israel Oriental Studies* 3 (1973): 261–68; and Al-Muḥibbi, *Tārīkh Khulāṣat al-āthār,* vol. 3, p. 475.

29. Al-Dajjāni, *Al-ʿiqd al-mufrad,* folio 1a. The same sense of deterioration is common to most writers on the subject, especially in this period. Note al-Amāsi's words at the end of the sixteenth century: "See, O wise one, how this ugly abomination spread and proliferated in this community during this time, in its Arabs and Persians *[ʿArabuha wa-ʿAjamuha],* learned and ignorant, the masses and the elite."

30. Ibid.

31. See also al-Wāsiṭi, *Al-ḥukm al-maẓbūṭ,* pp. 119–21.

32. See also Bell, *Love Theory,* p. 26.

33. See Schimmel, *Mystical Dimensions of Islam,* pp. 289–90; Bell, *Love Theory,* pp. 42–43; and Trimingham, *Sufi Orders,* p. 212 n. 1 (Trimingham defines the *ḥadīth* as "found or invented"). See al-Amāsi, *Tabyīn al-maḥārim,* folio 139b, where he claims that the attribution of a *ḥadīth* that permits sexual intercourse with one slave, attributed to Mālik, is apparently false; see also al-Wāsiṭi, *Al-ḥukm al-maẓbūṭ,* pp. 116–17.

34. Al-Dajjāni, *Al-ʿiqd al-mufrad,* folios 3b–4a.

35. Ibid., folios 4a–5a.

36. Al-Amāsi, *Tabyīn al-Maḥārim,* folio 139b; al-Wāsiṭi, *Al-ḥukm al-maẓbūṭ,* p. 99. The editor of the latter text, ʿUbaydallah al-Masri, says in the footnote that he could not find the source for this *ḥadīth,* and that many others are quoted from marginal sources.

37. Al-Dajjāni, *Al-ʿiqd al-mufrad,* folio 5a. The same story appears in earlier treatises (see al-Wāsiṭi, *Al-ḥukm al-maẓbūṭ,* p. 50) but seems to become much more widespread in the sixteenth century.

38. Al-Wāsiṭi, *Al-ḥukm al-maẓbūṭ*, pp. 54, 81; Franz Rosenthal, "Ar-Rāzī on the Hidden Illness," in *Science and Medicine in Islam: A Collection of Essays* (Aldershot: Variorum Reprints 1990), item IX.

39. Al-Wāsiṭi, *Al-ḥukm al-maẓbūṭ*, p. 51.

40. For the teachings of Birgivi on the prohibition of the gaze and homoerotic practices, see Efendi, *Cevhere-i Behiyye,* pp. 146, 153. See also Derin Terzioğlu, "Sufi and Dissident in the Ottoman Empire: Niyazī-i Misrī (1618–1694)" (Ph.D. dissertation, Harvard University, 1999), pp. 196–200.

41. Zilfi, *Politics of Piety,* p. 136. Terzioğlu, "Sufi and Dissident," pp. 213, 218–19.

42. Zilfi, *Politics of Piety*, pp. 140–45.

43. Ibid., p. 149.

44. Ibid.

45. See ʿAbd al-Rahmān al-Jabarti, *ʿAjāyib al-āthār fi al-tarājim wa'l-akhbār* (Beirut: Dar al-Jalīl, n.d.), pp. 83–86; and Rudolph Peters, "The Battered Dervishes of Bab Zuwayla: A Religious Riot in Eighteenth Century Cairo," in *Eighteenth Century Renewal and Reform in Islam,* ed. Nehemia Levtzion and John Voll (Syracuse, NY: Syracuse University Press, 1987), pp. 93–115.

46. Colin Imber, "Malmātiyya," in *Encyclopedia of Islam,* vol. 6, p. 223b.

47. John Obert Voll, *Islam: Continuity and Change in the Modern World* (Boulder, CO: Westview Press, 1982), p. 36.

48. Afsaneh Najmabadi, "That Fateful/Faithful Cup of Wine: Shaykh San'an and Heteronormalization of Love in Qajar Iran" (unpublished paper prepared for a workshop on New Trends in Arab and Ottoman Historiography, Istanbul, 1999); Najmabadi, *Women with Mustaches and Men without Beards: Gender and Sexual Anxieties of Iranian Modernity* (Berkeley and Los Angeles: University of California Press, 2005).

49. Najmabadi, "That Fateful/Faithful Cup of Wine," p. 16.

50. See chapter 6.

51. Gilsenan, *Saint and Sufi,* p. 189.

52. Snouck Hurgronje, "Les confreries religieuses, la Mecque et le Panislamisme," in *Verspreide Geschriften* (Bonn: Kurt Schroeder, 1923 [1900]), pp. iii, 189–206.

## CHAPTER 4. DREAM INTERPRETATION AND THE UNCONSCIOUS

1. For a list of dream interpretation books in the first centuries, see John Lamoreaux, "Dream Interpretation in the Early Medieval Near East" (Ph.D. dissertation, Duke University, 1999), pp. 355–61. For contemporary dream interpretation books, see notes 22 and 73 in this chapter.

2. See E. W. Lane, *An Account of the Manners and Customs of the Modern Egyptians* (London: East-West Publications, 1989 [1836]), p. 264.

3. G.E. von Grunebaum, "Introduction: The Cultural Function of the Dream as Illustrated by Classical Islam," in *The Dream and Human Societies,* ed. G.E. von Grunebaum and Roger Caillois (Berkeley and Los Angeles: University of California Press, 1966), pp. 16–17.

4. Ibid., pp. 6–7.

5. Steven M. Oberhelman, "Hierarchies of Gender, Ideology, and Power in Ancient and Medieval Greek and Arabic Dream Literature," in *Homoeroticism in Classical Arabic Literature,* ed. J. W. Wright Jr. and Everett K. Rowson (New York: Columbia University Press, 1997), pp. 58–59.

6. For meanings of the word *taʿbīr* in Arabic, see Lamoreaux, "Dream Interpretation in the Early Medieval Near East," p. 142.

7. Miklos Maroth, "The Science of Dreams in Islamic Culture," *Jerusalem Studies in Arabic and Islam* 20 (1996): 229–36; see mainly pp. 232–34. Ibn Khaldūn, who speaks of dream interpretation in the *Muqaddima* (Cairo, 1:6, 6,12–13), does a good job of explaining this. He enumerates three kinds of dreams: those inspired by God, those that originate with the Devil, and those of human origin. Ibn Khaldūn, *The Muqaddimah: An Introduction to History,* trans. Franz Rosenthal (Princeton, NJ: Princeton University Press, 1967), pp. 368–71.

8. William C. Chittick, *The Sufi Path of Knowledge* (Albany: State University of New York Press, 1989), p. 120.

9. See Fazlur Rahman, "Dream, Imagination and ʿĀlam al-Mithāl," in *The Dream and Human Societies,* ed. von Grunebaum and Caillois, pp. 409–19; Henri Corbin, "The Visionary Dream in Islamic Spirituality," in *The Dream and Human Societies,* ed. von Grunebaum and Caillois, pp. 381–408; Annemarie Schimmel, *Mystical Dimensions of Islam* (Chapel Hill: University of North Carolina Press, 1975), p. 270; and Ibn al-ʿArabi, "De la connaissance des songes," trans. Ali Ridha Arfa, *Aux sources de la sagesse* 1, part 2 (1994): 35–68; 1, part 3 (1994): 41–68.

10. Having written extensive commentaries on Ibn al-ʿArabi's work, ʿAbd al-Ghani al-Nābulusi was no doubt familiar with the concept of *ʿālam al-mithāl* and with other disputes concerning the origins of dreams. See W. A. S. Khalidi, "ʿAbd al-Ghani al-Nābulusi," in *Encyclopedia of Islam,* 2nd edition (Leiden: Brill, 1960–2002), vol. 1, pp. 60–61.

11. Very little is known about Artemidorus himself. He was a native of Daldis, a town in Lydia, Anatolia, and almost certainly lived in the second century A.D. See Artemidorus, *The Interpretation of Dreams: Oneirocritica,* trans. Robert J. White (Torrance, CA: Original Books, 1990). His work was already analyzed by Foucault in the framework of his monumental study of sexuality: Michel Foucault, *The History of Sexuality II: The Use of Pleasure* (London: Penguin Books, 1992 [1984]), pp. 5–20. Some of Foucault's observations will be discussed in the second part of this chapter. For the translation of Artemidorus's work into Arabic, see Ḥunayn Ibn Isḥāq, trans., *Kitāb Taʿbīr al-ru'yā: Awwal wa-ahamm al-kutub fi tafsir al-aḥlām* (translation of Artemidorus's *Oneirocritica*), ed. Abd al-munʿim al-Ḥifni (Cairo: Dar al-Rashad, 1991). The book includes a comparison of the texts of Artemidorus as translated by Ibn Isḥāq with dream interpretations by Ibn Sīrīn, al-Nābulusi, and Freud. See also T. Fahd, "Ru'yā," in *Encyclopedia of Islam,* vol. 8, p. 646; and De Lacy O'Leary, *How Greek Science Passed to the Arabs* (London: Routledge and Kegan Paul, 1964), pp. 164–70.

12. An interesting anecdote tells us that one of the things that convinced the caliph al-Ma'mūn to promote translations into Arabic of Greek philosophical texts, including the *Oneirocritica* itself, was a dream he had of a conversation

with Aristotle. Von Grunebaum, *Dream and Human Societies,* pp. 7–8 (quoted from the *Fihrist* of Ibn al-Nadim, Cairo 1348/1929–1930, p. 339).

13. Douglass Price-Williams, "Cultural Perspectives on Dreams and Consciousness," *Anthropology of Consciousness* 5, no. 3 (September 1994): 13–16.

14. See Lamoreaux, "Dream Interpretation in the Early Medieval Near East."

15. Ibid., pp. 228–84. See also Oberhelman, "Hierarchies of Gender," pp. 64–65.

16. Strohmaier, "Ḥuanyn Ibn Isḥaq," in *Encyclopedia of Islam,* vol. 3, pp. 578–81. In the original Greek version of *Oneirocritica,* deities of the Greek pantheon are omnipresent. See Artemidorus, *Interpretation of Dreams;* and Lamoreaux, "Dream Interpretation in the Early Medieval Near East," pp. 15, 80–81.

17. *"Fa-iʿtazilu al-nisa' fi'l-maḥīḍ."* "Surat al-baqara" (the cow), verse 222. See Abu al-Ḥasan ʿAli Ibn al-Qassār al-Khawlāni al-Qayrawāni, *Kitāb bulūgh al-marām fi taʿbīr al-ru'yā fi al-manām,* manuscript, Bibliothèque Nationale, Paris, Manuscrits Arabes 2746, folio 16b. For other examples, see folios 23, 26, 33b, and 35. See also Lamoreaux, "Dream Interpretation in the Early Medieval Near East," pp. 86–93.

18. *"Inna nursilū al-nāqa fitnatan lahum."* "Surat al-qamar" (the moon), verse 27. ʿAbd al-Ghani al-Nābulusi, *Taʿṭīr al-ānām fi taʿbīr al-manām* (Damascus: Dar al-khayr, 1998), p. 449. Examples in this book were checked against the Bulāq version of the book (Cairo: Bulāq, n.d.) and various manuscripts, notably al-Nābulusi, *Al-ʿAbīr fi'l-taʿbīr,* Princeton University, Garrett Collection, folios 91a–94b.

19. About koranic imagery, see also Oberhelman, "Hierarchies of Gender," p. 64.

20. On habitus, see Pierre Bourdieu, *Practical Reason: On the Theory of Action* (Cambridge: Polity Press, 1998), pp. 8, 81–82, 97–98; Richard Jenkins, "Habitus," in *The Social Science Encyclopedia,* 2nd edition (London: Routledge, 1996), pp. 354–55.

21. Khalidi, "ʿAbd al-Ghani bin Ismaʿīl al-Nābulusi," p. 60; Muḥammad Amīn Ibn Faḍlallah al-Muḥibbi, *Tārīkh Khulāṣat al-āthār fi Aʿyān al-qarn al-ḥādi ʿashar* (Cairo: Bulāq, 1284H), vol. 2, p. 433.

22. It is also interesting to note that at the end of the twentieth century, new, often censored, adaptations of this book as an encyclopedia flooded the Turkish market. See Şükrü Göknnar, *Rüya Tabirleri Ansiklopedisi* (Istanbul: Kitsan, n.d.); *Imam Nabulsi İslami Rüya Tabirleri Ansiklopedisi* (Istanbul: Eko Offset, n.d.); *Imam Nabulsi ve Diğer İmamlar İslami Rüya Tabirleri Ansiklopedisi* (Istanbul: Seda Yayinlari, n.d.).

23. This is based to a large extent on the science of *ḥadīth* and the apparatus used to verify the authenticity of the Prophet's traditions. The following discussion is based on ʿAbd al-Ghani al-Nābulusi, *Al-ʿAbīr fi al-taʿbīr fi uṣūl kayfiyat taʿbīr al-ru'yā fi al-manām* (Beirut: Mu'assasat ʿIzz al-Din, 1996), pp. 483–84. See also al-Nābulusi, *Al-ʿAbīr fi'l-taʿbīr,* Princeton University, Garrett Collection. See a similar discussion by Artemidorus on his own period in Ibn Isḥāq, *Kitāb Taʿbīr al-ru'yā,* pp. 27–30.

24. As Foucault points out, Artemidorus saw this principle of juxtaposition

of similarities as the basic principle governing the interpretation of dreams: Foucault, *Use of Pleasure,* p. 14.

25. Compare with Artemidorus in Ibn Isḥāq, *Kitāb Taʿbīr al-ru'yā,* p. 217. Artemidorus explains how the same symbol may mean a different thing when found in a chain of other symbols.

26. This example seems to have been a favorite of many interpreters. On the long history of the quince in the service of dream interpretation, see Lamoreaux, "Dream Interpretation in the Early Medieval Near East," p. 120.

27. Al-Nābulusi, *Al-ʿAbīr fi al-taʿbīr fi uṣūl kayfiyat taʿbīr al-ru'yā fi al-manām.* In this respect, see also Combs-Schilling, *Sacred Performances: Islam, Sexuality, and Sacrifice* (New York: Columbia University Press, 1989), p. 171. Another indication that dream interpreters saw interpretation as a science grounded in historical time and place is al-Nābulusi's description, based on *Tabaqāt al-muʿabbirīn* by Ḥasad bin Ḥusayn al-Khalāl, of a long chain of people—pagans, Jews, Christians, and Muslims—who contributed to knowledge of dreams and their meanings: al-Nābulusi, *Al-ʿAbīr fi al-taʿbīr fi uṣūl kayfiyat taʿbīr al-ru'yā fi al-manām,* p. 482. Al-Nābulusi's description may be compared to modern authors' analysis of symbolic language. See Erich Fromm, *The Forgotten Language: An Introduction to the Understanding of Dreams, Fairy Tales and Myths* (New York: Rinehart, 1951), p. 13. Fromm distinguishes among three kinds of symbols—conventional, accidental, and universal. A conventional one might be the name we have for a thing (table, chair), which has no intrinsic relation to the thing it symbolizes. An accidental one might be a landscape that triggers a certain mood in our minds because it is connected with a personal memory. A universal symbol is one that everyone identifies because it is connected with a sensory experience, such as fire signifying movement and energy.

28. Al-Qayrawāni, *Kitāb bulūgh al-marām,* folios 4–4b; Joseph de Somogyi, "The Interpretation of Dreams in Ad-Damīrī's Ḥayāt al-Ḥayawān," *Journal of the Royal Asiatic Society* pt. 1 (1940): 1–3; Muḥammad Ibn Sīrīn, *Tafsīr al-aḥlām al-kabīr* (Cairo: Maṭbaʿat al-Jalli, 1995), pp. 3–18.

29. See also interpretations for new phenomena such as coffee, guns, card games, or new musical instruments in Sayyid Süleyman al-Hüseyni, *Kenzülmenām* (Istanbul: Kitabhane-i Sevdi, 1340H), pp. 489, 715, 787, 801, 843, 840–46.

30. For comparisons between texts, see Lamoreaux, "Dream Interpretation in the Early Medieval Near East," pp. 146–72.

31. Oberhelman, "Hierarchies of Gender," p. 64.

32. Cemal Kafadar, *Between Two Worlds: The Construction of the Ottoman State* (Berkeley and Los Angeles: University of California Press, 1995), pp. 8–9, 30; Rudi Lidner, *Nomads and Ottomans in Medieval Anatolia* (Bloomington: Indiana University Press, 1983), p. 37.

33. On dreams as a unifying discourse, see Barbara Tedlock, "The Evidence from Dreams," in *Psychological Anthropology,* ed. Philip K. Bock (Westport, CT: Praeger, 1994), p. 286.

34. See Robert Dankoff, *The Intimate Life of an Ottoman Statesman* (Albany: State University of New York Press, 1991), pp. 16–17, 100–102, 185–86, 221–22. Dankoff suggests that both parties must have known that some of the

dreams were invented. About the possibility of shared dreams, see Stanley Krippner, "Waking Life, Dream Life, and the Construction of Reality," *Anthropology of Consciousness* 5, no. 3 (September 1994): 20–21. For an example of interpretation that uncovers deep psychological layers, see Evliya's dream about repairs in a decaying mosque, and Melek Paşa's very personal interpretation of the dream as referring to his own aging body, in Dankoff, *Intimate Life,* pp. 207–11. On dreams in nineteenth-century Egyptian culture, see Lane, *Account of the Manners and Customs,* p. 264: "The Egyptians place great faith in dreams, which often direct them in some of the most important actions of life. They have two large and celebrated works on the interpretation of dreams by Ibn-Shaheen and Ibn-Seereen, the latter of whom was the pupil of the former. These books are consulted even by many of the learned with implicit confidence."

35. Sigmund Freud, *The Interpretation of Dreams* (London: Allen and Unwin, 1913); Rosalind D. Cartwright, "Dreams," in *The Social Science Encyclopedia,* p. 197.

36. This is perhaps also true of some Islamic dream interpretation traditions today. Benjamin Kilborne, who presented some of the dreams Freud described to a group of Moroccan dream interpreters, discovered that they gave an entirely different meaning to the symbols in these dreams: B. Kilborne, "The Handling of Dream Symbolism: Aspects of Dream Interpretation in Morocco," *Psychoanalytic Study of Society* 9 (1981): 1–14.

37. Al-Nābulusi, *Taʿṭīr al-ānām* (Dar al-khayr edition), pp. 168 *(khātim)* and 187 *(khulkhāl).* A similar interpretation of rings can be found in Artemidorus in Ibn Isḥāq, *Kitāb Taʿbīr al-ru'yā,* p. 116. This is al-Nābulusi's analysis of a bracelet in a dream: "*Khulkhāl* [anklet, bracelet]—signifies a son in dreams. A man who sees a golden anklet on his body in a dream will fall ill, or commit a sin. And if the bracelet is on a woman's body she will be safe from harm and fear. If [the anklet] has no pair *[zawj]* she will marry a generous husband. Whoever sees an anklet of gold or silver on his body will have worries and grief, or will be arrested and tied up." See a similar interpretation in al-Hüseyni, *Kenzül-menām,* pp. 774–80.

38. Al-Nābulusi, *Taʿṭīr al-ānām* (Dar al-khayr edition), pp. 35, 165, 206, 234, 333, 427, 440; al-Qayrawāni, *Kitāb bulūgh al-marām,* folio 35: If one sees a snake coming out of his penis, he will provide for *(yarzuq)* a child. Compare with al-Hüseyni, *Kenzül-menām,* pp. 838–39.

39. Al-Nābulusi, *Taʿṭīr al-ānām.*

40. Ibid., p. 438.

41. Al-Nābulusi, *Taʿṭīr al-ānām* (Dar al-khayr edition), pp. 449, 457. See also Somogyi, "Interpretation of Dreams," pp. 4–10.

42. Al-Nābulusi, *Taʿṭīr al-ānām* (Dar al-khayr edition), pp. 58, 312.

43. Al-Qayrawāni, *Kitāb bulūgh al-marām,* folio 33b. Another alternative altogether is presented by Imam Jaʿfar's book of dream interpretation, in which animals are never symbols of men or women: M. Hidayet Hosain, "A Treatise on the Interpretation of Dreams," *Islamic Culture* 6 (1932): 578–82.

44. Al-Nābulusi, *Taʿṭīr al-ānām* (Dar al-khayr edition), pp. 60, 83, 159.

45. Artemidorus, *Interpretation of Dreams,* pp. 74–75.

46. Ibid., pp. 83, 85, 174, 304, 305, 387, 388; Aḥmad Mughniyya, *Tafsīr al-Aḥlām* (Beirut: Dar al-Hilal, 1979), pp. 220. See also Mughniyya, *Tafsīr al-Aḥlām,* pp. 279, 292, 294, 313, 350; and Artemidorus in Ibn Isḥāq, *Kitāb Taʿbīr al-ru'yā,* pp. 150–51, 163.

47. Janice Boddy, "Spirits and Selves in Northern Sudan: The Cultural Therapeutics of Possession and Trance," *American Ethnologist* 15, no. 1 (1988): 4–27. On women as receptacles for male sperm, see also Oberhelman, "Hierarchies of Gender," p. 69.

48. Boddy, "Spirits and Selves," pp. 5–6.

49. Artemidorus in Ibn Isḥāq, *Kitāb Taʿbīr al-ru'yā,* p. 78; Artemidorus, *Interpretation of Dreams,* pp. 66–67.

50. Al-Nābulusi, *Taʿṭīr al-ānām* (Dar al-khayr edition), p. 159. See also Mughniyya, *Tafsīr al-Aḥlām,* p. 98; al-Qayrawāni, *Kitāb bulūgh al-marām,* folio 22; and al-Hüseyni, *Kenzül-menām,* p. 540.

51. Al-Nābulusi, *Taʿṭīr al-ānām* (Dar al-khayr edition), p. 159.

52. Ibid., p. 160.

53. In late Ottoman and Arab folklore, the *ḥammām* is inhabited by Satan, just as mosques and graveyards are inhabited by angels.

54. Artemidorus in Ibn Isḥāq, *Kitāb Taʿbīr al-ru'yā,* pp. 93–105.

55. Artemidorus, *Interpretation of Dreams,* pp. 84–85.

56. In the original, this heading referred to sexual relations with gods and goddesses.

57. Artemidorus in Ibn Isḥāq, *Kitāb Taʿbīr al-ru'yā,* pp. 99–103; al-Hüseyni, *Kenzül-menām,* p. 437.

58. See Peter Brown, *The Body and Society: Men, Women, and Sexual Renunciation in Early Christianity* (New York: Columbia University Press, 1988), p. 432: "What had worried ancient Romans was that a free man might upset the stern civic hierarchy that separated him from a woman by indulging in oral sex with her, or by offering himself, like a woman, to be penetrated by his lover."

59. Oberhelman claims that this section on oral sex was not translated, but this part is clearly the translation, albeit considerably shortened and censored. "Hierarchies of Gender," p. 68.

60. Artemidorus in Ibn Isḥāq, *Kitāb Taʿbīr al-ru'yā,* pp. 103–6.

61. Ibid., pp. 106–7.

62. Brown, *Body and Society,* p. 19. See also Basim Musallam, *Sex and Society in Islam: Birth Control before the Nineteenth Century* (Cambridge: Cambridge University Press, 1983).

63. Ibn Sīrīn, *Tafsīr al-aḥlām al-kabīr.*

64. Hosain, "A Treatise on the Interpretation of Dreams"; al-Qayrawāni, *Kitāb bulūgh al-marām.*

65. Al-Nābulusi, *Taʿṭīr al-ānām* (Dar al-khayr edition), pp. 234, 236, 415, 458.

66. See Joseph Schacht, *An Introduction to Islamic Law* (Oxford: Clarendon Press, 1984 [1964]), pp. 120–22.

67. Al-Nābulusi, *Taʿṭīr al-ānām* (Dar al-khayr edition), p. 484.

68. Echoes of this are to be found in al-Hüseyni, *Kenzül-menām,* p. 437.

69. Here is part of al-Nābulusi's discussion of adultery:

*Zinā'* [adultery] in a dream is treason *[khiyānah]* and whoever sees himself fornicating has committed treason. An unknown woman is [in this respect] better and stronger than the known one. Adultery is also theft, because the adulterous hides like a thief. Whoever sees an adulterous woman coming to seduce him *[turāwiduhu 'an nafsihi]* has partaken of forbidden property. He who [dreams of having] committed adultery with a pretty girl *[shābbah ḥasnā']* has put his money in a safe place. A sultan dreaming of committing adultery and receiving the *ḥadd* punishment for it will strengthen his government. And if the dreamer anticipates a position of government, he will take office and the cloak shall be bestowed on him, and he will rule a province, but will rule it unjustly. And if one dreams of fornication with the wife of someone that he knows, [this indicates that the dreamer?] wants to take money from [the husband?]. Whoever dreams of having read the verse on the adulterer and the adulteress [in the Koran] is an adulterer himself. So also is the woman who has read this verse. Business with an adulterous woman in the dream signifies this world of sin and its seekers *[al-dunya waṭulābuha]*. (p. 234)

70. It is interesting to note that, perhaps for lack of a specific verb denoting homoerotic intercourse, al-Nābulusi uses the verb *nakaḥa* throughout this discussion of *liwāṭ*.

71. Al-Nābulusi, *Ta'ṭīr al-ānām* (Bulāq edition), p. 201. This heading was censored in the modern edition, and also in al-Hüseyni, *Kenzül-menām*, written at the beginning of the twentieth century.

72. Al-Nābulusi, *Ta'ṭīr al-ānām* (Bulāq edition), p. 483.

73. This is evident throughout books such as al-Hüseyni's *Kenzül-menām* and Mughniyya's *Tafsīr al-Aḥlām*, in which there is almost no mention of the long discussions of *liwāṭ*, for instance. See also 'Abd al-Fattāḥ al-Sayyid Al-Tūkhi, *Ta'bīr al-manām wa-tafsīr al-aḥlām* (Beirut: Al-Maktaba al-Thaqāfiyya, 1992).

## CHAPTER 5. BOYS IN THE HOOD

1. Mikhail Bakhtin, *Rabelais and His World* (Bloomington: Indiana University Press, 1984), p. 10; Bakhtin, *L'Oeuvre de François Rabelais et la culture populaire au Moyen Age et sous la Renaissance* (Paris: Gallimard, 1970).

2. Bakhtin, *Rabelais and His World*, p. 10.

3. Bakhtin, *L'Oeuvre de François Rabelais*, pp. 18–20.

4. For a good summary of critiques, see Peter Stallybrass and Allon White, *The Politics and Poetics of Transgression* (Ithaca, NY: Cornell University Press, 1986). For a thorough application of these approaches to an Islamic medieval culture, see Boaz Shoshan, *Popular Culture in Medieval Cairo* (Cambridge: Cambridge University Press, 1993), pp. 47–48.

5. Nicholas N. Martinovitch, *The Turkish Theatre* (New York: Benjamin Blom, 1968 [1933]), pp. 38–39. For descriptions of the stage and the screen, see also Sabri Esat Siyavuşgil, *Karagöz: Its History, Its Characters, Its Mystical and Satirical Spirit* (Istanbul: Milli Eğitim Basımevi, 1961), p. 2; Cevdet Kudret, *Karagöz* (Ankara: Bilgi Yayınevi, 1968), vol. 1, p. 48; and Metin And, *Karagöz: Theatre d'ombres Turc* (Ankara: Dost Yayınları, 1977), p. 75 (an English version exists as well). A detailed description is also given by Evliya Çelebi in the seventeenth century: *Seyahatname* (Istanbul: Ekdam Matbaasi, 1314H), vol. 1, p. 654.

6. The possibility of Jewish influence on, and participation in, the art of the shadow play is also suggested by Pocqueville, who traveled to the Ottoman Empire in the late eighteenth century: "Between the acts they often give the representation of a Jewish funeral, the procession of which is closed by a pieman announcing his commodities in the Portuguese language, which is that spoken by the Jews of Constantinople." F. C. H. L. Pocqueville, *Travels through the Morea, Albania, and Several Other Parts of the Ottoman Empire, to Constantinople* (London: Richard Philips, 1806), p. 134.

7. And, *Karagöz,* pp. 31–66. The passage is quoted from Ibn Iyās, *Kitāb tārīkh Miṣr al-mashhūr bi-badāyiʿ al-zuhūr fi waqā'iʿ al-duhūr* (Cairo: Bulāq, 1311–12H [1896]), vol. 3, pp. 125, 133. See also Kudret, *Karagöz,* vol. 1, pp. 7–11; Martinovitch, *Turkish Theatre,* pp. 31–32; Siyavuşgil, *Karagöz,* pp. 4–12; and Andreas Tietze, *The Turkish Shadow Theater and the Puppet Collection of the L. A. Mayer Memorial Foundation* (Berlin: Mann, 1977), p. 18.

8. J. Theodore Bent, ed., *Early Voyages and Travels in the Levant* (New York: Burt Franklin, 1893), p. 215.

9. Referring to Priapus, the Greek god known for his huge penis. In Lampsacus, a city in northwestern Anatolia, he was the most revered deity.

10. Pocqueville, *Travels,* p. 134. Even in the mid-nineteenth century, when most of the plays were censored, Charles White commented: "The pantomime and dialogue of the performers are beyond all endurance obscene. They would disgust the most abandoned of our most profligate classes. The tolerance of these spectacles, which abound during the nights of Ramazan, throw great discredit upon the Turkish police, and inspire strangers with a most degrading opinion of the morality of the people, the more so since half the spectators are youths or children; nay, the exhibition is sometimes demanded by and permitted in the harems of the wealthy." White, *Three Years in Constantinople* (London: Henry Colburn, 1846), vol. 1, pp. 121–22. A French traveler at around the same time expressed a similar opinion: "Cette pièce consacrée par la tradition, se mélange d'impudicités dégoûtantes et de mordantes railleries, est presque la seule manifestation du génie populaire en Turquie, et son unique création théâtrale." Charles Roland, *La Turquie contemporaine, hommes et choses* (Paris: Pagnerre, 1854), p. 144.

11. At the time of the story, Istanbul (Constantinople) was still held by the Byzantines.

12. Çelebi, *Seyāhatnāme,* vol. 1, pp. 652–53.

13. Selim Nüzhet, *Türk Temaşası: Meddah—Karagöz—Ortaoyunu* (Istanbul: Matbaai Ebüzziya, 1930), pp. 63–64. See also Tietze, *Turkish Shadow Theater,* pp. 18–19.

14. Kudret, *Karagöz,* p. 43.

15. Translation from Siyavuşgil, *Karagöz,* p. 30. See similar poems in Nüzhet, *Türk Temaşası,* p. 64.

16. One of the most famous poems was written by none other than Al-Nābulusi:

> I see shadow theater as the greatest lesson
> For him who excels in the science of truth.
> Apparitions and ghosts pass and disappear
> And vanish quickly while the puppeteer remains. (Nüzhet, *Türk Temaşası,* p. 64)

On the idea of the imaginal world *('ālam al-mithāl),* see chapter 4.

17. Siyavuşgil, *Karagöz;* Martinovitch, *Turkish Theatre,* pp. 35–36.

18. E.W. Lane, *Manners and Customs of the Modern Egyptians* (London: J.M. Dent and Sons, 1954), p. 397.

19. And, *Karagöz,* p. 73. There are several versions of *muhavere;* most popular is the "*gel-geç muhaveresi,*" in which Karagöz and Hacivat chase each other from one end of the screen to the other, exchanging puns. See also Tietze, *Turkish Shadow Theatre,* p. 25. Tietze suggests that *muhaveres* are relics of an older stage, when only short scenes were staged.

20. Tietze, *Turkish Shadow Theatre,* pp. 22–23.

21. Hellmut Ritter, *Karagös, Türkische Schattenspiele* (Hanover: Orient-Buchhandlung H. Lafaire, 1924).

22. Ignacz Kunos, *Három Karagöz-Játék* (Budapest: n.p., 1886); Ignacz Kunos, *Türk kavimleri halk edebiyatlarından örnekler* (Petersburg: n.p., 1899).

23. *Mecmua-i Hayāl* (Istanbul: Cihan matbaası, 1325 [1909]); *Letāif-i hayāl* (Istanbul: n.p., n.d.); *Şarkili ve kantolu Karagöz kitabı* (Istanbul: Asya Kütüphanesi, 1325 [1909]); Behriç ve Salıh Efendiler, *Hayal yahut Karagöz'ün son perdesi* (Istanbul: Kader matbaası, 1325 [1909]).

24. Hayalī Memduh, *Karagöz perdesi Kulliyātı* (Istanbul: Necm-i Istikbal matbaası, 1338–40 [1922]). Hayalī Küçük Ali also produced voice recordings with the help of Ilhan Başgöz (Ankara: Milli Kütüphane Müzik Bölümü Arşivi).

25. Having compared some the texts of Hellmut Ritter's *Karagös* and Cevdet Kudret's *Karagöz,* I concluded that there are no serious differences between them. I therefore decided to use Kudret's text, which was more easily accessible.

26. On the influence of Molière on Karagöz plays even in the 1840s, see Adolphe Thalasso, *Le théâtre turc: Molière et le théâtre de Karagueuz* (Paris: Editions de l'avenir dramatique et littéraire, n.d.).

27. Kudret, *Karagöz,* vol. 1, pp. 63–137, 169–214. *Abdal Bekçi* was translated by Tietze as "The Muddleheaded Night Watchman" (Tietze, *Turkish Shadow Theater,* pp. 41–60).

28. Kudret, *Karagöz,* vol. 1, pp. 178–79.

29. Ibid., p. 304; and *Karagöz,* pp. 85–86.

30. "A l'époque ou les règlements de police ordonnaient pour la première fois qu'on ne put sortir sans lanterne après la chute du jour, Karagöz parut avec une lanterne singulièrement suspendue, narguant impunément le pouvoir, parce que l'ordonnance n'avait pas dit que la lanterne dut enfermer une bougie. Arrêté par les gardes et relâché, d'après la légalité de son observation, on le vit reparaître avec une lanterne ornée d'une bougie, qu'il avait négligé d'allumer. Karagöz se permet la liberté de parole, il défie toujours l'injustice, le sabre et la corde." Gerard de Nerval, *Voyage en Orient* (Paris: Gallimard, 1998), p. 622. See also Sotiris Spatharis, *Behind the White Screen* (London: Magazine Editions, 1967), p. 27.

31. Kudret, *Karagöz,* vol. 1, p. 308 *(Büyük Evlenme).*

32. Ibid., pp. 308, 310. In the play *Ceşme,* the accusation that Karagöz's wife is a whore is made by Hacivat's wife: ibid., vol. 2, pp. 17–21. See also pp. 37, 137.

33. And, *Karagöz,* p. 86; Siyavuşgil, *Karagöz,* pp. 22–23; Tietze, *Turkish Shadow Theatre,* p. 27.

34. Martinovitch, *Turkish Theatre,* p. 41.
35. Siyavuşgil, *Karagöz,* pp. 20–29; And, *Karagöz,* pp. 26–34.
36. Siyavuşgil, *Karagöz,* pp. 20–21.
37. Ibid., p. 16.
38. *Kanunname-i Ceza* (1274H), manuscript, Süleymaniye Library, Hidiv Ismail Paşa no. 157.
39. Everett K. Rowson, "Two Homoerotic Narratives from Mamlūk Literature: Al-Safadi's Lawʿat al-shākī and Ibn Dāniyāl's al-Mutayyam," in *Homoeroticism in Classical Arabic Literature,* ed. J. W. Wright Jr. and Everett K. Rowson (New York: Columbia University Press, 1997), pp. 159–91. See also Amila Butrovic, "Sociology of Popular Drama in Medieval Egypt: Ibn Daniyal and His Shadow Plays" (Ph.D. dissertation, McGill University, 1994).
40. Stallybrass and White, *Politics and Poetics of Transgression,* p. 82.
41. Tietze, *Turkish Shadow Theater,* p. 20. Coffeehouses were established in the mid-sixteenth century. Tobacco smoking became popular at the beginning of the following century.
42. For an interesting description of a Karagöz play shown in a coffeehouse, see Siyavuşgil, *Karagöz,* pp. 16–17.
43. For a survey of medieval literature as it pertains to matters of gender and sex, see Fedwa Malti-Douglas, *Woman's Body, Woman's Word: Gender and Discourse in Arabo-Islamic Writing* (Princeton, NJ: Princeton University Press, 1991), chapters 2–5.
44. Annemarie Schimmel, "Eros—Heavenly and Not So Heavenly—in Sufi Literature and Life," in *Society and the Sexes in Medieval Islam,* ed. Afaf Marsot (Malibu, CA: Undena Publications, 1979), pp. 19–41.
45. Kudret, *Karagöz,* vol. 1, pp. 81–87.
46. Ibid., p. 247; vol. 2, pp. 119–20, 127, 310.
47. Ibid., vol. 1, p. 114 *(ağalık);* p. 208 *(Bahçe);* pp. 303, 323, 330 *(Buyük Evlenme)*; pp. 339–40, 352 *(Canbazlar);* vol. 2, pp. 26, 32 *(Çeşme);* pp. 127, 129 *(Ferhad ile Şirin);* pp. 311, 319–20 *(Kanlı Nigar);* p. 390 *(Kayık);* pp. 483, 488 *(Meyhane);* vol. 3, p. 38 *(Sahte Esirci);* pp. 113, 169 *(Sünnet);* p. 320 *(Timarhane).*
48. See also And, *Karagöz,* p. 80.
49. Kudret, *Karagöz,* vol. 1, pp. 323–24.
50. Rowson, "Two Homoerotic Narratives from Mamlūk Literature."
51. See Butrovic, "Sociology of Popular Drama," chapter 5.
52. Kudret, *Karagöz,* vol. 1, p. 163 *(Aşçılık);* pp. 197–98 *(Bahçe);* pp. 297–320 *(Büyük Evlenme);* vol. 2, pp. 197–232 *(Hamam);* vol. 3, pp. 9–46 *(Sahte Esirci);* pp. 269–303 *(Ters Evlenme).* See also Siyavuşgil, *Karagöz,* p. 37.
53. Dror Wahrman, "Percy's Prologue: From Gender Play to Gender Panic in Eighteenth Century England," *Past and Present* 159 (1998): 113–60.
54. Ibid., p. 121.
55. Ibid., pp. 164–67.
56. Tietze, *Turkish Shadow Theater,* p. 18; Kudret, *Karagöz,* vol. 1, p. 40.
57. Nerval, *Voyage en Orient,* pp. 619–20.
58. Théofile Gautier, *Constantinople,* trans. Robert Howe Gould (New York: Henry Holt, 1875), p. 170.

59. Kudret, *Karagöz,* vol. 1, p. 290 *(Bursalı Leyla);* vol. 2, p. 412 *(Kirginlar).*

60. Ibid., vol. 2, p. 36 *(Çeşme);* vol. 2, pp. 537–69 *(Ortaklar).*

61. Ibid., vol. 1, pp. 308–309 *(Büyük Evlenme).*

## CHAPTER 6. THE VIEW FROM WITHOUT

1. Unaware of the subtext of their own writing, many authors are oblivious to their own gender and sexual biases, which become evident through this way of categorizing East and West.

2. For a partial description of this literature, see Carter Vaughn Findley, "An Ottoman Occidentalist in Europe: Ahmed Midhat Meets Madame Gülnar," *American Historical Review* 103, no. 1 (February 1998): 15.

3. Irvin Cemil Schick, *The Erotic Margin: Sexuality and Spaciality in Alteritist Discourse* (London: Verso, 1999), p. 13. See also Rudi C. Bleys, *The Geography of Perversion: Male-to-Male Sexual Behavior Outside the West and the Ethnographic Imagination, 1750–1918* (New York: New York University Press, 1995), p. 269.

4. Edward Seymour Forster, trans., *The Letters of Ogier Ghiselin de Busbeq* (Oxford: Clarendon Press, 1968), p. 117.

5. George Sandys, *Sandys Travails, Containing a History of the Original and Present State of the Turkish Empire,* 5th edition (London: R. and W. Laybourn, 1657), p. 57.

6. J. Theodore Bent, ed., *Early Voyages and Travels in the Levant* (New York: Burt Franklin, 1893), p. 15. See also William Joseph Grelot, *A Late Voyage to Constantinople* (London: Printed by John Playford, 1683), p. 39.

7. Grelot, *A Late Voyage to Constantinople,* p. 9. See also Grelot's very impartial description of the *ḥammām,* pp. 190–96.

8. Bleys, *Geography of Perversion,* pp. 18–24.

9. Paul Rycaut, *The Present State of the Ottoman Empire* (1668; reprint, Frankfurt: Institute for the History of Arabic-Islamic Science, 1995), p. 33. See also p. 31.

10. See chapter 3.

11. Rycaut, *Present State,* pp. 33, 148–49.

12. Ibid., p. 153.

13. Billie Melman, *Women's Orients: English Women and the Middle East, 1718–1918* (Basingstoke: Macmillan, 1995), p. 62.

14. François, Baron de Tott, *Memoirs* (1785; facsimile, New York: Arno Press, 1973), vol. 2, p. 130.

15. Ibid., vol. 1, p. 162. For a description of male chauvinism and double standards, see F. C. H. L. Pocqueville, *Travels through the Morea, Albania, and Several Other Parts of the Ottoman Empire, to Constantinople* (London: Richard Philips, 1806), p. 135.

16. Melman, *Women's Orients,* pp. 77–98.

17. White, *Three Years in Constantinople* (London: Henry Colburn, 1846). For similar views, see Warrington W. Smyth, *A Year with the Turks* (New York: Redfield, 1854), pp. 234–35; J. V. C. Smith, *Turkey and the Turks* (Boston: James

French, 1854), pp. 24–26 (who also presents very different views in later pages); and James De Kay, *Sketches of Turkey in 1831 and 1832* (New York: J. and J. Harper, 1833), pp. 263–69. Such positive views about Ottoman morality seem to have been common among travelers from the United States of America. De Kay, for instance, an American who traveled to the Eastern Mediterranean in 1831, goes to the other extreme. Watching a performance of cross-dressing dancing boys, he compares them, without flinching, to old dances in England and Spain, completely ignoring the transgressive aspect of the dance (p. 330).

18. White, *Three Years in Constantinople,* vol. 1, p. 306.

19. For more on Slade, see Bernard Lewis, *The Emergence of Modern Turkey* (London: Oxford University Press, 1968), p. 125. Other travelers who express similar views include Walter Colton, *Land and Lee in the Bosphorus and Aegean* (New York: D. W. Evans, 1860). Though seemingly not perturbed by homoerotic discourse as Slade was, a recurring theme in French travelers' accounts concerns the deep immorality of Karagöz plays. See chapter 5.

20. Adolphus Slade, *Records of Travels in Turkey, Greece, etc., and of a Cruise in the Black Sea with the Capitan Pasha, in the Years 1829, 1830 and 1831* (London: Saunders and Otley, 1832), vol. 2, p. 243.

21. Ibid., vol. 2, p. 294.

22. Ibid., vol. 1, p. 209. King Henry III of France (1574–1588) was reputed to have had homosexual tendencies and to have kept a number of favorites on whom he showered lavish presents.

23. Slade refers here to the great Köprülü family of grand viziers, who ruled the Ottoman Empire from the 1650s to the beginning of the following century.

24. Slade, *Records of Travels,* vol. 1, p. 231.

25. Ibid., vol. 2, p. 395. A similar description of debauchery in the ranks of the bureaucracy is given in L. P. B. D'Aubignosc, *La Turquie nouvelle, jugée au point ou l'ont amenées les réformes du sultan Mahmoud* (Paris: Librairie de Delloye, 1839), pp. 277–97. D'Aubignosc discusses this debauchery in general terms, without referring to homeroticism. Being scandalized by male dancers was not limited to "righteous" travelers such as Slade. One excellent description of the shocked Western tourist confronted by *khawals* is provided by Nerval, traveling in 1843, who describes a dance performance, and only toward the end of the description reveals as masculine what up to that point was described as feminine: Gerard de Nerval, *Voyage en Orient* (Paris: Gallimard, 1998), pp. 202–4.

26. The *kapıcı başı,* or head gatekeeper, was a senior official in the Ottoman hierarchy.

27. Slade, *Records of Travels,* vol. 1, p. 473.

28. Colton, *Land and Lee,* pp. 159–60; another example is in D'Aubignosc, *La Turquie nouvelle,* pp. 319–30. For an almost diametrically opposed view, see De Kay, *Sketches of Turkey,* p. 266: "The advantage on the score of morality, to say nothing of propriety, is much in favor of the Moslem."

29. For another description of the Ottoman poor succumbing sexually to the power of the mighty, see R. Walsh, *A Residence at Constantinople* (London: Richard Bentley, 1838), p. 9. For a similar description of immorality related to Karagöz plays, see Charles Roland, *La Turquie contemporaine, hommes et choses* (Paris: Pagnerre, 1854), pp. 146–47.

30. Mohamad Tavakoli-Targhi, "Imagining Western Women: Occidentalism and Euro-Eroticism," *Radical America* 3, no. 24 (1994): 73–76. See also Afsaneh Najmabadi, *Women with Mustaches and Men without Beards: Gender and Sexual Anxieties of Iranian Modernity* (Berkeley and Los Angeles: University of California Press, 2005).

31. Tavakoli-Targhi, "Imagining Western Women," pp. 72–80.

32. See, for example, Fatima Müge Göçek, *East Encounters West: France and the Ottoman Empire in the Eighteenth Century* (New York: Oxford University Press, 1987), p. 25. For a later observation, see Cemal Kutay, *Sultan Abdülaziz'in Avrupa Siyahatı* (Istanbul, Bogazici Yayınları, 1991), p. 37. This is the travelogue of Ömer Faiz Efendi, who accompanied Sultan Abdülaziz on his trip to Europe in 1867. He frequently mentions his impressions of women and men mixing together in receptions and balls but never registers surprise or shock.

33. Göçek, *East Encounters West,* pp. 117–19.

34. Ibid., p. 45. Such views are repeated in many travelogues until the end of the nineteenth century. See Sadık Rıfat Paşa, "Avrupa Ahvaline Dair Risâle," in *Müntehabât-ı Âsâr* (Istanbul: Tatyos Divitçiyan Publishing, 1874), vol. 2, pp. 2–12; Mustafa Sami, *Avrupa Risalesi* (Istanbul: n.p., 1840), p. 40; and *Seyahatnâme-i Londra* (Istanbul: Ceride-i Havâdis Publishing, 1269 Rumî [1853]), p. 92.

35. Findley, "Ottoman Occidentalist," p. 17.

36. The printing press was introduced into the Ottoman Empire first during the Tulip era, in the early 1700s, but was soon discarded. Apart from enterprises by non-Muslims in other languages and a few local presses, mainly in Lebanon, stable, long-term printing presses were not established until the early nineteenth century in Istanbul and Cairo. See G. W. Shaw, "Maṭbʿa," in *Encyclopedia of Islam,* 2nd edition (Leiden: Brill, 1960–2002), vol. 6, p. 794b. Göçek, *East Encounters West,* pp. 108–15. The fact that many books were translated from English and French into Turkish is well known. For Lewis's remarks (based on N. W. Senior, *Journal Kept in Turkey and Greece in the Autumn of 1857 and the Beginning of 1858* [London: Longman, Brown, Green, Longmans and Roberts, 1859], p. 36) that Slade's book was read in Turkey at the time, see *Emergence of Modern Turkey,* pp. 144, 173.

37. Christoph Herzog and Raoul Motika, "Orientalism alla Turca: Late 19th/Early 20th Century Ottoman Voyages into the Muslim 'Outback,'" *Die Welt des Islams* 40, no. 2 (July 2000): 139–95.

38. Ahmet Midhat, *Avrupa'da bir Cevelan* (Istanbul: Tercüman-i Hakikat Publishing, 1308 Rumî [1892]). Findley, "Ottoman Occidentalist," p. 19.

39. Midhat, *Avrupa'da bir Cevelan,* p. 1017. See also Findley, "Ottoman Occidentalist," p. 46.

40. Jurji Zaydān, *Riḥlat Jurji Zaydān ila Urūba* (Cairo: Dār al-hilāl, 1923), pp. 41–42. A few years earlier, Fāris Shidyāq wrote similar things about European women, concluding that women in the Islamic world were far superior in morality and upbringing. See Nazik Saba Yared, *Arab Travellers and Western Civilization* (London: Saqi Books, 1996), p. 52. See also Qāsim Amīn, *Al-mar'a al-jadida* (Cairo: Maṭbaʿat al-maʿārif, 1900).

41. Muḥammad Kurd ʿAli, writing a few years later, has a more favorable

view of European women and their liberties, but admits that these values cannot, in the present state of affairs, be imitated by the Arab East. "This would be tantamount to a sick man, who is in need of medicine, but instead of a few grains, is given a whole *ruṭl* of it, which may kill him. We should adopt these customs gradually." *'Ajā'ib al-Gharb* (Cairo: Al-matba'a al-raḥmāniyya, 1923), p. 186.

42. Mehmed Enisi, *Avrupa Hatiratım* (Istanbul: Ebüziyya, 1327 [1911]), pp. 116–18.

43. Ibid. See also *Seyahatnâme-i Londra,* p. 92; and Celal Nuri, *Kutup Musahabeleri* (Istanbul: Yeni Osmanlı, 1331 [1915]), as quoted in Baki Asiltürk, *Osmanlı seyyahlarının Gozūyle Avrupa* (Istanbul: Kaknūs Yayınları, 2000), p. 434.

44. Bernard S. Cohn, *Colonialism and Its Forms of Knowledge: The British in India* (Princeton, NJ: Princeton University Press, 1996), p. 4.

45. Ibid., pp. 4, 162; Bernard Cohn, "The Census, Social Structure and Objectification in South East Asia," in *An Anthropologist among the Historians and Other Essays* (Delhi: Oxford University Press, 1987), pp. 228–31. See also Timothy Mitchell, "The Stage of Modernity," in *Questions of Modernity*, ed. Timothy Mitchell (Minneapolis: University of Minnesota Press, 2000), pp. 16–20.

46. Herzog and Motika, "Orientalism alla Turca," pp. 152–153, 179–80.

47. Ahmed Cevdet Paşa, *Ma'rūzāt,* ed. Yusuf Halaçoğlu (Istanbul: Çağrıı Yayıları, 1980), p. 9. Āli Paşa was grand vizier and a famous reformer.

48. Ibid.

# Bibliography

## MANUSCRIPTS

Al-Amāsi, Sinān al-Dīn Yūsuf. *Tabyīn al-maḥārim.* Princeton University, Firestone Library, Hitti Cat. no. 927.

Anon. *Asās sirr al-akyās.* Princeton University, Garrett Collection, Yahuda Section, folios 27b–41b.

*Ceza Kanunname-i Hümayun.* Arabic version, Süleymaniye Library, Hüsrev Paşa no. 826.

Al-Dajjāni, Abu al-Fatḥ. *Al-ʿiqd al-mufrad fi maḥabbat al-amrad.* Princeton University, Firestone Cat. no. 1952.

Ibn Sallūm, Ṣāliḥ Ibn Naṣrallah. *Ghāyat al-Itqān fi Tadbīr Badan al-Insān (The Greatest Thoroughness in Treatment of the Human Body).* Süleymaniye Library, Reşid Efendi 698 and Şehid Ali Paşa 2062.

Al-Isrā'īli, Al-Samaw'al bin Yaḥya al-Maghribi. *Nuzhat al-aṣḥāb fi muʿāsharat al-aḥbāb.* Bibliothèque Nationale, Paris, Manuscrits Arabes 3054, folios 1–185.

*Kanunname-i Ceza.* Süleymaniye Library, Hidiv Ismail Paşa no. 35, no. 157, and no. 121.

*Kiyafet Name.* Süleymaniye Library, B. Vehbi 918.

Muḥammad, Aḥmad bin. *Rushd al-labīb fi muʿāsharat al-ḥabīb.* Bibliothèque Nationale, Mss. Arabes 3051.

Al-Nābulusi, ʿAbd al-Ghani. *Al-ʿAbīr fi'l-taʿbīr.* Princeton University, Garrett Collection.

Al-Qayrawāni, Abu al-Ḥasan ʿAli Ibn al-Qassār al-Khawlāni. *Kitāb bulūgh al-marām fi taʿbīr al-ru'ya fi al-manām.* Bibliothèque Nationale, Paris, Manuscrits Arabes 2746.

PRINTED SOURCES

Adıvar, Adnan. *La science chez les turcs ottomans.* Paris: Maisonneuve, 1939.
———. *Osmanlı Türklerinde İlim.* Ankara: Remzi Kitabevi, 1982.
Ahmed, Leila. *Women and Gender in Islam.* New Haven, CT: Yale University Press, 1992.
Akgündüz, Ahmed. *Osmanlı Kanunnameler ve Hukuki Tahlileri.* Istanbul: Hilal Matbaası, 1992.
Algar, Hamid. "Reflections of Ibn ʿArabī in Early Nakshbandī Tradition." *Islami Araştırmalar* 5, no. 1 (January 1991): 1–20.
Ali, Muhammad Kurd. *ʿAjā'ib al-Gharb.* Cairo: Al-matbaʿa al-raḥmāniyya, 1923.
Ali, Mustafa. *Mevāʿidü n'nefa'is fi kavāʿidi l-mecālis.* Ed. C. Baysun. Istanbul: Osman Yalçın Matbaası, 1956.
Amīn, Qāsim. *Al-mar'a al-jadida.* Cairo: Maṭbaʿat al-maʿārif, 1900.
And, Metin. *Karagöz: Theatre d'ombres Turc.* Ankara: Dost Yayınları, 1977.
Artemidorus. *The Interpretation of Dreams: Oneirocritica.* Trans. Robert J. White. Torrance, CA: Original Books, 1975.
Asiltürk, Baki. *Osmanlı seyyahlarının Gozüyle Avrupa.* Istanbul: Kaknūs Yayınları, 2000.
ʿAwadalla, Ahmad al-Saba. *Dalil Tafsir al-aḥlam.* Cairo: N.p., 1949.
Bakhtin, Mikhail. *L'Oeuvre de François Rabelais et la culture populaire au Moyen Age et sous la Renaissance.* Paris: Gallimard, 1970.
———. *Rabelais and His World.* Bloomington: Indiana University Press, 1984.
Bardakçı, Murat. *Osmanlıda Seks: Sarayda Gece Dersleri.* Istanbul: Gür Yayınları, 1992.
Barkley, Henry C. *A Ride through Asia Minor and Armenia.* London: John Murray, 1891.
Al-Baṣri, Abi al-Ḥasan. *Al-ḥāwi al-kabīr fi fiqh madhhab al imām al-Shāfiʿi.* Beirut: Dār al-Kutub al-ʿIlmiyya, 1994.
Behriç ve Salıh, Efendiler. *Hayal yahut Karagöz'ün son perdesi.* Istanbul: Kader matbaası, 1325 [1909].
Bell, Joseph Norment. *Love Theory in Later Hanbalite Islam.* Albany: State University of New York Press, 1979.
Bellamy, James A. "Sex and Society in Islamic Popular Literature." In *Society and the Sexes in Medieval Islam,* ed. Afaf Marsot, pp. 23–42. Malibu, CA: Undena Publications, 1979.
Bent, J. Theodore, ed. *Early Voyages and Travels in the Levant.* New York: Burt Franklin, 1893.
Birge, John Kingsley. *The Bektashi Order of Dervishes.* London: Luzac, 1937.
Bleys, Rudi C. *The Geography of Perversion: Male-to-Male Sexual Behavior Outside the West and the Ethnographic Imagination, 1750–1918.* New York: New York University Press, 1995.
Bos, Gerrit. *Ibn al-Jazzār on Sexual Diseases and Their Treatment: A Critical Edition of Zad al-musāfir wa-qūt al-ḥādir.* London: Kegan Paul International, 1997.
Bosquet, G. H. *L'Ethique sexuelle de l'Islam.* Paris: G. P. Maisonneuve et Larousse, 1966.

Bouhdiba, Abdelwahab. *Sexuality in Islam.* London: Routledge and Kegan Paul, 1985.
Bourdieu, Pierre. *Outline of a Theory of Practice.* Cambridge: Cambridge University Press, 1992 [1972].
———. *Practical Reason: On the Theory of Action.* Cambridge: Polity Press, 1998.
Boyarin, Daniel. *Carnal Israel: Reading Sex in Talmudic Culture.* Berkeley and Los Angeles: University of California Press, 1995.
Brown, Peter. *The Body and Society: Men, Women, and Sexual Renunciation in Early Christianity.* New York: Columbia University Press, 1988.
———. *Power and Persuasion in Late Antiquity: Toward a Christian Empire.* Madison: University of Wisconsin Press, 1992.
Butrovic, Amila. "Sociology of Popular Drama in Medieval Egypt: Ibn Daniyal and His Shadow Plays." Ph.D. dissertation, McGill University, 1994.
Cadden, Joan. *Meanings of Sex Difference in the Middle Ages: Medicine, Science and Culture.* New York: Cambridge University Press, 1993.
Celentano, Giuseppe. *Due Scritti Medici di Al-Kindi.* Naples: Instituto Orientale di Napoli, 1979.
Cevdet Paşa, Ahmed. *Maʿrūzāt.* Ed. Yusuf Halaçoğlu. Istanbul: Çağri Yayınları, 1980.
Chittick, William C. *The Self-Disclosure of God: Principles of Ibn al-ʿArabi's Cosmology.* Albany: State University of New York Press, 1998.
———. *The Sufi Path of Knowledge.* Albany: State University of New York Press, 1989.
Cohn, Bernard S. "The Census, Social Structure and Objectification in South East Asia." In *An Anthropologist among the Historians and Other Essays*, pp. 228–31. Delhi: Oxford University Press, 1987.
———. *Colonialism and Its Forms of Knowledge: The British in India.* Princeton, NJ: Princeton University Press, 1996.
Colton, Walter. *Land and Lee in the Bosphorus and Aegean.* New York: D. W. Evans, 1860.
Combs-Schilling, M. E. *Sacred Performances: Islam, Sexuality, and Sacrifice.* New York: Columbia University Press, 1989.
Coulson, Noel J. "Regualtion of Sexual Behavior under Traditional Islamic Law." In *Society and the Sexes in Medieval Islam*, ed. Afaf Marsot, pp. 23–42. Malibu, CA: Undena Publications, 1979.
Dankoff, Robert. *The Intimate Life of an Ottoman Statesman.* Albany: State University of New York Press, 1991.
D'Aubignosc, L. P. B. *La Turquie nouvelle, jugée au point ou l'ont amenées les réformes du sultan Mahmoud.* Paris: Librairie de Delloye, 1839.
De Kay, James. *Sketches of Turkey in 1831 and 1832.* New York: J. and J. Harper, 1833.
Enisi, Mehmed. *Avrupa Hatiratım.* Istanbul: Ebüziyya,1327 [1911].
Erdoğan, Selma Nilgün. *Sexual Life in Ottoman Society.* Istanbul: Dönence, 1996.
Eşref bin Muḥammed. *Hazāʾinü's-saʿādāt.* Ankara: Türk Tarih Kurumu, 1960.
Evliya Çelebi. *Narrative of Travels in Europe, Asia and Africa in the Seventeenth* Century. Trans. Joseph von Hammer. London: Parbury, Allen, 1834.
———. *Seyāhatnāme.* Istanbul: Ekdam Matbaasi, 1314H.

Fahd, Toufy. *La divination Arabe*. Leiden: Brill, 1966.

Findley, Carter Vaughn. "An Ottoman Occidentalist in Europe: Ahmed Midhat Meets Madame Gülnar." *American Historical Review* 103, no. 1 (February 1998): 15–49.

Fleischer, Cornell. *Bureaucrat and Intellectual in the Ottoman Empire: The Historian Mustafa Ali (1541–1600)*. Princeton, NJ: Princeton University Press, 1986.

Forster, Edward Seymour, trans. *The Letters of Ogier Ghiselin de Busbeq*. Oxford: Clarendon Press, 1968.

Foucault, Michel. *The Birth of the Clinic*. London: Tavistock, 1973.

———. *The History of Sexuality*. New York: Pantheon Books, 1978.

———. *The History of Sexuality II: The Use of Pleasure*. London: Penguin Books, 1992 [1984].

Freud, Sigmund. *The Interpretation of Dreams*. London: Allen and Unwin, 1913.

Fromm, Erich. *The Forgotten Language: An Introduction to the Understanding of Dreams, Fairy Tales and Myths*. New York: Rinehart, 1951.

Gagnon, John. *Human Sexualities*. Glenview, IL: Scott, Foresman, 1977.

Gautier, Théofile. *Constantinople*. Trans. Robert Howe Gould. New York: Henry Holt, 1875.

Gerber, Haim. *State, Society and Law in Islam: Ottoman Law in Comparative Perspective*. Upper Saddle River, NJ: Pearson Addison Wesley, 2000.

Gilsenan, Michael. *Saint and Sufi in Modern Egypt: An Essay in the Sociology of Religion*. Oxford: Clarendon Press, 1973.

Göçek, Fatima Müge. *East Encounters West: France and the Ottoman Empire in the Eighteenth Century*. New York: Oxford University Press, 1987.

Gölpinarlı, Abdulbaki. *Melamilik ve Melamiler*. Istanbul: Devlet Matbaası, 1931.

Gorlin, Moris, ed. *Maimonides "On Sexual Discourse."* New York: Rambash Publishing, 1961.

Grelot, William Joseph. *A Late Voyage to Constantinople*. London: Printed by John Playford, 1683.

Haci Paşa. *Müntehab-ı Şifa*. Ed. Zafer Önler. Ankara: Türk Dil Korumu, 1990.

Hajji Khalifa. *Kashf al-ẓunūn. Lexicon bibliographicum et encyclopaedicum*. Arabic text with Latin translation by G. Flügle. 7 vols. Leipzig: R. Bentley for the Oriental Translation Fund of Great Britain and Ireland, 1835–58.

Al-Ḥalabi, Ibrāhim. *Multaqa al-abḥur*. Beirut: Mu'assassat al-Risāla, 1989.

Hallaq, Wael. "The Qadi's Diwan (Sijill) before the Ottomans." *Bulletin of the School of Oriental and African Studies* 61, no. 3 (1998): 416–36.

Halperin, David. "Is There a History of Sexuality?" *History and Theory* 23, no. 3 (1989): 257–74.

Hammoudi, Abdellah. *Master and Disciple: The Cultural Foundations of Moroccan Authoritarianism*. Chicago: University of Chicago Press, 1997.

Herzog, Christoph, and Raoul Motika. "Orientalism alla Turca: Late 19th/Early 20th Century Ottoman Voyages into the Muslim 'Outback.'" *Die Welt des Islams* 40, no. 2 (July 2000): 139–95.

Heyd, Uriel. "Kanun and Sharīʿa in Old Ottoman Criminal Justice." *Proceedings of the Israel Academy of Sciences and Humanities* 3, no. 1 (1967): 1–8.

———. *Studies in Old Ottoman Criminal Law.* Ed. V.L. Menage. Oxford: Clarendon Press, 1973.

Hiçyılmaz, Ergün. *Eski Istanbulda "Muhabbet."* Istanbul: Cep Kitapları, 1991.

Hodgson, Marshall G. S. *The Venture of Islam: Conscience and History in a World Civilization.* Chicago: University of Chicago Press, 1976.

Hosain, Hidayet M. "A Treatise on Interpretation of Dreams." *Islamic Culture* 6 (1932): 568–85.

Hurgronje, Snouck. "Les confreries religieuses, la Mecque et le Panislamisme." In *Verspreide Geschriften,* pp. 189–206. Bonn: Kurt Schroeder, 1923 [1900].

Al-Hüseyni, Sayyid Süleyman. *Kanzül-menām.* Istanbul: Kitabhane-i Sevdi, 1340H.

El-Hüseynī, Seyyid Süleyman (Cami ve müellifi). *Kenzü'l-Havass.* Istanbul: Demir Kitabevi, n.d.

Ibn ʿĀbidīn, *Radd al-muḥtār ʿala al-darr al-mukhtār.* Beirut: Dār Iḥya al-Turāth al-ʿArabi, n.d.

Ibn al-ʿArabi. "De la connaissance des songes." Trans. Ali Ridha Arfa. *Aux sources de la sagesse* 1, part 2 (1994): 35–68; 1, part 3 (1994): 41–68.

Ibn Isḥāq, Ḥunayn, trans. *Kitāb Taʿbīr al-ru'yā: Awwal wa-ahamm al-kutub fi tafsir al-aḥlām* (translation of Artemidorus's *Oneirocritica*). Ed. ʿAbd al-munʿim al-Ḥifni. Cairo: Dar al-Rashad, 1991.

Ibn Iyās. *Kitāb tārīkh Miṣr al-mashhūr bi-badāyiʿ al-zuhūr fi waqā'iʿ al-duhūr.* Cairo: Bulāq, 1311–12H [1896].

Ibn al-Jawzi, ʿAbd al-Raḥmān Ibn ʿAli. *Al-Nafīs fi takhrīj aḥādīth ṭalbīs iblīs.* Ed. Yaḥya bin Khālid bin Tawfīq. Cairo: Maktabat al-tarbiya al-Islāmīya, 1994.

Ibn Kamāl Pasha (Kemal Paşa Zade). *Rujūʿ al-shaykh ila sibāh fi al-quwwa ʿala al-bāh.* Cairo: Bulāq, 1309H.

Ibn Khaldūn. *The Muqaddimah: An Introduction to History.* Trans. Franz Rosenthal. Princeton, NJ: Princeton University Press, 1967.

Ibn Sīrīn, Muḥammad. *L'Interpretation des songes.* Beirut: Dar al-fikr, n.d.

———. *Tafsīr al-aḥlām al-kabīr.* Cairo: Maṭbaʿat al-Jalli, 1995.

Ibn Taymiyya, Taqi al-Dīn Aḥmad ʿAbd al-Ḥalīm. *Ḥijāb al-mar'a wa-libāsuha fi'l-Islām.* Cairo: n.p., [1974].

———. *Majmuʿ fatāwa shaykh al-islām Ahmad ibn Taymiyya.* Ed. ʿAbd al-Raḥmān Muḥammad Ibn Qāsim. Saudi Arabia: n.p., n.d.

Iloğlu (derleyen), Mustafa. *Gizli Ilimler Hazinesi.* Istanbul: Aktaş Matbaası, 1968.

Imber, Colin. *Ebu's-Su'ud: The Islamic Legal Tradition.* Stanford, CA: Stanford University Press, 1997.

———. "Zina in Ottoman Law." In *Studies in Ottoman History and Law,* pp. 174–206. Istanbul: Isis Press, 1996.

Al-ʿItāqi, Shams al-Dīn. *The Treatise on Anatomy of Human Body and Interpretation of Philosophers (Tashrīḥ al-abdān).* Trans. Esin Kahya. Islamabad: National Hijra Council, 1990.

Al-Jabarti, ʿAbd al-Rahmān. *ʿAjāyib al-āthār fi al-tarājim wa'l-akhbār.* Beirut: Dar al-Jalīl, n.d.

Al-Jawzīyya, Ibn Qayyim. *Akhbār Al-Nisā'.* Beirut: Dar Al-Fikr Al-Lubnani, 1990.

Kadizade Islamboli, Ahmed bin Muhammed Emin. *Cevhere-i Behiyye-i Ahmediyye fi şerhi vasiyet al Muhammediyye.* Üsküdar: n.p., 1218.

Kafadar, Cemal. *Between Two Worlds: The Construction of the Ottoman State.* Berkeley and Los Angeles: University of California Press, 1995.

Kahya, Esin, and Ayşegül D. Erdemir, *Bilimin Işiğinda Osmanlıdan Cumhuriyete Tıp ve Sağlık Kurumlari.* Ankara: Türkiye Diyanet Vakfi Yayinlari, 2000.

Katib Çelebi. *The Balance of Truth (Mizanül hakk).* Trans. G. L. Lewis. London: George Allen and Unwin, 1957.

Keykavus (Ilyasoğlu Mercimek, Ahmet). *Kābusname.* Ed. Atilla Özkırımlı. Istanbul: Milli Eğitim Basimevi, 1974.

Kilborne, B. "The Handling of Dream Symbolism: Aspects of Dream Interpretation in Morocco." *Psychoanalytic Study of Society* 9 (1981): 1–14.

Klūt, Antūn Bartīlīmī. *Durar al-Ghawal fi amrāḍ al-aṭfāl.* Cairo: Bulāq, 1260H [1844].

Klūt Bayk, Antun. *Kunūz al-Siḥḥa wa-yawāqīt al-minḥa.* Beirut: Dar Lubnan li'l-ṭibāʿa wa'l-nashr, 2004.

Knysh, Alexander. *Islamic Mysticism: A Short History.* Leiden: Brill, 2000.

Krippner, Stanley. "Waking Life, Dream Life, and the Construction of Reality." *Anthropology of Consciousness* 5, no. 3 (September 1994): 17–23.

Kudret, Cevdet. *Karagöz.* 3 vols. Ankara: Bilgi Yayınevi, 1992.

Kunos, Ignacz. *Három Karagöz-Játék.* Budapest: n.p., 1886.

———. *Türk kavimleri halk edebiyatlarından örnekler.* Petersburg: n.p., 1899.

Kurd ʿAli, Muḥammad. *ʿAjā'ib al-Gharb.* Cairo: Al-maṭbaʿa al-raḥmāniyya, 1923.

Kuru, Selim S. "A Sixteenth Century Scholar, Deli Birader, and his Dāfi'ü'l gumūm ve rafi'ü'l humūm." Ph.D. dissertation, Harvard University, May 2000.

Kutay, Cemal. *Sultan Abdülaziz'in Avrupa Siyahatı.* Istanbul: Boğazici Yayınları, 1991. (Travelogue of Ömer Faiz Efendi.)

Lamoreaux, John. "Dream Interpretation in the Early Medieval Near East." Ph.D. dissertation, Duke University, 1999.

Lane, E. W. *An Account of the Manners and Customs of the Modern Egyptians.* London: East-West Publications, 1989 [1836].

———. *Manners and Customs of the Modern Egyptians.* London: J. M. Dent and Sons, 1954.

Laqueur, Thomas. *Making Sex: Body and Gender from the Greeks to Freud.* Cambridge, MA: Harvard University Press, 1990.

*Letāif-i hayāl.* Istanbul: n.p., n.d.

Levtzion, Nehemia, and John Voll, eds. *Eighteenth-Century Renewal and Reform in Islam.* Syracuse, NY: Syracuse University Press, 1987.

Lewis, Bernard. *The Emergence of Modern Turkey.* London: Oxford University Press, 1968.

Lidner, Rudi. *Nomads and Ottomans in Medieval Anatolia.* Bloomington: Indiana University Press, 1983.

Lifchez, Raymond, ed. *The Dervish Lodge: Architecture, Art, and Sufism in Ottoman Turkey.* Berkeley and Los Angeles: University of California Press, 1992.

*Majmūʿ fatāwa shaykh al-islām Aḥmad ibn Taymiyya.* Collected by Abd al-Rahman Muhammad Ibn Qāsim. n.p., n.d.

Malti-Douglas, Fedwa. *Woman's Body, Woman's Word: Gender and Discourse in Arabo-Islamic Writing.* Princeton, NJ: Princeton University Press, 1991.

Maroth, Miklos. "The Science of Dreams in Islamic Culture." *Jerusalem Studies in Arabic and Islam* 20 (1996): 229–36.
Marsot, Afaf, ed. *Society and the Sexes in Medieval Islam.* Malibu, CA: Undena Publications, 1979.
Martinovitch, Nicholas N. *The Turkish Theatre.* New York: Benjamin Blom, 1968 [1933].
Al-Masri, Y. *Le drame sexuel de la femme dans l'Orient Arabe.* Paris: Lafont, 1962.
Matsuda, Matt K. *The Memory of the Modern.* New York: Oxford University Press, 1996.
Mawārdi, Ali Ibn Muḥammad. *Al-ḥāwi al-kabīr fi fiqh madhhab al-Imām al-Shāfiʿi, wahuwwa sharḥ mukhtār al-muzani.* Beirut: Dār Al-Kutub al-ʿIlmiyya, 1994.
*Mecmua-i Hayāl.* Istanbul: Cihan matbaası, 1325 [1909].
Melman, Billie. *Women's Orients: English Women and the Middle East, 1718–1918.* Basingstoke: Macmillan, 1995.
Memduh, Hayalī. *Karagöz perdesi Kulliyātı.* Istanbul: Necm-i Istikbal matbaası, 1338–40 [1922].
Mernissi, Fatima. *Al-sulūk al-jinsi fi mujtamaʿ Islāmi ra'smāli.* Beirut: Dār al-Ḥadātha, 1982.
Meyan, A. Faruk, ed. *Birgivi Vasiyetnamesi (Kadizade Şerhi).* Istanbul: Bedir Publishing, 1977.
Midhat, Ahmet. *Avrupa'da bir Cevelan.* Istanbul: Tercüman-i Hakikat Publishing, 1308 [1892].
Milson, M. *A Sufi Rule for Novices: Kitāb ādāb al-murīdīn of Abu al-Najīb al-Suhrawardi.* Cambridge, MA: Harvard University Press, 1975.
Mitchell, Timothy. "The Stage of Modernity." In *Questions of Modernity,* ed. Timothy Mitchell, pp. 16–20. Minneapolis: University of Minnesota Press, 2000.
Mourad, Youssef. *La physiognomie arabe et le kitāb al-firāsa de Fakhr al-Dīn al-Rāzi.* Paris: Librairie Orientaliste Paul Geuthner, 1939.
Mughniyya, Aḥmad. *Tafsīr al-Aḥlām.* Beirut: Dar al-Hilal, 1979.
Al-Muḥibbi, Muḥammad Amīn Ibn Faḍlallah. *Tārīkh Khulāṣat al-āthār fi Aʿyān al-qarn al-ḥādi ʿashar.* Cairo: Bulāq. 1284H.
*Muʿjam al-fiqh al-ḥanbali: Muʿjam al-mughni fi al-fiqh al-ḥanbali, mustakhlas min kitāb al-mughni li'ibn Qudāma.* Beirut: Dār al-Kutub al-ʿIlmiyya, 1973.
Al-Munajjid, Salāḥ al-Din. *Al-ḥayāt al-jinsiyya ʿind al-ʿArab.* Beirut: Dār al-kitāb al-jadīd, 1975 [1958].
Murray, Stephen O., and Will Roscoe, eds. *Islamic Homosexualities: Culture, History, and Literature.* New York: New York University Press, 1997.
Musallam, Basim. *Sex and Society in Islam: Birth Control before the Nineteenth Century.* Cambridge: Cambridge University Press, 1983.
Al-Nābulusi, ʿAbd al-Ghani. *Al-ʿAbīr fi al-taʿbīr fi uṣūl kayfiyat taʿbīr al-ru'ya fi al-manām.* Beirut: Mu'assasat ʿIzz al-Dīn, 1996.
———. *Taʿṭīr al-ānām fi taʿbīr al-manām.* Damascus: Dar al-khayr, 1998.
———. *Taʿṭīr al-ānām fi taʿbīr al-manām.* Cairo: Bulāq, n.d.
Al-Nafzawi, Al-Shaykh. *Al-Rawḍ al-ʿāṭir fi nuzhat al-khātir.* Ed. Jamāl Jumʿa. London: Riyad El-Rayyes Books, 1993.

Najmabadi, Afsaneh. *Women with Mustaches and Men without Beards: Gender and Sexual Anxieties of Iranian Modernity.* Berkeley and Los Angeles: University of California Press, 2005.

Al-Nawawi, Muḥyi al-Dīn Abu Zakariyya. *Kitāb al-majmūʿ: Sharḥ al-muhadhdhab li'l-Shirāzi.* Beirut: Dār al-Turāth al-ʿArabi, 1990.

Nerval, Gerard de. *Voyage en Orient.* Paris: Gallimard, 1998.

Niemeyer, Felix von. *Ilm-i emraz dahiliye.* Istanbul: Mekteb-i tibbiye-i askeriye matbaasi, 1300 [1882].

Nüzhet, Selim. *Türk Temaşası: Meddah—Karagöz—Ortaoyunu.* Istanbul: Matbaai Ebüzziya, 1930.

Ocak, Ahmet Yaşar. "Oppositions au soufisme dans l'empire ottoman aux quinzième et seizième siècles." In *Islamic Mysticism Contested: Thirteen Centuries of Controversies and Polemics,* ed. F. de Jong and B. Radtke, pp. 603–13. Leiden: Brill, 1999.

O'Leary, De Lacy. *How Greek Science Passed to the Arabs.* London: Routledge and Kegan Paul, 1964.

Ortayli, Ilber. "The Family in Ottoman Society." In *Analecta Isisiana X: Studies on Ottoman Transformation,* ed. Ilber Ortayli, pp. 93–105. Istanbul: Isis Press, 1994.

Osman Saib. *Ahkamül-emraz.* Istanbul: Matbaa-i amire, 1252 [1836].

Panzac, Daniel. *La Peste dans l'empire ottoman, 1700–1850.* Louvain: Peeters Editions, 1992.

Partner, Nancy. "No Sex, No Gender." *Speculum* 68 (1993): 419–43.

Peirce, Leslie P. "Beyond Harem Walls: Ottoman Royal Women and the Exercise of Power." In *Gendered Domains: Rethinking Public and Private in Women's History,* ed. Dorothy O. Heliy and Susan M. Reverby, pp. 40–55. Ithaca, NY: Cornell University Press, 1992.

———. "Fatma's Dilemma: Sexual Crime and Legal Culture in an Early Modern Ottoman Court." *Annales—Histoire, Sciences Sociales* 53, no. 2 (1998): 291–346.

———. *Morality Tales: Law and Gender in the Ottoman Court of Aintab.* Berkeley and Los Angeles: University of California Press, 2003.

———. "Seniority, Sexuality and Social Order: The Vocabulary of Gender in Early Modern Ottoman Society." In *Women in the Ottoman Empire: Middle Eastern Women in the Early Modern Era,* ed. Madeline Zilfi, pp. 169–96. Leiden: Brill, 1997.

Perlman, Moshe. "A Seventeenth-Century Exhortation Concerning Al-Aqsā." *Israel Oriental Studies* 3 (1973): 261–68.

Pocqueville, F. C. H. L. *Travels through the Morea, Albania, and Several Other Parts of the Ottoman Empire, to Constantinople.* London: Richard Philips, 1806.

Price-Williams, Douglass. "Cultural Perspectives on Dreams and Consciousness." *Anthropology of Consciousness* 5, no. 3 (September 1994): 13–16.

Al-Ramli, Khayr al-Dīn. *Al-fatāwa al-Khayriyya li-nafʿ al-bariyya.* Cairo: Bulāq, 1300H.

Raşit Efendi. *Tarih-i Raşit.* 6 vols. Istanbul: Matbaa-yı Âmire, 1282H.

Repp, Richard C. *The Müfti of Istanbul: A Study in the Development of the Ottoman Learned Hierarchy.* London: Ithaca Press, 1986.

Ritter, Hellmut. *Karagös, Türkische Schattenspiele.* Hanover: Orient-Buchhandlung H. Lafaire, 1924–53.
Roland, Charles. *La Turquie contemporaine, hommes et choses.* Paris: Pagnerre, 1854.
Rosenthal, Franz. "Ar-Rāzī on the Hidden Illness." In *Science and Medicine in Islam: A Collection of Essays.* Aldershot: Variorum Reprints, 1990.
Ruggiero, Guido. *The Boundaries of Eros: Sex Crime and Sexuality in Renaissance Italy.* New York: Oxford University Press, 1985.
Rycaut, Paul. *The Present State of the Ottoman Empire.* 1668; reprint, Frankfurt: Institute for the History of Arabic-Islamic Science, 1995.
Sabuncuoğlu, Şerefeddin. *Cerrāhiyyetü'l-haniyye.* Ed. Ilter Uzel. Ankara: Dil ve Tarih Yüksek Kurumu, 1992.
Sadık Rıfat, Paşa. "Avrupa Ahvaline Dair Risâle." In *Müntehabât-ı Âsâr,* vol. 2, pp. 2–12. Istanbul: Tatyos Divitçiyan Publishing, 1874.
Sahlins, Marshall. *Islands of History.* Chicago: University of Chicago Press, 1985.
Sami, Mustafa. *Avrupa Risalesi.* Istanbul: n.p., 1840.
Sanders, Paula. "Gendering the Ungendered Body: Hermaphrodites in Medieval Islamic Law." In *Women in Middle Eastern History: Shifting Boundaries in Sex and Gender,* ed. Nikki R. Keddie and Beth Baron, pp. 74–95. New Haven, CT: Yale University Press, 1992.
Sandys, George. *Sandys Travails, Containing a History of the Original and Present State of the Turkish Empire.* 5th edition. London: R. and W. Leybourn, 1657.
Şanizade, Mehmet Ataullah. *Hamse-i şanizade.* Istanbul: Darüt-Tibaatü'l-Amire, 1235 [1820].
Sarı, Nil. "Osmanlı sağlık hayatında kadının yerine kısa bir bakış." In *Sağlık alanında Türk kadını,* ed. Nuran Yıldırım, pp. 451–65. Istanbul: Novartis, 1998.
*Şarkili ve kantolu Karagöz kitabı.* Istanbul: Asya Kütüphanesi, 1325 [1909].
Schacht, Joseph. *An Introduction to Islamic Law.* Oxford: Clarendon Press, 1984 [1964].
Schick, Irvin Cemil. *The Erotic Margin: Sexuality and Spaciality in Alteritist Discourse.* London: Verso, 1999.
Schimmel, Annemarie. *Mystical Dimensions of Islam.* Chapel Hill: University of North Carolina Press, 1975.
Scott, Joan Wallach. *Gender and the Politics of History.* New York: Columbia University Press, 1988.
*Şer'iye Sicilleri.* Istanbul: Türk Dünyası Araştırmaları Vakfı, 1989.
*Seyahatnâme-i Londra.* Istanbul: Ceride-i Havâdis Publishing, 1853.
Shoshan, Boaz. *Popular Culture in Medieval Cairo.* Cambridge: Cambridge University Press, 1993.
Siyavuşgil, Sabri Esat. *Karagöz: Its History, Its Characters, Its Mystical and Satirical Spirit.* Istanbul: Milli Eğitim Basimevi, 1961.
Slade, Adolphus. *Records of Travels in Turkey, Greece, etc., and of a Cruise in the Black Sea with the Capitan Pasha, in the Years 1829, 1830 and 1831.* 2 vols. London: Saunders and Otley, 1832.
Smith, J. V. C. *Turkey and the Turks.* Boston: James French, 1854.
Smyth, Warrington W. *A Year with the Turks.* New York: Redfield, 1854.

Somogyi, Joseph de. "The Interpretation of Dreams in Ad-Damīrī's Ḥayāt al-Ḥayawān." *Journal of the Royal Asiatic Society* pt. 1 (1940): 1–20.

Spatharis, Sotiris. *Behind the White Screen*. London: Magazine Editions, 1967.

Stallybrass, Peter, and Allon White. *The Politics and Poetics of Transgression*. Ithaca, NY: Cornell University Press, 1986.

Surieu, Robert. *Sarv-é Naz: An Essay on Love and Representation of Erotic Themes in Ancient Iran*. Geneva: Nagel Publishers, 1967.

Sviri, Sara. "Hakīm Tirmidhī and the Malāmatī Movement in Early Sufism." In *The Heritage of Sufism*, ed. L. Lewisohn, vol. 1, pp. 583–613. Boston: Oneworld Publications, 1999.

Tavakoli-Targhi, Mohamad. "Imagining Western Women: Occidentalism and Euro-Eroticism." *Radical America* 3, no. 24 (1994): 73–87.

Tedlock, Barbara. "The Evidence from Dreams." In *Psychological Anthropology*, ed. Philip K. Bock, pp. 279–95. Westport, CT: Praeger, 1994.

Terzioğlu, Derin. "Sufi and Dissident in the Ottoman Empire: Niyazī-i Misrī (1618–1694)." Ph.D. dissertation, Harvard University, 1999.

Thalasso, Adolphe. *Le théâtre turc: Molière et le théâtre de Karagueuz*. Paris: Editions de l'avenir dramatique et littéraire, n.d.

Tietze, Andreas. *The Turkish Shadow Theater and the Puppet Collection of the L. A. Mayer Memorial Foundation*. Berlin: Mann, 1977.

Al-Tifāshi, Shihāb Al-Dīn Aḥmad. *Nuzhat al-albāb fima la yūjad fi kitāb*. Ed. Jamāl Jumʿa. London: Riyad El-Rayyes Books, 1992.

Al-Tijāni, Muḥammad Ibn Aḥmad. *Tuḥfat al-ʿarūs wamutʿat al-nufūs*. Ed. Jalīl Al-Atiyya. London: Riyad El-Rayyes Books, 1992.

Toledano, Ehud R. *The Ottoman Slave Trade and Its Suppression*. Princeton, NJ: Princeton University Press, 1980.

Tott, François, Baron de. *Memoirs*. 1785; facsimile, New York: Arno Press, 1973.

Trimingham, J. Spencer. *The Sufi Orders in Islam*. London: Oxford University Press, 1973.

Al-Tūkhi, ʿAbd al-Fattāḥ al-Sayyid. *Taʿbīr al-manām wa-tafsīr al-aḥlām*. Beirut: Al-Maktaba al-Thaqāfiyya, 1992.

Ullman, Manfred. *Islamic Medicine*. Edinburgh: Edinburgh University Press, 1978.

Uludağ, Osman Şevki. *Beşbuçuk asırlık Türk tababeti tarihi*. Ankara: Kültür Bakanlığı Yayınları, 1991 [1925].

Voll, John Obert. *Islam: Continuity and Change in the Modern World*. Boulder, CO: Westview Press, 1982.

Von Grunebaum, G. E., and Roger Caillois, eds. *The Dream and Human Societies*. Berkeley and Los Angeles: University of California Press, 1966.

Wahrman, Dror. "Percy's Prologue: From Gender Play to Gender Panic in Eighteenth Century England." *Past and Present* 159 (1998): 113–60.

Walsh, R. *A Residence at Constantinople*. London: Richard Bentley, 1838.

Al-Wansharīsi, Aḥmad. *Al-Miʿyār al-muʿrib wa'l-jāmiʿ al-mughrib fi fatāwa ʿulamā' Ifriqya wa'l-Andalus wa'l-Maghrib*. Rabāt, Morocco: Dār al-Gharb al-Islāmi, 1981.

Al-Wāsiṭi, Shams al-Dīn Muḥammad Ibn ʿUmar al-Ghamri. *Al-ḥukm al-maẓbūṭ fi taḥrīm fiʿl qawm Lūṭ*. Ed. ʿUbaydallah al-Masri. Cairo: Dar al-Saḥāba li'l-Turath, 1988.

Weeks, Jeffrey. *Sex, Politics and Society: The Regulation of Sexuality since 1800*. London: Longman, 1989.

———. *Sexuality*. London: Tavistock Publications and Ellis Horwood, 1986.

White, Charles. *Three Years in Constantinople*. London: Henry Colburn, 1846.

Wittman, William. *Travels in Asia Minor, Syria, and across the Desert into Egypt during the Years 1799, 1800 and 1801*. London: Richard Philips, 1803.

Wright, J. W., Jr., and Everett K. Rowson. *Homoeroticism in Classical Arabic Literature*. New York: Columbia University Press, 1997.

Yared, Nazik Saba. *Arab Travellers and Western Civilization*. London: Saqi Books, 1996.

Zaydān, Jurji. *Riḥlat Jurji Zaydān ila Urūba*. Cairo: Dār al-hilāl, 1923.

Ze'evi, Dror. "*Kul* and Getting Cooler: The Dissolution of an Elite Collective Identity in the Ottoman Empire." *Mediterranean Historical Review* 11, no. 2 (December 1996): 177–99.

———. *An Ottoman Century: The District of Jerusalem in the 1600s*. Albany: State University of New York Press, 1996.

———. "Sex, Society and State: An Examination of Legal Systems in the Ottoman Empire." *Continuity and Change* 16, no. 2 (2001): 219–42.

Zilfi, Madeline C. *The Politics of Piety: The Ottoman Ulema in the Postclassical Age (1600–1800)*. Minneapolis: Bibliotheca Islamica, 1988.

# Index

*Page numbers in italics refer to illustrations.*


Abbasid period: homosexuality in, 38; oral sex in, 115; poetry of, 8
*Abdal Bekçi* (shadow play), 133–34, 141
ʿAbd al-Qays, 1
Abdülhamid II, Sultan, 164–65
Abdülmecid, Sultan, 71, 76
Abstinence, sexual, 32
Abu Ḥanīfa, 55, 85
Abu Nuwās, 8
Adıvar, Adnan, 20
Adultery. See *Zinā'*
Ahmed, Fazıl, 94
Aksarayı, Cemaluddin, 19
*ʿĀlam al-mithāl* (imaginal world), 102, 131, 187n10, 194n16
Alexandros, on dream interpretation, 101
Āli Paşa (vizier), 198n47
Amāsi, Sinān al-Dīn al- (al-Wāʿiẓ), 88, 185n29
*Amrad. See* Boys, beautiful
Anatomy: in Islamicate medicine, 12; Western models of, 39, 45–46
Angels, sexual intercourse with, 113, 115
Anthropomorphy, 79
Arab literature, modern, 6
Aristotle, 188n12; *De divinatione ex insomniis,* 101; on semen, 178n46
Artemidorus, biography of, 187n11
Asāl (hero), 5
*Aşçılık* (shadow play), 145
*Askeri* (aristocracy), responsibilities of, 66, 67
ʿAyntāb (Anatolia), court archives of, 174n13

*Bahçe* (shadow play), 134
Bakhtin, Mikhail, 139, 192n4; on high and low culture, 126–27
Bathing, public, 112
Battle of the Trench, 109
Bektashi *(ṭarīqa),* 80, 97, 153
Birds, symbolism of, 111
Birgivi *(ʿālim),* 93, 186n40
Bleys, Rudy: *Geography of Perversion,* 154–55
Blood: oaths, 37; in Ottoman genetics, 36–37
Boddy, Janet, 111
Body: autonomous, 22; Christian rejection of, 35; Galenic concept of, 47; humoral balance of, 22; juridico-discursive mechanisms of, 12; one-sex model of, 22–23, 168; script of, 12; surface of, 26–31; two-sex model of, 24, 44, 46–47, 168
Boerhaave, Herman, 20
Bouhdiba, Abdelwahab, 7; *Sexuality in Islam,* 3–4, 183n1
Boyarin, Daniel, 52

STUDIES ON THE HISTORY OF SOCIETY AND CULTURE

Victoria E. Bonnell and Lynn Hunt, Editors

1. *Politics, Culture, and Class in the French Revolution,* by Lynn Hunt
2. *The People of Paris: An Essay in Popular Culture in the 18th Century,* by Daniel Roche
3. *Pont-St-Pierre, 1398–1789: Lordship, Community, and Capitalism in Early Modern France,* by Jonathan Dewald
4. *The Wedding of the Dead: Ritual, Poetics, and Popular Culture in Transylvania,* by Gail Kligman
5. *Students, Professors, and the State in Tsarist Russia,* by Samuel D. Kassow
6. *The New Cultural History,* edited by Lynn Hunt
7. *Art Nouveau in Fin-de-Siècle France: Politics, Psychology, and Style,* by Debora L. Silverman
8. *Histories of a Plague Year: The Social and the Imaginary in Baroque Florence,* by Giulia Maria Calvi
9. *Culture of the Future: The Proletkult Movement in Revolutionary Russia,* by Lynn Mally
10. *Bread and Authority in Russia, 1914–1921,* by Lars T. Lih
11. *Territories of Grace: Cultural Change in the Seventeenth-Century Diocese of Grenoble,* by Keith P. Luria
12. *Publishing and Cultural Politics in Revolutionary Paris, 1789–1810,* by Carla Hesse
13. *Limited Livelihoods: Gender and Class in Nineteenth-Century England,* by Sonya O. Rose
14. *Moral Communities: The Culture of Class Relations in the Russian Printing Industry, 1867–1907,* by Mark D. Steinberg
15. *Bolshevik Festivals, 1917–1920,* by James von Geldern
16. *Venice's Hidden Enemies: Italian Heretics in a Renaissance City,* by John Martin
17. *Wondrous in His Saints: Counter-Reformation Propaganda in Bavaria,* by Philip M. Soergel
18. *Private Lives and Public Affairs: The Causes Célèbres of Prerevolutionary France,* by Sarah Maza
19. *Hooliganism: Crime, Culture, and Power in St. Petersburg, 1900–1914,* by Joan Neuberger
20. *Possessing Nature: Museums, Collecting, and Scientific Culture in Early Modern Italy,* by Paula Findlen
21. *Listening in Paris: A Cultural History,* by James H. Johnson

22. *The Fabrication of Labor: Germany and Britain, 1640–1914*, by Richard Biernacki
23. *The Struggle for the Breeches: Gender and the Making of the British Working Class*, by Anna Clark
24. *Taste and Power: Furnishing Modern France*, by Leora Auslander
25. *Cholera in Post-Revolutionary Paris: A Cultural History*, by Catherine J. Kudlick
26. *The Women of Paris and Their French Revolution*, by Dominique Godineau
27. *Iconography of Power: Soviet Political Posters under Lenin and Stalin*, by Victoria E. Bonnell
28. *Fascist Spectacle: The Aesthetics of Power in Mussolini's Italy*, by Simonetta Falasca-Zamponi
29. *Passions of the Tongue: Language Devotion in Tamil India, 1891–1970*, by Sumathi Ramaswamy
30. *Crescendo of the Virtuoso: Spectacle, Skill, and Self-Promotion in Paris during the Age of Revolution*, by Paul Metzner
31. *Crime, Cultural Conflict, and Justice in Rural Russia, 1856–1914*, by Stephen P. Frank
32. *The Collective and the Individual in Russia: A Study of Practices*, by Oleg Kharkhordin
33. *What Difference Does a Husband Make? Women and Marital Status in Nazi and Postwar Germany*, by Elizabeth D. Heineman
34. *Beyond the Cultural Turn: New Directions in the Study of Society and Culture*, edited by Victoria E. Bonnell and Lynn Hunt
35. *Jazz, Rock, and Rebels: Cold War Politics and American Culture in a Divided Germany*, by Uta G. Poiger
36. *The Frail Social Body: Pornography, Homosexuality, and Other Fantasies in Interwar France*, by Carolyn J. Dean
37. *Blood and Fire: Rumor and History in Colonial Africa*, by Luise White
38. *The New Biography: Performing Femininity in Nineteenth-Century France*, edited by Jo Burr Margadant
39. *France and the Cult of the Sacred Heart: An Epic Tale for Modern Times*, by Raymond Jonas
40. *Politics and Theater: The Crisis of Legitimacy in Restoration France, 1815–1830*, by Sheryl Kroen
41. *On the Postcolony*, by Achille Mbembe
42. *Fascist Modernities: Italy, 1922–1945*, by Ruth Ben-Ghiat
43. *Women Writing Opera: Creativity and Controversy in the Age of the French Revolution*, by Jacqueline Letzter and Robert Adelson
44. *Popular Theater and Society in Tsarist Russia*, by E. Anthony Swift

45. *Beyond the Pale: The Jewish Encounter with Late Imperial Russia,* by Benjamin Nathans
46. *The View from Vesuvius: Italian Culture and the Southern Question,* by Nelson J. Moe
47. *The Three-Piece Suit and Modern Masculinity: England, 1550–1850,* by David Kuchta
48. *The Emancipation of Writing: German Civil Society in the Making, 1790s–1820s,* by Ian F. McNeely
49. *Obstinate Hebrews: Representations of Jews in France, 1715–1815,* by Ronald Schechter
50. *An Ottoman Tragedy: History and Historiography at Play,* by Gabriel Piterberg
51. *The Family on Trial in Revolutionary France,* by Suzanne Desan
52. *Producing Desire: Changing Sexual Discourse in the Ottoman Middle East, 1500–1900,* by Dror Ze'evi
53. *The Emerging Female Citizen: Gender and Enlightenment in Spain,* by Theresa Ann Smith

Text: 10/13 Sabon
Display: Sabon
Compositor: Integrated Composition Systems